Local Governments and Rural Development

Local Governments and Rural Development

Comparing Lessons from Brazil, Chile, Mexico, and Peru

Krister Andersson
Gustavo Gordillo de Anda
Frank van Laerhoven

The University of Arizona Press   Tucson

The University of Arizona Press
www.uapress.arizona.edu

© 2009 The Arizona Board of Regents
All rights reserved. Published 2009
First paperback edition 2015

Printed in the United States of America
20　19　18　17　16　15　　7　6　5　4　3　2

ISBN-13: 978-0-8165-2701-4 (cloth)
ISBN-13: 978-0-8165-3206-3 (paper)

Cover design by Tasja van der Veen, Bingo! Graphic Design / www.bingo-graphicdesign.com

Library of Congress Cataloging-in-Publication Data
Andersson, Krister, 1965–
　Local governments and rural development : comparing lessons from Brazil, Chile, Mexico, and Peru / Krister Andersson, Gustavo Gordillo de Anda, Frank van Laerhoven.
　　p. cm.
　Includes bibliographical references and index.
　ISBN 978-0-8165-2701-4 (hardcover : alk. paper)
　1. Local government—Latin America. 2. Rural development—Latin America. 3. Decentralization in government—Latin America. I. Gordillo, Gustavo. II. Laerhoven, Frank van, 1968– III. Title.
　JS2061.A53 2009
　307.1'412098—dc22

2008032117

♾ This paper meets the requirements of ANSI/NISO Z39.48-1992 (Permanence of Paper).

Contents

List of Figures   vii
List of Maps   ix
List of Tables   xi
Acknowledgments   xiii
List of Abbreviations   xv

1 Poverty, Rural Development, and Local Governance in Latin America   3

2 Framing the Comparative Study of Decentralization in Latin America   22

3 The Role of Local Governments in Rural Development in Brazil, Chile, Mexico, and Peru   30

4 Brazil: At the Decentralization Forefront
Frank van Laerhoven   42

5 Chile: A Free-Market Model of Decentralization
With Paul Lewin   69

6 Mexico: A Case of Limited Decentralization
With Fabián González and Juan José Ochoa   91

7 Peru: The Pre-Decentralization Baseline Case
Miguel Jaramillo Baanante   113

8 Comparative Analysis of the Institutional Conditions for Effective Rural-Development Services   139

9 Does Decentralization Promote Participatory Governance? A Comparative Analysis   161

10 Conclusions   184

   Notes   203

   References   209

   Index   225

Figures

1.1 Theoretical framework 16
4.1 Local-government involvement in Brazil 52
5.1 Number of hired agricultural staff in Chile 79
6.1 Indicators of service quality in Mexico 98
7.1 Structure of Ministry of Agriculture in Peru 120
8.1 Performance of municipal agricultural system 145
8.2 Statistics of three dependent variables 147
9.1 Participatory municipal governance 175

Maps

4.1 Sampled municipalities in Brazil   50
5.1 Sampled municipalities in Chile   77
6.1 Sampled municipalities in Mexico   96
7.1 Sampled municipalities in Peru   127

Tables

3.1 Comparison of local-government mandates in rural development   32
4.1 Description of the statistical models   54
4.2 Description of the independent variables   56
4.3 Logit regression results   58
5.1 Description of variables used in the analysis   80
5.2 Descriptive statistic of variables   81
5.3 Econometric analysis results   83
6.1 Description of variables   100
6.2 Binary logit results   103
7.1 Annual average national and agricultural GDP and population growth   116
7.2 Determinants of the existence of at least one agricultural service/technical-assistance service   130
7.3 Determinants of the probability of observing satisfaction with the services provided   133
8.1 Description of variables used in the analysis   148
8.2 Descriptive statistic of the variables   150
8.3 Regression results   151
8.4 Changing probabilities for predicted outcomes   152
9.1 Description of variables included in the statistical analysis   172
9.2 Descriptive statistics   174
9.3 Determinants of participatory municipal governance   176
9.4 Changing probabilities for statistically significant coefficients   177

Acknowledgments

This book is the fruit of a truly collaborative effort, involving many individuals and organizations in all four countries of the study. First, we would like to extend our gratitude to our field assistants who helped us gather the interview data in the 390 municipal territories. These individuals were trained and supervised by our colleagues at Centro IDEAS and Instituto Apoyo in Peru, El Instituto de Gestión y Liderazgo Social para el Futuro (INDESO) and Instituto Maya in Mexico, Gestión y Desarrollo in Chile, as well as by the Department of Rural Socioeconomic Studies (DESER) and the Superintendência de Estudos Econômicos e Sociais da Bahia (SEI) in Brazil.

Adriana de Groote translated most of the chapters in the book from Spanish to English, for which we are very grateful. We acknowledge Sage Publications, who granted us permission to include chapter 9, which was previously published as an article in their journal *Comparative Political Studies*. Thanks also to Patty Lezotte and David Price and the editors at the University of Arizona Press, especially Patti Hartmann and Mary Rodarte, for all their help with reviewing and editing this book. Several colleagues provided us with valuable comments and suggestions on earlier versions of the various chapters in the book, and we are particularly grateful for input from Elinor and Vincent Ostrom, Alain de Janvry, Merilee Grindle, Carlos Icaza, Laura Noguer, Catherine Tucker, and Glenn Wright.

We are most indebted, however, to the more than 1,200 men and women in the rural areas of Brazil, Chile, Mexico, and Peru who agreed to be interviewed for this study. Finally, we gratefully acknowledge the financial support from the Food and Agriculture Organization of the United Nations; the Ford Foundation; the National Science Foundation (BCS0527165 and SES0648447); USAID (SANREM-CRSP LTR1), the Sustainability Science Program at Harvard University, and the Workshop in Political Theory and Policy Analysis at Indiana University.

Abbreviations

ABCAR	Associação Brasileira de Crédito e Assistência Rural (Brazilian Association for Credit and Rural Support)
AGROASEMEX	Institución Nacional de Seguros (National Insurance Institution)
ASBRAER	Associação Brasileira das Entidades Estaduais de Asistencia Técnica e Extensão Rural (Brazilian Association of State Entities for Technical Support and Rural Extension)
ASERCA	Apoyos y Servicios a la Comercialización Agropecuaria (Support and Services for the Agriculture and Livestock Commericialization)
BANRURAL	Banco Nacional de Crédito Rural, SNC
CBETAS	Centros de Bachillerato Tecnológicos Agropecuarios (Vocational Training Centers for Agricultural Technology, high school equivalent).
CBO	Community-Based Organization
CEASA	Centro de Abastecimiento del Estado de Santa Catarina (Food Supply Center of the State of Santa Catarina)
CESAEGRO	Colegio Superior Agropecuario del Estado de Guerrero (Superior College for Agiculture and Livestock for the State of Guerrero)
CESCO	Consejo Económico y Social Comunal (Communal Social and Economic Council)
CIDASC	Compañía Integrada de Desarrollo Agrícola de Santa Catarina(Integrated Agricultural Development Company of Santa Catarina)
CMDR	Conselho Municipal de Desenvolvimento Rural (Municipal Council for Rural Development)

CNDRS	Consejo Nacional de Desarrollo Rural Sostenible (Council on Rural Sustainable Development)
CNR	Comisión Nacional de Riego (National Irrigation Commission)
CONAB	Compañía Nacional de Abastecimiento (National Food Supply Company)
CONACS	Consejo Nacional de Camélidos Sudamericanos (National Council on South American Camelids)
CONAF	Corporación Nacional Forestal (National Forestry Corporation)
CONAPESCA	Comisión Nacional de Acuacultura y Pesca (National Commission for Aquaculture and Fishery)
CONAZA	Comisión Nacional de las Zonas Áridas (National Commission for Dry Areas)
COPLADEMUN	Comité de Planeación para el Desarrollo Municipal (Committee for Municipal Development Planning)
COREDE	Consejos Regionales de Desarrollo (Regional Development Councils)
CTAR	Consejos Transitorios de Administración Regional (Transitory Regional Administration Councils)
DEFAB	Departamento de Floresta y Areas Protegidas (Forests and Protected Areas Department)
DESER	Departamento de Estudos Sócio-Econômicos Rurais (The Department of Rural Socioeconomic Studies)
DRH	Departamento de Recursos Hídricos (Department of Water Resources)
EMATER	Empresa de Asistencia Técnica (Technical Assistance Company)
EMBRAPA	Empresa Brasileña de Investigación Agropecuaria (Brazilian Agricultural Research Company)
EMBRATER	Empresa Brasileira de Assistência Técnica e Extensão Rural (Brazilian Company for Technical Support and Rural Extension)
EPAGRI	Empresa de Investigación Agropecuaria y Extensión Rural de Santa Catarina (Agricultural Research and Rural Extension Enterprise of Santa Catarina)
FAO	Food and Agriculture Organization of the United Nations

FATMA	Fundación del Medio Ambiente (Environmental Foundation)
FEAS	Fomento del Mercado de Servicios de Asistencia Técnica en la Sierra Peruana (Technology Transfer to the Peasant Communities of the Highlands of Peru)
FEPAGRO	Fundación Estatal de Investigación Agropecuaria (State Foundation for Agricultural Research)
FEPAM	Fundación Estatal de Protección Ambiental (State Foundation of Environmental Protection)
FIRA	Fideicomisos Instituidos en Relación con la Agricultura (Agriculture Trust Funds)
FIRCO	Fideicomisos de Riesgo Compartido (Shared Risk Trust Funds)
FNDR	Fondo Nacional de Desarrollo Regional (The National Fund for Regional Development)
FNMA	Fondo Nacional del Medio Ambiente (National Environmental Fund)
FOCIR	Fondo de Capitalización e Inversión del Sector Rural (Fund for Capitalization and Investment in the Rural Sector)
FZB	Fundación Zoobotánica (Zoo-Botanical Foundation)
GDP	Gross Domestic Procuct
HDI	Human development index
IAD	Institutional Analysis and Development framework
IAP	Instituto Ambiental de Paraná (Environmental Institute of Paraná)
IBGE	Instituto Brasileiro de Geografia e Estatística (Brazilian Institute of Geography and Statistics)
ICEPA	Instituto de Planeamiento y Economía Agrícola de Santa Catarina (Institute of Planning and Agrarian Economy of Santa Catarina)
IMTA	Instituto Mexicano de Tecnología del Agua (Mexican Institute of Water Technology)
INCA Rural	Instituto Nacional para el Desarrollo de Capacidades del Sector Rural (National Institute for Skills Development in the Rural Sector)

INCRA	Instituto Nacional de Colonização e Reforma Agrária (Nacional Institute for Colonization and Agricultural Reform)
INDAP	Instituto de Desarrollo Agropecuario (Agriculture and Livestock Development Institute)
INDESO	El Instituto de Gestión y Liderazgo Social para el Futuro (Institute for Social Governance and Leadership for the Future)
INEGI	Instituto Nacional de Estadística Geografía e Informática (National Institute of Geographic Statistics and Informatics)
INFOR	Instituto Forestal (Forestry Institute)
INI	Instituto Nacional Indigenista (National Institute for Indigenous Affairs)
INIA	Instituto Nacional de Investigaciones Agropecuarias (Agriculture and Livestock Research Institute)
INIA	Instituto Nacional de Investigación Agraria (National Institute for Agrarian Research)
INIFAP	Instituto Nacional de Investigaciones Forestales, Agricolas y Pecuarias (National Institute of Forestry, Agricultural and Animal Research)
INRENA	Instituto Nacional de Recursos Naturales (National Institute of Natural Resources)
IP	Instituto de Pesca (Fisheries Institute)
ITA	Instituto de Tecnología Agropecuaria (Institute of Agricultural Technology)
LOM	Ley Orgánica Municipal (Organic Law of Municipalities)
MAPA	Ministerio de Abastecimiento y Producción Agropecuaria (Ministry of Agricultural Production and Storage)
MDA	Ministerio de Dessarrollo Agrario (Ministry of Agrarian Development)
MMA	Ministerio de Medio Ambiente (Ministry of the Environment)
NAFIN	Nacional Financiera (National Finance Organization)

NEAD	Nucleo de Estudios Agrarios (Nucleus of Agrarian Studies)
NGO	Nongovernmental Organization
OECD	Organization for Economic Co-operation and Development
OLS	Ordinary Least Square
OPD	Organismo Público Descentralizado (Decentralized Public Organization)
PAN	Partido de Acción Nacional (National Action Party)
PEA	Población Económicamente Activa (Economically Active Population)
PETT	Proyecto Especial de Titulación de Tierras (Special Land Titling and Cadastral Project)
PMDRS	Planos Municipais de Desenvolvimento Rural Sustentável (Annual Municipal Work Plan)
PRI	Partido Revolucionario Institucional (Institutional Revolutionary Party)
PROCAMPO	Farmers Direct Support Program
PROCEDE	Programa de Certificación de Derechos Ejidales y Titulación de Solares Urbanos (Program for the Certification of Ejido Rights and Titling of Urban Property Rights)
PRODEFOR	Programa de Desarrollo Forestal (Forestry Development Program)
PRODEPLAN	Programa para el Desarrollo de Plantaciones Forestales Comerciales (Program for the Development of Commercial Forest Plantations)
PROGER	Programa de Geração de Emprego e Renda (Program for the Generation of Employment and Income)
PROGRESA	Programa de Educacion, Salud y Alimentacion (Education, Health and Food Program)
PROMPEX	Oficina de Promoción de las Exportaciones (Export Promotion Commission)
PRONAF	Programa Nacional de Fortalecimento da Agricultura Familiar (National Program for Strengthening Family Farming)

PRONAMACHS	Programa Nacional de Manejo de Cuencas Hidrográficas y Conservación de Suelos (National Program of Watershed Management and Soil Conservation)
PRONERA	Programa Nacional de Educación de la Reforma Agraria (National Agrarian Reform Education Program)
PSI	Programa Subsectorial de Irrigaciones (Subsectorial Program of Irrigation)
SAG	Servicio Agrícola y Ganadero (Agriculture and Livestock Service)
SAGARPA	Secretaria de Agricultura, Ganadería, Desarrollo Rural, Pesca y Alimentación (Secretariat of Agriculture, Livestock, Rural Development, Fisheries, and Food)
SCT	Secretaría de Comunicaciones y Transportes (Ministry of Communications and Transport)
SEDESOL	Subsecretaría de Desarrollo Social y Humano (Subsecretariat for Social and Human Development)
SEI	Superintendência de Estudos Econômicos e Sociais da Bahia (Superintendence of Socioeconomic Studies of Bahia)
SEMARNAT	Secretaría de medio ambiente y recursos naturales (Ministry of the Environment and Natural Resources)
SENASA	Servicio Nacional de Sanidad Agropecuaria (National Agrarian Health Service)
SEREMI	Secretarías Regionales Ministeriales (Regional Ministerial Secretariats)
SERPLAC	Secretarías Regionales de Planificación y Coordinación (Regional Secretariats for Planning and Coordination)
SNIM	Sistema Nacional de Indicadores Municipales (National System of Municipal Indicators)
SUBDERE	Subsecretaría de Desarrollo Regional y Administrativo (Subsecretariat for Regional and Administrative Development)

SUDERHSA	Superintendencia de Desarrollo de Recursos Hídricos y Saneamiento Ambiental (Superintendency of Water Resources Development and Environmental Sanitation)
UA	Unidades Agropecuaria (Farming unit)
UAAAN	Universidad Autónoma Agraria Antonio Narro (Autonomous Agrarian University Antonio Narro)
UACH	Universidad Autónoma de Chihuahua (Autonomous University of Chihuahua)
UNDP	United Nations Development Program
UOPE	Unidad Operativa de Proyectos Especiales (Operational Unit for Special Projects)
ZEE	Programa de Zonificación Ecológica y Económica (Ecological and Economic Zoning Program)

Local Governments and Rural Development

1
Poverty, Rural Development, and Local Governance in Latin America

This book analyzes recent efforts to address problems of rural poverty in Latin America. We focus our inquiry on the ways in which the decentralization of formal policy functions from central to local governments affect the governance arrangements for rural development at the local level. Our premise is that the quality of public services aiming at reducing rural poverty is ultimately the result of a local-governance process in which a variety of actors under very different circumstances are involved. Granting local government more autonomy and formal responsibilities through decentralization reforms may alter the governance dynamics at the local level, but if and when this will lead to improved public policy outcomes remains an open question. It is precisely this question that we explore in this book.

The concept of "good governance" has sprung to the forefront of the development debate, especially among development aid organizations (Doornbos 2001; Rhodes 1996; Meso et al. 2006). This new emphasis of many donor-supported development programs largely originated from the perception among many development workers and scholars that the public sector in most developing countries performed rather badly (Tendler 1997). In the 1970s and 1980s, one of the main frustrations for those concerned with development issues were the centralized bureaucracies that were not able to respond to the development needs of poor people (Riddell 2007; Gibson, Andersson et al. 2005). One of the most popular responses to nonresponsive, "bad" governance in the region has been decentralization reform. The empirical literature on decentralization is largely optimistic about the ability of empowered local governments to contribute to the overall improvement of governance performance. This view has become dominant in the development studies field despite theoretical work that points to the risks associated with decentralization (Musgrave 1997; Peterson 1995; Bartley et al. 2008). For Latin America, success stories about the effect of decentralization on the quality of local governments are not hard to come by. For example, there are numerous studies that analyze the participatory budgeting experience in Porto Alegre, Brazil (Avritzer 2002; Bruce 2004; Baiocchi 2001, 2005; Gret and Sintomer 2005; Koonings 2004). The case studies indicate the broader trend in the empirical literature on decentralization to focus the analysis on specific successful experiences and formulate "lessons learned" from the selected success stories. It is, however, much more difficult to find examples in the empirical literature that tell a story of local governments failing to translate their newfound autonomy into better public-service performance (but see work on elite capture: Platteau 2004; Schönwälder 1997; Khadiagala 2001). Might this unbalanced account be because positive outcomes for public-service quality are more prevalent in Latin America? We do not think so. In fact, our own field observations in Brazil, Mexico, Chile, and Peru tell a rather different story. One of the most important findings of our study is the enormous variation in the quality of public services within decentralized regimes. Some municipalities fare quite well, but arguably even more show no performance improvement at all after local governments were granted increased autonomy through decentralization.

The finding that decentralization does not automatically result in better performance of the public sector does not come as a big surprise to most governance scholars. For example, Kooiman and van Vliet (1993, 64) state that "the governance concept points to the creation of a structure or an order which cannot be externally imposed but is the result of the interaction of a multiplicity of governing and each other influencing actors." According to this view, governance does not necessarily require a single center of power, and *the* government need not always claim an exclusive responsibility for resolving policy issues (see also McGinnis 1999a and b on polycentricity). To be sure, granting more autonomy to *local governments* through decentralization will undoubtedly alter the dynamics and possibilities of *local governance*. However, the local government is only one piece of the local-governance puzzle. The ultimate outcome of interactions and exchanges in the local polity also depends on the place-specific biophysical environment, the preferences and roles of other policy actors as determined by the specific socioeconomic context, and the dynamics of the existing local institutional arrangements, as well as the degree of nestedness of the local-policy arena within a broader institutional setting.

Hence, to understand the diversity of decentralization outcomes, it seems necessary to start by analyzing to what extent local-governance actors within both decentralized and centralized structures interact and decide to engage themselves in rural-development problem solving at the local level. To the extent that decentralization reforms strengthen the downward accountability of government, and thus improve local people's access to decisions that directly impact their daily lives (Fox and Aranda 1998; Ribot 2002; Agrawal and Ostrom 2001) it seems plausible that decentralization reforms could very well alter local-governance structures so that policy goals, such as poverty alleviation and rural development, would be achieved. At the same time, however, it is important to consider that we are far from understanding exactly how and when decentralization will have a positive impact on public-sector performance. This book is an attempt to address this current lack of understanding.

In this book we explore the links between poverty, rural development, decentralization, and local governance in different national policy contexts in Latin America. Particularly, we look at the provision and production of agricultural services in rural municipalities in Brazil, Chile, Mexico, and Peru. According to the International Fund for Agricultural Development (2001), whereas 44 percent of Latin America's total population lives below the poverty line, approximately 64 percent of the *rural* population can be categorized as being poor. This means that in Brazil, Mexico, Peru, and Chile—the four countries this book focuses on—42 million people living in rural areas have to get by on less than a dollar per day (United Nations Development Program 2004).[1] Between 1980 and 2000, rural poverty in Latin America increased in both absolute and relative terms (IFAD 2001), and while most countries in the region experienced vigorous economic growth in GDP per capita during the first decade of the century, aggregate rural poverty has remained largely unchanged (World Bank, 2008).

Although we recognize the growing significance of nonrural employment as a strategy to escape poverty in Latin American rural areas (Reardon et al. 2001), it cannot be denied that agriculture remains a leading sector in Latin America's rural areas: Although exact numbers are not available regarding the relevance of agriculture for rural economies for all four countries, census data does reveal a close relationship between the number of people reported to live in rural areas and the total number of people occupied in the agricultural sector (UNDP 2004).

We focus on the local provision and production of agricultural services in particular because of the demonstrated importance of this sector in efforts to reduce rural poverty. In India, Thirtle et al. (2002) compare the poverty effect of a 1 percent productivity gain in agriculture, industry, and services, respectively. Whereas the impact on poverty of an increase of productivity in the service sector is actually negative and in the industrial sector is negligible, they find that investment in productivity improvement in the agricultural sector had led to a significant positive impact on poverty alleviation. For Latin America, they estimate that a 1 percent increase in yield would lead to an 8 percent decrease in the number of people living on a dollar or less per day. Scholars associated with the International Food Policy Research Institute reached similar conclusions by examining the relationship between public investment in agriculture and the number of malnourished children for a sample of thirty-six developing nations (Rosegrant et al. 2001). Creating a simulation model based on past relationships between a series of factors related to agricultural productivity, they find that there is a strong negative relationship between public-investment levels in agriculture and the number of malnourished children (Rosegrant et al. 2001). In sum, public policies aimed at the agricultural sector have the potential to be an important ally in the fight against extreme rural poverty in Latin America.

We argue that the success of agricultural policies as a tool to fight rural poverty is importantly linked to how the current wave of decentralization reforms in the region will eventually affect local-governance structures. The recent proliferation of decentralization reforms has placed the performance of local governments at the center of the public-policy debate in Latin America. Although most countries in the region grant limited political and fiscal authority to their local governments, the role of local governments in public policy processes is of increasing importance. Despite the often limited mandate as well as the widespread lack of human and financial resources, municipal governments play a particularly important role in the delivery of public services related to agriculture and rural development because in the rural areas of Latin America, the municipal government is often the only public organization with a continuous physical presence. Theory suggests that because local government officials are "closer to the people" they are in a better position than central-government actors to assess and address the farmers' most urgent needs, to incorporate local farmers' capabilities and resources in policy responses, and to guarantee that their responses will ultimately result in public-service delivery that is both effective and efficient. In reality, however, the observed outcomes of decentralized governance have been less clear-cut. The purpose of this book is to sort out why some municipal governments perform better than others, and to explore how national- and international-policy efforts might be developed to support local governments to excel in their new roles.

There are a growing number of studies that speak to these issues. Most of these are case studies that undertake profound and qualitative analyses of particular cases of local governments in particular countries. To date, however, very few studies compare the decentralized governance of public services among local governments in different countries (but see Crook and Manor 1998; Andersson et al. 2006). By studying the experience of a single country during a single time period, it is not possible to analyze the effects that national policy reforms, such as decentralization and property-rights reforms, might have had on local-governance performance. Our study is an attempt to do just that. We use data gathered through personal interviews with several actors involved in the provision, production, and use of agricultural public services in 390 municipalities in Brazil, Chile, Mexico, and Peru. Using a mix of qualitative and quantitative methods, we analyze how and to what extent municipal institutional arrangements affect the probability of achieving successful public services related to small-scale agriculture and rural development.

One of the main lessons of this study is that the effects of decentralization reforms on local governance are neither uniformly positive nor uniformly negative. We find that the effects of these reforms depend to a great extent on the particular context, not just in each country but in each locality. We find that, regardless of the degree of decentralization present in the agricultural sector of each country, the quality of public services is closely linked to the operation of the local institutional arrangements for coprovision and coproduction. Municipalities with a high degree of inclusive and participatory processes for decision making (coprovision) and implementation (coproduction)—which involve local farmers, NGOs, and officials at the local, regional, and central-government levels—are more likely to deliver effective agricultural services.

Contrary to the conventional wisdom in this field, we find that it is not the technical skills, administrative capacity, or financial resources of the individual organization at any particular level of governance that make the biggest difference. Rather, in this book we argue that positive governance outcomes related to public service performance are related to the degree of association between actors at different governance levels. This means that successful decentralization of the governance of agricultural services requires, first and foremost, the development of robust local institutions capable of managing *cooperation* and *coordination* among different actors with different interests but with a clear stake in the delivery of those services at the local level.

Our study also finds that most municipalities in the four countries have failed to make such cooperation work smoothly. We propose that the lack of institutions for local cooperation is due in part to perverse incentives—e.g., related to corruption, clientelistic networks, and their interactions with a paternalistic state—that affect some actors. The study identifies the sources of these perverse incentives and provides suggestions as to how future public rural development policies could contribute to advance positive incentives in support of coprovision and coproduction arrangements between public-service stakeholders.

The following two sections present our theoretical approach and define the essential challenge of decentralized governance as the task of overcoming three dilemmas that we argue complicate collective action: motivation, information, and power issues. The fourth section presents the main arguments and hypotheses of the study. We conclude the chapter by offering a glimpse of some of our analytical results and then lay out the structure for the rest of the book.

The Theoretical Foundation of the Study

In the literature on decentralization, we find many useful proposals for how to approach the study of decentralization and local governance. A number of these approaches take into consideration institutional arrangements affecting the characteristics of exchange and interactions between policy actors, including central government, local government, and civil-society representatives. For example, Agrawal and Ribot (1999) propose a framework that takes into account the actors in decentralization, the type of powers they respectively exercise, and the institutions for accountability in place. Fox (1996), recognizing the importance of civil society for the success of local governance, stresses the relevance of social capital for the meaningful participation of citizens in democratic local governance. Ames (1987) suggests that public-sector expenditure in Latin America can be understood by looking at interaction between providers, producers, and consumers of public goods and services (See also Oakerson 1999). Geddes (1994) applies rational-choice theory to map the incentives to which politicians are more likely to respond, in order to understand under what circumstances public-sector performance can be expected to bloom or falter. Grindle (2000) also focuses on incentives experienced by policy makers in explaining why, in the interaction between policy actors, governments decide to put into effect participatory institutional arrangements. Ward and Rodriguez (1999) examine the interaction of legislative, executive, and judicial branches in Mexico, and the gradual formalization of those relations, in order to explain the opening of government. Booth and Seligson (2005) speak of the importance of a "political community" and "trust in local governments" to explain the success or failure of participation and citizen engagement in provision and production of public services.

In sum, a significant literature studies decentralization, and not exclusively in terms of its likely impact on local government. The literature specifically emphasizes the effect of increased autonomy of local governments on local-governance arrangements. The insights that emerge from this tradition raise several new questions for research: How are relations between local-policy actors altered by decentralization? How do local institutional arrangements—such as formal rules, historical relations, and other factors such as norms and trust—affect the way in which exchange relations and interactions between local government, central government, and civil-society representatives pan out after the implementation of reforms? How does all of this combine to result in good or bad governance outcomes? As we seek to address these questions, we situate our own endeavor within this tradition.

We posit that an effective public-service system has an important demand-driven aspect to it. By this we mean that the types of public goods and services that an effective governance system produces reflect the particularities of citizens' needs, preferences, and specific circumstances. In a public economy, "provision units" make decisions about what types of collective goods and services should be produced, how they should be financed, and what rules should govern their delivery. The "production units" make decisions concerning the alternative ways of implementing the activities related to the goods and services. An effective municipal system, then, requires citizens' active participation in both provision and production unit decisions. We call this participation coprovision and coproduction. Provision refers to the decision-making processes regarding the levying of taxes; public expenditure; the selection of what services to provide; the most adequate level of supply for these services; the monitoring of service performance; and the production itself. Production refers to the process of transforming a set of inputs into the final products or services (output) (See Oakerson 1999).

Provision units are developed in accordance with a given territorial cluster of individual preferences regarding certain public services. Depending on the characteristics of a local-governance structure, other policy actors, besides the local government, participate in these provision units. Together, actors engage in coprovision. Provision units deliberate about and decide on questions like: What services need to be provided by the central or local government? What is left in the hands of private entities social organizations, nongovernmental organizations (NGOs), etc.? What private-sector activities need to be regulated? What amount of resources needs to be collected in order to finance the provision? How will these resources be collected (taxes, duties, consumer prices)? What quantity and quality standard should be applied to the provision? How will services that have been agreed upon be produced and by whom?

The more centralized a regime is, the more these provision decisions are made exclusively by central-government agency officials without the participation of the local governments of the territories where the services are to be produced, and less with the participation of the potential beneficiaries of those services. Decentralization reforms can, however, alter the composition of provision units by offering the opportunity to municipalities and representatives of grassroot organizations to participate in the decision-making processes regarding the provision of services.

The same distinction can be made between production units and coproduction. Production units are developed by those officials in charge of public-service implementation. These can be the same individuals who participate in the provision unit, should they decide it is convenient to unilaterally produce public services on their own. If not, they may decide it makes more sense to outsource these services to an independent contractor. A production unit can include agricultural-extension government agency staff, municipal technicians, independent consultants, and producer organizations, among others. If the production unit includes the end users, it becomes a coproduction unit. In a well-developed public economy, production units are organized in such a way as to capture economies of scale and thus increase service efficiency. Production organization is also best when it creates a division of tasks that closely matches the specific expertise of each producer (Oakerson 1999).

The degree of public-economy decentralization determines who has the authority to define the organization of the provision and production units. For instance, in a completely decentralized public economy, local governments decide how to set up the provision and production units. As per the proponents of decentralization reforms, such restitution of responsibilities to local governments can foster an improvement in public administration through the democratization of local governments (Crook and Manor 1998; Ribot 2002); greater popular participation in decision-making processes related to the provision of public goods and services (Tocqueville 1840 [2003]; Chambers 1994; Blair 2000; Fiszbein 1997); and the promotion of institutions involved in the coproduction of public services (Ostrom 1996a; Oakerson 1999). However, these same authors acknowledge the existence of several obstacles preventing the successful attainment of this transformation. Next, we examine some of these obstacles more closely.

Collective Dilemmas in Decentralized Governance

Institutions for coprovision and coproduction are the result of numerous and repeated interactions between a variety of actors involved in the municipal decision making, such as farmers, municipal staff, local politicians, and private agricultural-extension agents, as well as central-government staff and officials. All of these actors have their own interests related to the public services to be delivered, their own sources of information, and their own level of political and economic clout. An effective coprovision and coproduction of public services requires these actors to overcome the temptation to satisfy only their own particular interests, and instead, work toward outcomes that will benefit the collective group the most. In this sense, the challenge of creating effective public services has to do with the negotiation, agreement, and enforcement of specific collective-action agreements among the different actors involved in the provision and production of collective goods and services. That is what decentralized public administration is all about. For the effective creation and implementation of each agricultural service, we argue that the institutions that encourage collective action play a decisive role.[2] The decentralized governance of agricultural services requires numerous instances of collective action that quite frequently pose difficulties for the participants, hindering their cooperation efforts. We categorize these difficulties into three types of collective action problems: motivational dilemmas, information problems, and power asymmetries.

Motivational Dilemmas

Let us assume that officials in a given municipality have been vested with the mandate (either from their constituency or central government) to provide certain public services. Notwithstanding their official commitment to their principal, the officials will face the temptation to ignore or shirk on this commitment, especially under imperfect monitoring. When the resources of a municipal administration are scarce, and the personal well-being of the local officials is not directly related to the existence of these agricultural services, the temptation to neglect their official commitments becomes particularly strong (Gibson, Andersson et al. 2005). For some municipal governments, the demands for public services in areas of education, health, and water supply—voiced by both the local population and the central government—are so pressing that an agricultural-extension service might be considered by some administrators as a secondary priority or even as a luxury on which they cannot justify spending scarce resources (Andersson 2003).

Another element working against the local politicians' motivation to provide municipal agricultural services is the political weakness of the primary beneficiaries of agricultural services: the small-scale producers. From a political survival perspective, a rational mayor invests municipal resources so as to be re-elected and to obtain economic returns. Therefore, he or she responds to the needs of those groups that are in a position to return the favor in the manner of electoral votes or economic benefits. It follows, then, that community-based organizations can expect to be served by their respective municipal governments only if they become a critical electoral mass or if they are able to create an economic stake for the municipal executives. It is not always evident when municipal executives would be sufficiently motivated to invest in the provision and production of public services in the agricultural sector. Consequently, how to motivate actors involved in the municipal-governance system becomes a key issue when analyzing those elements that empower the success of agricultural municipal governance.

Prior research has found that the existence of a legal mandate is no guarantee of its effective implementation, especially if the mandate is not linked to the presence of several institutional incentives (Andersson et al. 2004; Andersson and van Laerhoven 2007; Andersson 2003; Gibson and Lehoucq 2003). These studies suggest that municipal action is motivated by the relative force of (1) effective central-government monitoring of municipal commitments (Pacheco 2000; Andersson 2003), (2) the potential for financial gain (Pacheco and Kaimowitz 1998; Kaimowitz, Flores, et al. 2000; Gibson and Lehoucq 2003), and (3) the demands from an organized electorate (Ribot 1999a; Blair 2000). These three potential sources of motivation represent positive incentives for the municipal provision of agricultural services.[3]

Since these incentives emerge from the relationship between the municipal administration and the different actors involved in the local governance, actors' awareness of such incentives is more likely when local actors interact more frequently. Our study suggests that the creation of agricultural coprovision institutions is one way to enhance the motivation of local politicians to invest in public services for rural development. However, the creation of these same coprovision institutions is far from an automatic process. It is in itself a collective-action dilemma since it requires the willingness of all the actors to invest time and effort to negotiate and enforce the terms of the provision process. What may appear as a straightforward public administration procedure is actually a fairly complex collective decision process (See also Geddes 1994; Grindle 2000).

Even though motivation could be a decisive factor in successful decentralized governance, this does not mean that motivation will be a sufficient condition to guarantee success. A public administration that is motivated to provide a service still faces the challenge of organizing itself in ways that allow it to perform its tasks in an effective and efficient manner. This organization process is complicated by information problems and power asymmetries.

Information Problems

Several decentralization policy analysts argue that the capacity of local actors to exchange essential information is one of the factors with the greatest impact on the outcome of the reforms themselves (Ostrom, Schroeder, and Wynne 1993; Fiszbein 1997; Blair 2000; Andersson 2004). Without communication mechanisms, the actors involved in municipal governance will not have sufficient information to tailor public goods and services to the specific needs and preferences of the citizens of a given area, and to the characteristics of its resources. In addition, an asymmetric distribution of information about government activities and decisions frustrates the efforts made by the citizens to enforce accountability upon their political representatives. Here we propose that an effective exchange of information is essential for (1) the operation of accountability mechanisms (Agrawal and Ostrom 2001; Ribot 1999a, 2002); (2) the adaptation of political interventions to the local conditions and needs (O'Riordan 2001; Light et al. 2002; Hayek 1948); and (3) the coordination and exchange of learning experiences with other actors (Litvack et al. 1998; Lee 1993; Johnson 1999).

If actors involved in municipal governance meet frequently in coprovision forums or through coproduction arrangements, opportunities to communicate their intentions, target their commitments to the common good, and exchange information essential for municipal-governance performance are much greater. Even though the presence of coprovision and coproduction institutions does not ensure that the exchange of information will produce high-quality public services, we suggest that, all other things being equal, it will increase the probability of a successful public administration.

Power Asymmetries

The distribution of the political and economic power is another key factor influencing the municipal organization, particularly those decisions related to the provision of agricultural services. If an elite group is in control of the political and economic scene at the municipal level, it is highly unlikely that the members of such a group will allow the incorporation of outsiders into the public administration's decision-making processes. Even in the presence of participatory planning forums involving a diversity of actors, these power asymmetries limit the true weight that representatives of groups outside the local elite can exert. The creation of coprovision and coproduction institutions is not enough, in itself, to solve such asymmetries, but those municipalities that have them are better equipped to mitigate their negative effects.

Several studies have suggested that the authority of these local elites may actually be strengthened by a decentralization process, since the decentralized context usually lacks institutions capable of making them fulfill their obligations toward citizens (Crook and Manor 1998; Kaimowitz et al. 2000; Smoke 2003). The possible ascendancy of these elites over the municipal administration has significant repercussions on rural development, since local elites tend to favor municipal investments in the urban environment where they normally reside. An unorganized rural population that does not represent a critical electoral mass has very limited means of trying to redistribute the existing political power (Gordillo and Andersson 2004). Nonetheless, the political power of small-scale farmers and indigenous organizations is increasing in the region. For instance, in Brazil, Bolivia, and Ecuador, rural peasants have gained a significant political space thanks to the organizational improvements implemented by their community-based organizations and, particularly, to their relationships with producer associations at regional, national, and even international levels (Bebbington and Carroll 2000; Birk 2000; Urioste and Pacheco 2001).

The success of the decentralized-governance approach is not guaranteed by the mere presence of coprovision and coproduction institutions. Their presence means only that the conditions will be more suitable for dealing with social dilemmas. Coprovision and coproduction institutions represent necessary but insufficient factors to remedy the governmental flaws produced by the information gap commonly present between public administration and civil society. These institutions may also help to compensate for some capacity flaws of the government by creating strategic alliances with actors with greater technical capacity and by opening the door to the hiring of specialists for the production of public services. Finally, the institutions for coprovision and coproduction may also mitigate the appearance of *perverse incentives* in the public administration (such as corruption and clientelistic relationships, etc.) thanks to ongoing social supervision and control of public expenditures, hence improving both transparency and accountability.

The underlying causes for collective-action dilemmas will never vanish completely; they will continue to put institutions for collective action to the test, creating great challenges for coprovision and coproduction. Several empirical studies on social dilemmas in public administration have shown that there are neither perfect nor permanent solutions to these dilemmas (Miller 1992; Singleton 1998; Ostrom et al. 2002). Gary Miller (1992:198, 232) points out that "there is no way to transform an organization of diverse individuals into a machine. . . . Individuals in hierarchic structures are inevitably in situations in which their individual interests are in clear conflict with the efficiency of the organization."[4]

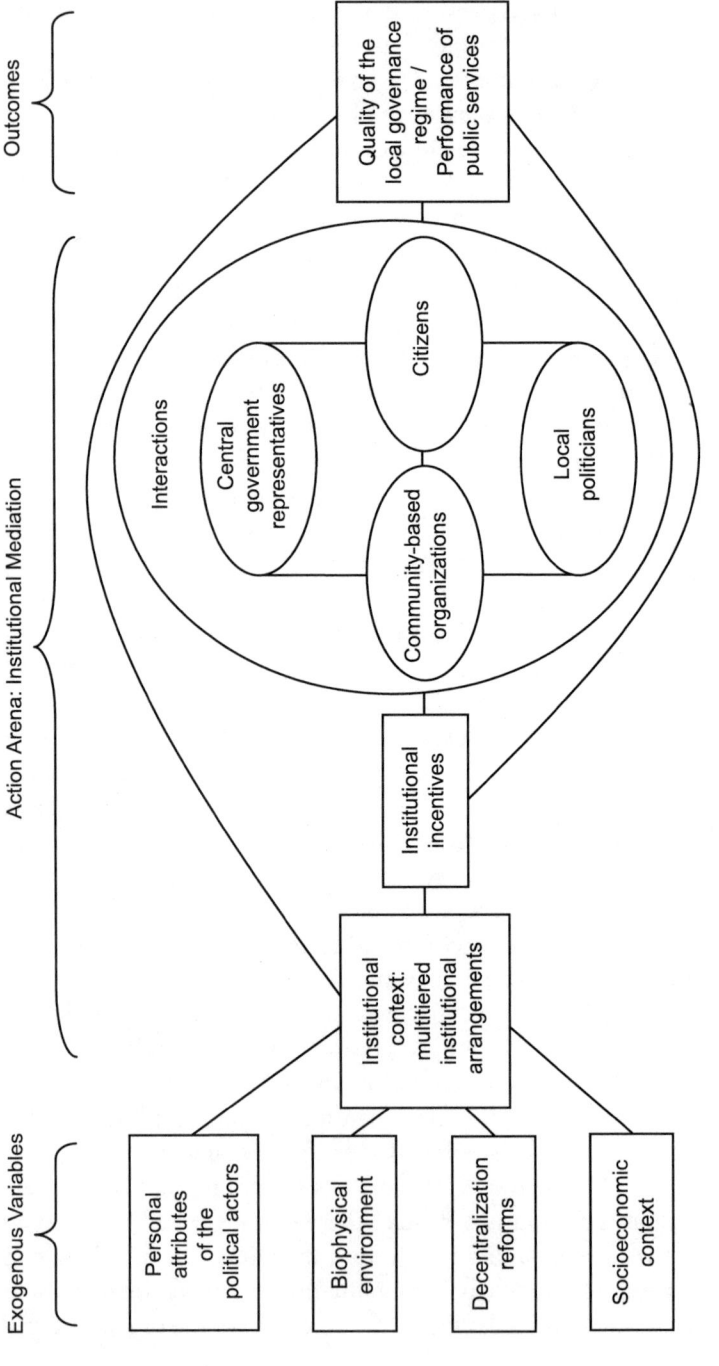

Figure 1.1 An adaptation of the Institutional Analysis and Development (IAD) framework (adapted from Ostrom 2005).

We argue that local politicians play a crucial role in determining the outcomes of decentralized-governance activities. Because it is to the local politicians that power and resources are being devolved to through the reforms, they constitute the "linchpins" of the decentralized regime. Because local politicians worry about staying in power, they are unlikely to follow blindly what the central government asks them to do and will perform only those tasks that are congruent with their interests. Our approach recognizes that citizens may or may not demand inclusion in the political decision-making process, central governments may or may not encourage participation, and local governments may or may not pay attention to these signals. Understanding these parallel and partially intertwined incentive structures then becomes crucial for disentangling the relationship between decentralization reforms, local contexts, institutions, and local-governance outcomes.

One of the advantages of the institutional approach that we use in this book is that it is based on an explicit theoretical framework—the Institutional Analysis and Development (IAD) framework (see fig. 1.1)—which helps the researcher structure the context-specific analysis of institutions and the incentives they generate (for reviews, see Ostrom 2005; Gibson, Andersson et al. 2005). In this analytical approach, we emphasize a contextually grounded analysis of incentives—the idea that incentives emerge within human interactions that take place in particular biophysical, socioeconomic, and institutional contexts. In other words, the effects of decentralization reforms are affected by a filter of institutional mediation.

We view the decisions of local politicians as shaped by both national- and local-level institutions, as illustrated by figure 1.1. The local politicians' incentive structures are composed of the perceived rewards and penalties from political as well as financial arenas. These incentives emerge from the patterns of interactions between local politicians and a variety of actors, such as resource users, central-government representatives, and private-interest groups who operate under varying contextual conditions. We propose that the characteristics of these interactions in the local context will in part depend on national-level institutions, such as the particular mandate given to local governments and their experience in governing in a particular policy domain, such as agricultural-extension or rural-development programs. Following this logic, local politicians will invest their time and resources into public services when they perceive the potential for political and/or financial rewards from doing so. Investing in a municipal rural-development service program may, for example, enhance or constrain their official powers, their municipality's revenues, or their electoral chances.

We further hypothesize that local politicians are more likely to express interest in public services related to agriculture and rural development if they are granted more fiscal and regulatory powers by the central government. Local politicians are always searching for increases in revenues, and having more authority will improve their opportunities for raising such revenue.

In a nutshell, our arguments boil down to a central hypothesis about what factors best explain the observed variation in governance performance within the decentralized regimes in Latin America. The core hypothesis is that the performance of public services—with regard to their effectiveness in alleviating poverty, halting environmental degradation, and promoting agricultural development—is associated with the institutional arrangements for coprovision and coproduction at the municipal level. More specifically, we expect to see more participatory institutions for decision making related to provision and production of services in those municipal-governance systems where the local politicians have strong electoral and economic incentives to share their power and resources with local farmers. We also expect to see more effective service provision in municipalities that have strong institutions for coprovision and coproduction. Our empirical analysis puts these arguments about the determinants of successful municipal governance to the test and proposes that the quality of public services mirrors the efficiency of municipal institutions in solving issues of motivation, information, and power asymmetries. These three elements—motivation, information, and power—thus emerge as necessary requirements for the local government to move in a certain direction regarding the public expenditure. In which direction and how far local government can move (its maneuverability margin) depend on the decentralization system itself. Because our analysis compares local governments in four countries that have varying degrees of decentralization of the governance over public services related to rural development, our results speak to the continuing debate about the effects of decentralization policies on governance outcomes.

We would like to stress that an endeavor like this, by definition, must deal with the inherent tension between the search for general tendencies and the recognition of the importance of time-and-place particularities and the fact that "context matters." Clean, theoretical models tend to focus on the first, while the "messy" reality that we encounter in "the field" reminds us of the latter. Our field experience has taught us to be cautious when it comes to formulating water-tight theoretical models that seek to explain and make predictions about the kind of situations we describe. Hence, in the individual-country chapters that follow, we will try to strike a balance between not overgeneralizing our theoretical claims on the one hand, and still being able to engage in a comparative analysis, on the other.

Main Findings

The 1,210 people interviewed represent the great diversity that characterizes the decentralization processes in the agricultural sectors of Brazil, Chile, Mexico, and Peru. In Brazil, for instance, all southern municipalities have their own agricultural technical units, and more than 80 percent of them organize consensus-building forums where different actors participate in the provision of agricultural services in the municipal territory. Conversely, only 5 percent of the Peruvian municipalities have an agricultural technical unit. Almost all the mayors in Chile, Mexico, and Brazil state that they have seen evidence of the recent decentralization reforms in the agricultural sector, while only 10 percent of their Peruvian counterparts state the same.

One of the main concerns of the technical and financial organizations that support the empowerment of municipal governments in Latin America is the limited municipal technical capacity in the agricultural sector. The interviews confirm, to a certain extent, this overall technical weakness, but at the same time show that the availability of qualified agricultural staff at the municipal level is quite varied between and within countries. Our analysis shows that Chile is the only country in which most municipalities have a professional agronomist. The variation in the number of professionals that work for the municipalities in these countries raises the question as to why a mayor or municipal chairman would decide to invest scarce resources to pay an agronomist. This is the first question that we strive to answer in this book.

The results of interviews with community-based organization representatives show that most of them are not too satisfied with the quality of locally available agricultural services: in Brazil, the country where community-based organizations rated the performance of the services higher, less than half of them considered that said quality was up to par. In Chile, Mexico, and Peru, only 40 percent, 22 percent, and 4 percent, respectively, of the community-based organizations considered that the locally available agricultural services were good-quality services. This observation gives rise to the second fundamental question raised in this book: Why is the level of performance in some municipalities much higher than in others? The study shows that the answer to both questions has to do with the specific organizational characteristics of the cluster of actors involved in the municipal-governance system. Municipalities with institutions that are capable of dealing with the three social collective-action dilemmas are better positioned to deliver high-quality agricultural public services.

In summary, the study suggests that the creation of coprovision and coproduction institutions can go a long way toward improving the conditions for governance performance of rural-development services. One of the main lessons from this book is that municipal governments that are endowed with increased levels of autonomy are, potentially, important players in the local-policy arena for the provision and production of public policies that would foster rural development and poverty alleviation. However, their potential to positively contribute to local-governance outcomes is importantly shaped by the nature of local institutional arrangements. In general, participation helps the cause of good governance; but the creation of institutions promoting the inclusion of participatory publics in local-governance arrangements represents a complicated collective-action problem in itself. By paying attention to the incentive structures of local politicians, one can begin to appreciate under which conditions local politicians will be more likely to pursue more participatory forms of governance. Such knowledge will be an important element in any effort—decentralized or not—that aims at improving the effectiveness of rural-development policies.

The Structure of the Book

The book is divided into three parts. The first part consists of the first three chapters. After this introductory chapter, we outline the research design of the study. Chapter 3 provides essential background information on the role of municipal governments when it comes to agricultural-related services in the four countries. The second part of the book contains four chapters—each one presenting the case studies of Brazil, Chile,

Mexico, and Peru. These chapters offer an in-depth analysis of the role of local institutions as a determinant municipal performance. In the third part, two chapters scale up the analysis to the regional level by carrying out comparative analyses of the municipal governance of agricultural services in the four countries. Finally, in the tenth chapter, we conclude by summarizing our findings, outlining a series of implications for public policies on rural development, and identifying key topics for future research.

2
Framing the Comparative Study of Decentralization in Latin America

The first chapter raised a challenging question for individuals interested in public policies that support rural development efforts in Latin America: Under which conditions are local governments likely to contribute to an effective delivery of public services for the rural poor? In this chapter, we describe our strategy for analyzing that question empirically. We lay out our study's main design features—including our logic for choosing the four countries included in the study, and the reasons for using local-government arenas as our main units of analysis. Here, we also describe our methods for gathering data in the field as well as the methods used for analyzing that data in subsequent empirical chapters.

The Research Design

This book uses comparative analysis to learn about the ways in which national policies and local institutional arrangements affect local-government involvement in public services for rural populations. The comparative method relies on the establishment of natural experiments in which researchers carefully select and compare cases that represent stark contrasts regarding a series of predefined characteristics of interest. In our study, we are interested in explaining varying outcomes when it comes to the performance of rural-development programs in Latin America, and the extent to which the degrees of decentralization and local-governance arrangements may help explain such variation. With this analytical goal in mind, we selected four contrasting cases for our comparative analysis. Such purposeful selection helps us to test the potential influence that decentralization might have on rural-development outcomes. Such an analysis would be very difficult, if not impossible, if we were to study four randomly (rather than purposefully) selected cases (Diamond 2004; King, Keohane, and Verba 1994).

More specifically, our comparative research approach seeks to answer questions about the causes and consequences of local-government involvement in public services related to rural development. There are two types of causes that we are particularly interested in analyzing: the influence of (1) national-level decentralization policies and (2) local-governance arrangements on the performance of public services related to rural development. In this section, we briefly lay out our strategy for analyzing these processes.

National decentralization policies denote the degree to which central governments assign rights, resources, and responsibilities to local governments in the realm of rural development and agriculture. Using comparative analysis to explain the influence of decentralization on the performance of rural development–related public services requires a careful selection of the cases to be compared. We applied two selection criteria to this procedure. According to our first criterion, the cases included in the sample should be as *different as possible* regarding the degrees of decentralization. That meant seeking out countries that ranged from "highly decentralized" to "very centralized" regarding their rural development policies. However, to avoid the risk of selecting a set of countries that are not only different when it comes to the degree of decentralization but also regarding other factors that may simultaneously affect the observed outcomes, we applied a second selection criterion. According to this second criterion, the set of countries to be included in the sample should also be *as similar as possible* when it comes to nondecentralization factors that may also influence the outcomes of interest. Such factors include the relative importance of agricultural production for the country's economy, the importance of smallholder agriculture as the main source of livelihood for the majority of the rural population, government recognition of the existence of rural poverty, and the existence of government programs that target the agricultural production of the rural poor.

After careful study of these criteria in all Latin American countries, we chose four countries that satisfy both: Brazil, Chile, Mexico, and Peru. These countries may be placed along a continuum of decentralization, where Brazil is located at one extreme representing a federal nation with a high degree of decentralization. At the other extreme of this continuum we find Peru. At the time of our fieldwork for this study (January–April 2002) Peru had a heavily centralized governance structure and had not carried out any decentralization reforms in any sectors. Chile and Mexico are situated in the middle of this continuum, in between the two extremes. As far as these countries' similarities go, we found that smallholder agriculture is a predominant feature in all four countries. In Brazil, 85.2 percent of all farms belong to smallholder farmers (INCRA/SADE 2000). In Mexico, according to the Agricultural Sector Plan, 54 percent of all farms are smaller than five hectares, and 30 percent are smaller than two hectares (SAGARPA 2001). In Chile, there are 270,000 *campesino* smallholder farms, accounting for 31 percent of total arable land in the country (INDAP 2005). Finally, in Peru there are about one million farms that measure less than two hectares, representing 58 percent of the total number of farms in that country (Nagayets 2005).

The second set of causal variables that we are interested in are related to the potential influence of local-governance arrangements (formal and informal) at the municipal level on the effectiveness of public services offered to rural populations. Our strategy for analyzing the effect of this variable is to make use of the variation between different institutional arrangements for rural development activities at the municipal level within each country. Because we had no previous, systematic knowledge of what these institutional arrangements looked like in all municipalities of the four countries, we faced the challenge of choosing an appropriate sample for the comparative analysis. To make sure we collected data that had sufficiently large variation regarding the institutional arrangements for public-service provision, we randomly selected a large number of municipal governments in each of the four countries. Moreover, to increase the comparability of the local contexts in the sample, we decided to limit our sample to small rural municipalities, as these exhibit similar contextual traits across all four countries. We started our selection procedure by randomly sampling from a pool of municipalities in each country that fulfilled two criteria: (1) a total population of less than 20,000 in the latest available census and (2) more than 50 percent of the total population living outside the municipal capital. From this pool we selected a statistically representative number of rural municipalities in each country, ending up with a total sample size of 390 local-government territories distributed across the four countries (one hundred in Brazil, forty in Chile, 150 in Mexico, and one hundred in Peru).[1]

We believe this careful selection of countries and type of local governments increases the comparability of the empirical observations. This framing of our comparative analysis enables us to conduct more robust empirical tests of the potential effects of national policies and local institutions on rural development outcomes across countries and municipalities.

Fieldwork

Our research teams conducted fieldwork in a total of 390 municipal governments. The fieldwork started in late 2001 in Mexico and concluded in northeastern Brazil two years and 1,210 interviews later. In each municipality, the teams, which were sponsored by the Food and Agriculture Organization (FAO) of the United Nations, conducted a face-to-face interview with the municipal-government mayor using a semistructured survey that solicited the mayor's perceptions regarding relationships with farmers, citizens at large, central-government organizations and individuals, as well as nongovernmental, community-based organizations (CBOs).[2]

In every municipality visited, the teams also interviewed representatives from two different community-based organizations whose principal activities are related to small-scale agriculture.[3] To the extent possible, the field teams identified these organizations through conversations with local people affiliated with nonpartisan organizations that were involved in rural development work of some sort. In Chile and Peru, members of irrigation associations were good sources of such information and, in Mexico, representatives of the Catholic Church helped the field teams to identify appropriate CBOs for interviews. Conducting these in-depth interviews with three different individuals in all municipalities—each individual reflecting a unique and independent perspective on existing local-governance arrangements, public policies, and the needs of the rural poor in the area—enables us to use triangulation of responses to enhance the reliability of our field observations. Each interview took approximately two hours to complete.

Measurement Issues

Our analysis of the causes and consequences of local-government involvement in rural development relies on two principal sources of data. Our measures of local institutional arrangements for the provision and production of rural development services come from the recorded responses from the three interviewed local-governance actors described in the previous section. We also use interview responses to measure other contextual factors that are known to influence rural development outcomes, such as the mayor's level of education, the share of municipal employees that have a professional degree in agriculture, the mayor's perception of constituent demands, and the number of CBOs that carry out rural-development activities in the municipal territory. In each individual chapter's empirical analysis we provide a detailed account of how we measure each of the variables of interest. There is, however, one set of measurements that is particularly challenging to deal with: appropriate measures for outcome variables. This topic merits a discussion of its own.

One of the most difficult tasks facing public-policy scholars is to create and use appropriate outcome measures when conducting empirical analyses. For any given policy, it is rare that there is a readily identifiable outcome variable that completely captures the effectiveness of that policy (Martin and Sanderson 1999; McGlynn 1997; Weimer and Vining 2004). Because of this constraint, researchers rely on *proxy measures* of policy outcomes. Such measures are imperfect indicators of the outcome that the researchers are really interested in, but this imperfection may be partially overcome by selecting a set of different proxy measures that capture *complementary* aspects of the policy outcome of interest.

In our study of decentralized rural development policy in Latin America, the outcomes we are interested in are related to the role, responsiveness, and overall capacity of the local-government authority in the area of rural development. Since we do not have any readily available indicators that measure these outcomes directly, we employ a set of indirect proxy measures of such outcomes.

Our main outcome variable is a proxy measure for the *quality of services* related to rural development. We calculate this measure by considering the interview responses by community-based organization (CBO) representatives. In our interviews with these representatives in each municipality, we asked them to rate the quality of available public services related to small-scale agricultural production in their locality using a five-point Likert scale.

As with all proxy measures, relying on user ratings obtained through interviews is a strategy that has both advantages and disadvantages. One advantage is that user ratings are comparable outcome measures across all local-government territories because they are based on the opinions of the primary intended users of the public services (the farmers). If the farmers are not satisfied, it seems reasonable to assume that these services are not performing as they should. In addition, by combining the independent assessments of service quality made by the different CBO representatives in each municipality we increase the validity of this outcome measure. On the negative side, if a CBO does not have access to the actual service (or that service simply has no relevance for the CBO), the CBO representatives are not likely to have reliable information about that service's quality. Because of this limitation, we employ several complementary outcome measures. These capture other aspects of the role, responsiveness, and capacity of local governments in rural development activities—such as the number of local-government staff involved in delivering public services related to rural development and agriculture, the extent to which CBOs and local-government staff coproduce public services, and the degree to which the local government responds to CBO requests for intervention. Precisely because we are looking at a variety of outcome measures that reflect different aspects of the conditions for rural development—not just one measure of outcomes—we can be more confident in the validity of our analysis.

Analytical Methods

Our empirical analysis of the relationships between different local-governance arrangements and rural development outcomes makes use of a combination of qualitative and quantitative methods. We rely on qualitative observations primarily to describe the types of public services that central- and local-government actors offer to rural populations. In each of the country case-study chapters (chapters 4 through 7), we draw on fieldwork observations to describe concrete rural-development experiences, focusing in particular on the involvement of local governments in the delivery of public services for the rural poor. These qualitative observations provide the reader with examples of both successes and failures of local-government involvement in public services for rural development. Moreover, our empirical work provides illustrations of the types of public services that are offered within particular local contexts in each country and how the human institutions shape the opportunities for constructive interactions between representatives from local governments and community-based organizations, as well as other local-governance actors concerned with rural development. As such, the qualitative analysis generates several hypotheses about what specific contextual variables may be contributing to the observed success or failure of local-government involvement in rural-development activities.

As useful as this qualitative analysis is, however, it will take us only so far. When it comes to testing the extent to which our hypotheses help us explain the conditions under which local governments are effective facilitators of rural development more generally, we need a different set of analytical methods. We therefore choose to complement the qualitative analysis with quantitative, statistical analysis.

In each of the empirical chapters, we use multiple regression techniques to test the effect of our main explanatory variables. One of the advantages of multivariate statistical techniques is that they allow the researcher to control for other variables that may also influence the variation in outcomes. Hence, multiple regression methods help the researcher to isolate the effect of particular variables of interest. By combining the two analytical approaches, we believe we are able to offset some of the imperfections inherent in both approaches.

Conclusion

This chapter frames the empirical study of decentralization, local governance, and rural development. We argue that the reliability and validity of our analytical results in subsequent chapters are intrinsically linked to our initial decisions regarding the research design, the scope and methods of fieldwork, and types of measures and analytical methods. One might argue that some of the most important decisions that end up determining much of the quality of the final analytical results are made long before the data analysis stage, and even before data collection begins.

We utilize a comparative-research design that exploits the variation in local-governance conditions both within and across national-policy regimes. Our unit of analysis is the local-governance system, and we study a random sample of 390 local-government territories in four different national regimes with varying degrees of decentralization: one highly decentralized, one highly centralized, and two semidecentralized.

We collected comparable observations for all 390 municipal territories through personal, in-depth interviews for a wide array of variables related to the governance of rural-development activities and their observed outcomes. This data allows us to use rigorous analytical methods —both quantitative and qualitative—to test the hypotheses about the effects of decentralization and local-governance arrangements—as laid out in the first chapter—and interpret the results of those tests more broadly.

It is our hope that by framing the study in this way, we will be in a better position to contribute to a deeper understanding of the conditions under which decentralization may help to produce more effective programs and public services for the rural poor. The next chapter is the first in a series of chapters that engages in empirical analysis of these conditions.

3
The Role of Local Governments in Rural Development in Brazil, Chile, Mexico, and Peru

One of the main issues that we are interested in is the influence of decentralization on local efforts to address rural-development problems. We believe a word of caution is warranted here: the purpose of our comparative analysis is *not* to identify a "recipe" for the best decentralization policy. We acknowledge that there is no such thing as a "best policy," or at least that we would not be able to identify it through a comparison of this nature. The same policy may be a success in one national context, but a complete failure in the country right next door. That said, we do believe that the diversity of experiences in the governance of public services for rural development in Latin America lends itself very well to a comparative analysis. As discussed at length in chapter 2, the existence of differences in formal governance structures is the main reason we chose to compare these particular countries. Such a comparison has the potential to increase our understanding of the conditions under which decentralization can have a positive impact on the performance of rural public services at the local level. In this chapter, we provide a detailed description of the formal governmental mandates to local governments in the area of rural development.

Historically, the roles of local governments have been defined quite differently in the countries of Brazil, Chile, Mexico, and Peru. These differences are apparent when studying the nature of public decision making related to the allocation of public funds for rural development in the four countries.

For example, while Mexico and Brazil are both federal systems, their governance structures for rural-development services are quite different. During the past 10 to 15 years, Brazil has experimented a great deal with channeling public funds earmarked to rural development through municipal-based participatory councils. Mexico, on the other hand, only recently started to implement a more decentralized governance structure for programs targeting the decentralized rural development. In Chile, a unitary political system, the allocation of public funds for rural development is partly arranged through market instruments, such as competitive technical-assistance funds to which farmers may apply. Although private operators play an important role, funding is primarily decided upon by the central government. At the time of our fieldwork in 2001 and 2002, Peru was the country with the most centralized decision-making structure regarding public service provision and production related to rural development. Shortly after we finished the data collection for this study, however, a series of decentralization reforms were also introduced formally in Peru.

The chapter is organized into five sections. The first four lay out the role of local governments in public services for the rural poor in Brazil, Chile, Mexico, and Peru, and the last section, the conclusion, compares these formal mandates and roles. We begin with the country that vests most authority in its local governments in the area of rural development and agriculture: Brazil.

Brazil

Brazil is a federal republic with a presidential system. It is administratively divided into twenty-six states and one federal district and almost 5,500 municipalities throughout the country. The municipalities are vested with the power to legislate (Article 30) on matters of local interest; complement the federal and state legislation; establish and collect taxes under their jurisdiction; organize and provide local-interest services; and develop with the technical and financial cooperation of the federation and the state preschool and elementary-education programs, as well as healthcare services.

Its formal mandate in matters of rural development and agricultural promotion does not allow municipalities much room to maneuver. Most services and programs deemed relevant for rural development fall under federal jurisdiction. Only a limited few fall under the jurisdiction of state governments

The municipalities of Brazil—even though their formal mandate in the area of agricultural promotion and rural development is somewhat limited—play a significant role in the decision-making processes related to the use of public resources. A large quantity of public funds is channeled through several Municipal Councils (for health, education, social outreach, children and teenagers, rural development) where all stakeholders can participate. Brazil has an average of five councils per municipality. Municipal Councils for Rural Development (a structure with counterparts at both the federal and state levels) are citizen par-

Table 3.1
Comparison of local-government mandates in rural development

Attributes	Brazil	Chile	Mexico	Peru
Separate mayoral elections	Yes	No	No	No
Election rule executive power (mayor)	Simple plurality vote	Closed list system. Winning party provides mayor.	Closed list system. Winning party provides mayor.	Closed list system. Winning party provides mayor.
Election rule legislative power (council)	Closed list system, proportional rep.	Closed list system, proportional rep.	Closed list system, proportional rep.	Closed list system. Winning party gets 51% of seats.
Length of term	4 years	4 years	3 years	5 years
Possibility of re-election	Yes (since 2000)	Yes	No	Yes
Authority to levy taxes and service fees	Yes	Yes	Yes	Yes (but very small amounts)
Responsibility in health and education	Yes	Some deconcentrated tasks	No	No
Responsibility for infrastructure	Yes	Yes	Yes	Yes
Responsibility in natural resource management	Yes	No	Yes (since 2002)	No

Source: Authors' elaboration based on national governments' legal documents as well as Nickson 1995 and Zaz Friz Burga 2001.

ticipatory forums that allow the participation of all those community-based organizations with a stake in the matter. A consensus (reflected in a Municipal Work Plan) is reached annually within the council, and this becomes the foundation from which to establish municipal development priorities. Based on this agreed-upon Work Plan, the municipality applies for the funds available at the federal level, at state level, and with (international) donors and private foundations in order to finance a variety of projects.

Municipal Plans tend to have the characteristics of a "shopping list," often lacking internal coherence (IPARDES 2001). The consensus-building efforts among the different stakeholder groups frequently result in coordination problems. What is good for all groups is not necessarily good for any given individual group (Abramovay 2001).

Consequently, the previously described process imposes the obligation to promote the creation of Municipal Councils on the mayors, encourages community-based organizations to participate in such councils, and attempts to develop consensual Work Plans. Compliance with this obligation is reinforced by the fact that the only way to access significant external funds is by complying with the federal directive to organize Municipal Councils. In theory, this mechanism seems to generate positive incentives that could motivate the local-government intervention in rural development.

Through the Municipal Councils, issues of representation regarding budget allocation are theoretically solved in the decision-making process. Even though the municipal level may not be the optimum level for service provision and production in terms of economies of scale, the probability that community-based organizations will participate in monitoring their common interests is higher. One can expect to find that a decision-making process within an open council would improve the access to relevant information for all parties. In theory, it should be easier to create institutional arrangements to avoid information dilemmas. Of course, there is always the risk that power struggles within the municipality are also fought out in the Municipal Councils or that the decisions made by the councils will not be particularly favorable for already marginalized groups. However, the inclusion of groups that have been traditionally marginalized represents in itself a significant step forward in the fight to overcome historic political and economic power asymmetries. Table 3.1 summarizes the local-government mandates in rural development for Brazil as well as for the other three countries included in the study.

Chile

Currently, the Chilean national territory—in matters of administrative and governmental responsibilities—is divided into thirteen regions that in turn are divided into fifty-one provinces. For local administrative purposes, provinces are divided into 341 communes (*comunas*). Regional governments serve as an intermediate body of public administration. Their main responsibilities include regional-development planning, spatial planning, promoting productive activities, and social and cultural development. These responsibilities are quite broad, and most of them are shared with other public entities.

At the community level, municipal governments play a role in state administration. Municipalities are defined as public law corporations, vested with autonomy, legal status, and rights to raise their own funds for the purpose of promoting the economic, social, and cultural development of the locality, with the participation of the local community. The responsibilities of the municipalities are explicitly prescribed and defined and are shared—for the most part—with other public entities.

The municipalities have competence in matters related to sports and recreation, and are responsible for managing a segment of the sports infrastructure for popular use; in matters of social welfare, the municipalities can promote their own projects to support low-income sectors, also fulfilling a significant role in the allocation of monetary subsidies to families living in extreme poverty; in matters of housing, they fulfill executive roles in the Ministry of Interior's program known as "serviced lands." Finally, as shown in table 3.1, municipal authorities share responsibilities with the central governments in matters of education and health, and they are in charge of the front-line management of school facilities and primary healthcare centers with funding provided by the central government (Espinoza and Marcel 1993).

Community participation is institutionalized in the Communal Economic and Social Council, "El Consejo Económico y Social Comunal" (CESCO), presided by the mayor and constituted by representatives of the major citizen, business, and labor organizations of the commune. They are vested only with consultative powers: the mayor's sole obligation is to submit the budget and the development plan to this council for comment and review.

In Chile, as in the other three countries of our study, the central government provides most public services related to rural development, and municipalities are devoid of a leadership role in both their design and in their implementation. These public services are produced through a diverse mixture of state interventions and market mechanisms. These attempts to match demand for services with public-resource allocations are made by having beneficiaries apply for so-called competitive funds. Consequently, the Chilean public policy, in this context, is characterized by an almost direct correlation between service and beneficiary.

The following is a summary related to the Chilean local-government mandate in the agricultural sector:

- The local government does not seem particularly motivated to become actively involved in the deployment of rural public services. On the other hand, information exchange is substantial. Beneficiaries have to provide the information needed to comply with the competitive funds' requirements.
- Organization of stakeholder groups is not an issue. Stakeholder groups do not have to engage in a consensus-building effort in order to access public resources. Producers, independently or in an organized effort, can deal directly with providers.
- Access to public resources depends on the outcome of bilateral and front-line negotiations between beneficiary and public service.

Mexico

The "new federalism" in Mexico is characterized by the full exercise of state sovereignty combined with municipal freedom. This concept implies the need to enhance the administrative and political power of local governments in order to achieve a true decision-making autonomy through the administration of municipalities' own resources and the effective application of measures needed to satisfy the population's demands. At community level, this principle takes shape in Article 115 of the Constitution, which vests the municipality with political powers, and not just with the administrative powers that all states have. *Ramos* (budget lines) 26 and 33 of the national budget—pertaining to the federal contributions to municipal and federative entities—are specifically designed to embody this concept.

In reality, however, all of these formal manifestations in matters of rural development, support of agricultural activities, and the fight against hunger and poverty do not seem to have endowed municipal governments with a major role in these areas. There are, however, remarkable differences among states. Even though municipal responsibilities include those related to the environment, the agricultural sector, and social welfare, most social investment for rural development stems directly from the federal level, without the local level participating either in the design or in the implementation of policies.

As for public services targeting productive development, the Secretariat of Agriculture, Livestock, Rural Development, Fisheries, and Food (SAGARPA) has transferred nearly 80 percent of its responsibilities and most of its financial resources to state governments and producers. The mechanism used in this process is the "Coordination Agreement" between SAGARPA and the executive of each federative entity. The resource amount to be contributed annually by each party is precisely detailed and established. All resources are allocated through a state trust fund. As part of these Coordination Agreements, the state executive is bound to organize and participate in an "Agricultural State Council." This council is chaired by the state executive and conformed by social and producer organizations in the agricultural sector. A representative of SAGARPA serves as the council's technical secretary. To complement the Agricultural State Council, a "Foundation for Technology Transfer" has been created in each federative entity.

These Coordination Agreements are connected to the main federal program for agricultural production and rural development, known as "Alianza para el Campo"—a program directly managed by the different states. "Alianza" accounts for more than 50 percent of public expenditures in rural areas. The budgetary resources of "Alianza para el Campo" are allocated through a trust plan that takes into consideration the priorities formulated by participants in the Agricultural State Councils (Mohar 1998).

As evidenced by this relatively large-sized program, the decisions related to the provision and production of public services related to "Alianza" are made at the state level. This generates a series of questions:

- Will this administrative figure motivate municipal governments to take action to promote the agricultural development at the municipal level? There is neither a formal mandate nor enough resources for the active participation of local governments. Consequently, one would not expect them to take a prominent role in promoting rural initiatives.
- Is the state level the most appropriate level for the creation of social

and producer organizations in the agricultural sector? Due to economies of scale and in order to create alternative channels for the delivery of services, the organization of stakeholder groups at the state level might be a legitimate proposal. However, the size of such groups could generate issues of representation that, at the same time, might hinder collective action among members.
- Is the state level the most favorable level for an optimum flow of information? Is the state the optimum level at which actors can exert pressure in favor of transparency and accountability?

Peru

At the time of our study, the administrative structure of Peru comprises twenty-four departments administrated by the Transitory Regional Administration Councils, "Consejos Transitorios de Administración Regional" (CTAR), 193 provinces plus the "Constitucional del Callao" province, and 1,828 districts (municipalities). Regional governments are responsible for coordinating and implementing regional socioeconomic plans and programs. They also perform the duties asked of them by the central government. The regions are also supposed to provide support to local governments. In the case of municipalities, their competencies are established as follows: (1) approve their internal organization and budget; (2) manage their assets and revenues; (3) create, modify, and lift levies, rates, tolls, municipal taxes and duties, and licenses; (4) organize, regulate, and administrate local public services under their jurisdiction; (5) plan the urban and rural development in their territory and implement related plans and programs; (6) participate in the development of activities and services inherent to the state; and (7) other matters determined by law (Casas 1997).

The Peruvian constitution of 1979 was a daring attempt to advance a decentralization policy by endowing regional entities with governmental responsibilities. Between 1988 and 1990, twelve regional democratically elected governments came to power. In 1992, however, the executive branch—in addition to dissolving the National Congress—also dissolved the regional governments and replaced them with Transitory Regional Administration Councils (CTAR) appointed at the central level and devoid of all decision-making powers and autonomy in the handling of resources. Since then, sectorial competencies reverted to the central ministries (Santa Cruz 1999).

In order to establish said competencies, the basic criterion applied was to separate, on the one hand, the normative and regulatory roles of the sector's major competency areas (agriculture, livestock, forestry, natural resource conservation, and agro industry) into a relatively small central nucleus in the Ministry of Agriculture, and to transfer the executive responsibilities related to research, health, and natural-resource management to entities known as Decentralized Public Agencies, "Organismos Públicos Descentralizados" (OPD), and so-called special projects for the delivery of services and achievement of specific goals.

In addition, Regional and Subregional Agrarian Departments were created as deconcentrated entities that assumed the roles and competencies of the Ministry of Agriculture at the regional level, promoting productive agricultural activities. The Agrarian Agencies and Centers are present at the local level (Santa Cruz 1999).

At the municipal level, the strong presence of the national administration competes with municipal governments and reduces their authority. Municipal governments lack the ability to play a strong intermediary role between citizens and central government, both due to a lack of resources and due to the impossibility of making decisions without the intervention of the national government. There have been, however, a few isolated experiences that demonstrate an effort to become effective local governments. In this context, the most remarkable experiences are the "Mesas de Concertación" (multistakeholder roundtables). These "Mesas" (which are civil-society initiatives) were created, often by nongovernmental organizations, to articulate the work of different state-level agencies and programs and NGOs with the demands of civil society (Nicod 1999).

In summary, in Peru,

- The local government is not particularly motivated to promote agriculture-related initiatives.
- The direct relationship between national services and their beneficiaries—without the intervention of local political actors—has an arguably negative impact on the flow of information.
- Of all the countries studied, Peru is the most centralist. Even though, at present, civil society seems to express a political will of its own reflected by promising initiatives, the administrative structure that defines agricultural policies still bears the stigma of its clientelistic past, a factor that usually works against marginalized groups.

Conclusions

During the last few decades, an assortment of decentralization policies has impacted the performance of the local-governance systems in the four countries. Reforms affecting fiscal policies altered the budgetary foundation of local governments. In addition, the amount of resources available at the municipal level was impacted by changes made to rules regarding the transfer of funds from the capital. Municipalities are also challenged by expanding or altering jurisdictions. The number of political arenas where local governments can or should intervene has changed. New mandates and tools determine the manner in which municipalities can function. At times, municipalities are vested with discretionary powers in matters related to the design of public policy or to the adaptation of existing policies to local conditions. Moreover, public services that were previously administered by their respective central-government ministries have opened local offices that can cooperate with the local government or, alternatively, operate on their own. Many public services —whose provision and/or production fall under the jurisdiction of the local government—are partially privatized or are challenged by the incorporation of market components. Also, different citizen participatory mechanisms, both formal and informal, have been created at the local level, producing great variations in the degree and manner of responsiveness of both local politicians and technical officials.

The new institutional scenario in which local actors find themselves after the implementation of decentralization policies in the four countries affords them different margins for political maneuvering. These new institutions have an impact on the degree of citizen motivation to search for solutions to the problems in their local political arena or, conversely, to raise their demands to other governmental levels or entities. The Chilean farmer can be expected to seek a solution to his or her problems through direct contact with the national government's agricultural agency (INDAP), while his or her Brazilian counterpart will turn to the Municipal Council to solve his or hers. Furthermore, these new institutions determine the extent to which local political actors feel motivated to assume responsibility for addressing certain issues. Chilean law provides that the mayor should create a Communal Economic and Social Council in his or her municipality to institutionalize citizen participation. This legal stipulation provides the Chilean mayor with a tool that his or her Peruvian counterpart is lacking. And last, said institutions, to a large extent, also determine the quality of public services, particularly through the emergence of institutions for the generation and dissemination of information. In Brazil, the legal framework imposes upon the mayor the obligation to create a Rural Development Council in his or her municipality. In Peru, the existence of those instances known as "Mesas de Concertación" (multistakeholder roundtables) is greatly dependent upon NGOs. Each country has a different administrative framework, a fact that will exert an impact on whether and how information is generated and disseminated. We expect that the presence of institutions of collective action will positively influence the performance level of the services produced therein. The greater the success of local actors in solving collective-action dilemmas, the better the performance of public services will be.

By way of comparison, Peru turns out to be the most centralized of our four cases regarding the provision and production of agricultural services. One would predict that this will have a negative impact on the motivation that both the citizens and the local political actors might have to tackle their problems in the local political arena. In Mexico, decisions related to budgetary and thematic planning in the agricultural sector are taken at the federal and state government levels. In Brazil, local governments—through the Municipal Councils—seem to allow both beneficiaries and local governments to exert greater influence on decisions related to the provision and production of agricultural services. Finally, the Chilean process for the provision and production of agricultural services, through certain market mechanisms such as competitive funds and the role of private consultants, seems to depend more upon the relation between the service in question and the individual producers, and not so much upon municipal actions. However, this does not mean that Chilean municipalities are devoid of a mandate to influence the sector.

The purpose of the set of studies presented here is to enhance our understanding of how the different decentralization policies currently under implementation are most likely to impact local-governance systems. To what extent will the new, more relevant role of local actors in the public policy decision-making processes provide them with new opportunities to promote rural development? Under what circumstances are they more likely to capitalize on these opportunities? Why do some local-governance systems perform well while others perform poorly? We will attempt to determine whether the differences observed among municipalities demonstrate any systematic patterns. We will put to the test several possible explanations for the level of motivation found among local political actors and the quality of the public services delivered and produced in the four countries.

This study's description of the local governments' mandates related to the agricultural sector provides the constitutional-level rules framework for local-government involvement in rural development activities in each national context. It portrays the context into which the local governments in each country are embedded. As such, the degree of decentralization is only one of the many potential influences on the performance of public services for the rural poor. The variation in public service outcomes is likely to depend on many other factors, all of which are filtered through the decision-making process at the local level. In the next four chapters we analyze how differences in these local decision-making processes at the local level help determine the varying quality of public services offered to rural populations (the analysis of the influence of the varying degrees of decentralization is the topic of chapters 8 and 9).

The next four chapters tell the story of how local governments in different national contexts are coping with their mandates to serve the rural poor. These individual country chapters are organized in a similar fashion. Each chapter starts out with a qualitative description of several concrete local-government experiences in rural-development efforts. The authors then examine the evidence concerning discrepancies between the formal local-government mandate and actual activities in the rural-development sectors. After a review of previous research on the factors that have been demonstrated to influence local-government involvement and performance in public-service delivery, the authors present the descriptive results of the fieldwork, followed by findings from the empirical analyses on the relationships between local institutions and other contextual factors and different rural development outcomes.

4
Brazil
At the Decentralization Forefront

Frank van Laerhoven

Both national governments and organizations of international cooperation around the world perceive decentralization as a promising strategy to improve the effectiveness and efficiency of conventional systems of public administration (Burki et al. 1999; Maro 1990; Ribot 1999a, 1999b; World Bank 1988). Thanks to a series of innovative reforms, municipal authorities in Brazil have a great deal more decision-making autonomy than their counterparts in neighboring countries. Has this consolidation of the local political power in Brazil produced an overall improvement in the performance of public services, particularly in rural areas? We argue that decentralization of political power may have been necessary for the improvement of governance performance in many developing countries, but it is generally not sufficient.

Our skepticism about the purported benefits of decentralization policies for rural development in Brazil originates from field observations in one hundred rural municipalities in northeastern and southeastern Brazil. There, we observed a great deal of variation between municipalities, not so much in terms of the existence or not of services for the rural poor as for the types of services being offered and the level of quality. The following two examples give a glimpse of the reality that many rural municipalities in Brazil face today.

In Cândido de Abreu, in the state of Paraná, 75 percent of the population depends on farming and ranching. About 50 percent of all pastureland and 20 percent of all other agricultural land is subject to soil degradation. Although agricultural productivity has increased considerably during the last five years—mainly due to technical innovations—it is felt that it is still not optimal, because of the use of inappropriate crop varieties. None of the interviewees had ever formally requested support from the local government. Farmers had, however, engaged in the implementation (coproduction) of certain municipal projects. Overall, the farmers we spoke with met about once per month with municipal representatives, either during field visits by municipal agents or scheduled meetings. The municipality has a so-called participatory rural development council (which is mandatory), and both the farmer organizations we interviewed reported to be a part of this council. However, at the time of the interview, none of them had ever presented a project in the council.

In Mariana Pimentel, in Rio Grande do Sul, 95 percent of the population depends on farming and forestry. Soil degradation, inappropriate crop varieties, poor market access, and pollution are considered important problems by the farmers we interviewed. In general, municipal technical assistance was reported to be inept. Although farmers did bring up the issue of soil degradation with their municipal representatives, they never formally requested municipal support. One of the two community-based organizations (CBOs) that we interviewed reported to have collaborated with the municipality in a project. The other CBO, however, had never been involved in what we call coproduction in this book. Both CBOs varied quite a bit in their interaction with local authorities. One of them—an organization involved in agricultural credit—reported to meet twice per month with municipal authorities, mainly through scheduled meetings. The other CBO—involved in social assistance to farmers—met only three times per year with representatives of the municipality, mainly via the rural development council (the CBO in question never initiated a project in the council). Municipal agents did not seem to engage in so-called field visits. At least, none of the CBOs interviewed mentioned this as a form of interaction with local authorities.

As suggested by the variation captured by these two contrasting cases of municipal involvement in rural development, we question the causal claim that there is a simple and direct positive relation between the transfer of power to lower levels of government and the overall quality of public administration. We explore the degrees to which the impact of decentralization reforms on public services is mitigated by a series of local institutional variables. The analysis particularly targets the process of the provision and production of agricultural services aimed at small-scale farmers in rural municipalities in Brazil.

In this chapter, we analyze several questions derived from the literature on decentralization and natural-resource management. First, which factors (co-)determine the probability of a local government contributing time, effort, and resources to support small-scale agriculture within its jurisdiction? Our prediction is that a mayor will respond to a mixed set of incentives coming from a multitiered system of institutional arrangements, including central-government agencies, local electorates, and social movements. The first hypothesis that this study seeks to corroborate is the following: The stronger the incentives a mayor perceives from both higher levels of government and local-level constituents and community-based organizations (CBOs), the higher the probability that he or she will dedicate time, effort, and resources to address their demands.

Second, what conditions contribute to the improvement of the performance of municipal agricultural services? We argue that even if a mayor is responsive to the incentives to act, this will not automatically lead to high-quality public services. The likelihood that local-government action results in "good governance," we argue, depends on both the quality of information and the ability to cooperate. The second hypothesis guiding this analysis is that the probability of encountering high-quality public services in a municipality will increase when there are institutions in place that facilitate communication and cooperation between local-policy actors.

Our empirical analysis is based on a series of logit regression models. The data was gathered between 2002 and 2003 in one hundred Brazilian rural municipalities, half of them located in the southern region and the other half in the northeastern region of the country. In the next section, we provide some background information on decentralization and local government in Brazil. The section on the empirical analysis follows, which we start out by describing the statistical methods used. We then present the results of the analysis, and a discussion thereof. We conclude by discussing implications for future research and make some (modest) policy recommendations.

Background

This section provides background information regarding local governance in Brazil's rural areas. What are the characteristics of the agricultural sector, what are the local-governments' mandates, and what opportunities do citizens formally have to participate in local policy making?

Agricultura Familiar in Brazil

Up until the last decade of the previous century, the main target of Brazilian agricultural policies was the "modernization" of the sector and the gradual eradication of peasant agriculture. The acknowledgment of (family-based) peasant farming as a viable economic sector gained ground in the political debate during the 1990s. Farming is the economic activity segment that provides most employment in Brazil. About 85 percent of the rural population is involved in what is known as *agricultura familiar*. Agricultura familiar is commonly defined as a form of farming in which the farmer makes the majority of the decisions related to farm management, and in which the family members constitute a larger proportion of the farm's workforce than hired labor. Additionally, the maximum size of a property pertaining to the agricultura familiar sector is formally established by criteria that vary per region.[1] Overall, this sector produces about 40 percent of Brazil's total agricultural production. In addition to being a significant source of employment, family farming constitutes an important buffer against uncontrolled urban expansion (INCRA/FAO 2000).

The northeastern region (one area looked at in this study) has the highest percentage of family farms in the country. Almost half (49.7 percent) of all family-based farms in Brazil are located in this region. The three southern states of Paraná, Santa Catarina, and Rio Grande do Sul (the other region of interest to this analysis) represent 21.9 percent of the total number of family farms in Brazil.

Decentralization and Local Government in Brazil

The Brazilian process of decentralization is importantly linked to the struggle against authoritarianism during the military regime and to the process of redemocratization. Affonso (1996) points out that democracy first materialized at the subnational level with the election of governors and prefects during the early 1980s. Electoral democracy eventually reached the upper echelons of the central government in 1989 with the election of the president of the republic. However, it would be misleading to characterize the democratization and the associated decentralization process exclusively as a bottom-up process. A significant motivation to transfer power to the lower levels of the administrative hierarchy was that the "developmentalist" state, which traditionally assumed responsibility for the structural economic transformations in Brazil since the 1950s, lost a significant portion of its intervention capacity during the fiscal and financial crisis that began in the 1980s.

The Constitution of 1988 acknowledges the political-administrative autonomy of the municipalities, broadens their competencies in matters of planning and executing services, endows them with more opportunities to collect local taxes, and increases their participation in the national tax formulas. However, small municipalities, mainly those predominantly engaged in agricultural activities, remain highly dependent upon the constitutional transfers from the capital. In general, some policy areas, such as health and education, depend on resources that are predefined by law, while others remain dependent upon the federal and state governments' budget approval. This fact limits municipal autonomy and may thus hinder the design and execution of certain projects at the local level.

In Brazil, the mayor is elected by direct vote. Mayoral and legislative (municipal council) elections are separated. More so than in neighboring countries, where in practice there is no clear distinction between mayor and council, municipal councilmen in Brazil represent a more antagonistic political power (the legislature) that does not necessarily coincide with the executive power in the hands of the mayor. The local-government regime can be characterized as being "presidentialist." The local government's elected officials serve a four-year term.[2] City hall usually includes a body of elected officials plus permanent, temporary, and outsourced staff. In Brazilian municipalities, about one-third of the bureaucratic personnel hold political rather than bureaucratic positions that are filled directly by the mayor. This ability to hire and fire sets the limits for the mayor's autonomy in deciding how to allocate resources (Zaz Friz Burga 2001; Nickson 1995).

Participatory Publics

All Brazilian municipalities have one or several so-called Municipal Participatory Councils covering areas such as health, education, employment, and rural development.[3] In 1999, there were almost twenty-seven thousand councils operating in the country, meaning that each town had on average about five such councils (Favareto and de Marco 2002). In 2000, about 68 percent of the Brazilian municipalities had what is known as a Municipal Council for Rural Development (Conselho Municipal de Desenvolvimento Rural, or CMDR).[4]

By law, CMDRs are to be created by the local authorities. All those organizations with a stake in the subject of rural development are invited to participate in these councils. Representatives of the local authorities, farmer organizations, community-based social organizations, and the private sector use the CMDR to discuss and prioritize public expenditure areas in the locality. Ideally, the multilaterally negotiated consensus reflects in an integrated way the diverse local preferences and demands (Bittencourt 2000; Abramovay 2001; Abramovay and da Vega 1999; Belik 1999; Favareto and de Marco 2002).

The CMDR prepares the Annual Municipal Work Plan (PMDRS). Once mutually agreed upon and accepted, this plan enables the prioritization of the municipal investments in the rural sector. The activities stipulated in the PMDRS are converted into a series of specific projects that are then submitted to several competitive funds, both private and public. The National Program for Strengthening Family Farming (PRONAF), particularly the "infrastructure and services" component of this program, is the largest source of funding for these projects. To access PRONAF resources, it is mandatory for a municipality to have a CMDR in which at least 50 percent of the family farmers in the area are represented (Ortega and Corréa 2002). Although participation takes place on a voluntary basis, it is implicitly assumed that access to public funds, such as those provided by PRONAF, will serve as an incentive to attract all relevant stakeholders with an interest in rural development in a certain locality.

Once PRONAF approves a project application submitted by a CMDR, it provides the funding to hire the counterparts required to implement the planned activities. Contractors can be either public or private entities and are selected by those who developed the project in question. Primarily, the activities involve a combination of infrastructure construction (roads and processing, storage, transportation, and marketing facilities), the development of new technologies, the exploration of new economic niches, and professional training.

According to the rationale behind PRONAF's particular way of disbursing federal funding, in theory, the typical information gap between government and citizens is bridged, which would guarantee a more efficient investment of scarce public resources, allowing for time and place particularities to be taken into consideration. Moreover, the multistakeholder and transparent nature of the negotiations that take place within the CMDR would prevent the capture of public funds by local elites. The democratic involvement of all relevant interest groups is supposed to enhance downward accountability. Finally, the collective action exercised in the councils could foster organizational learning and increase "social capital." Shared experiences in solving common problems could gradually boost the community's self-confidence and establish, nurture, and increase trust among the interest groups involved. Abramovay (2001), however, points out that the most significant weakness of CMDRs is precisely their reliance on collective action.

Public Services for Rural Development and the Role of Municipalities

In 1974, the Brazilian Company for Technical Support and Rural Extension (EMBRATER) replaced the ABCAR (Brazilian Association for Credit and Rural Support) system. This system was based on a technological model and had a centralized structure. The fiscal and financial crisis that affected the Brazilian state in the 1980s marked the end of EMBRATER at the beginning of the 1990s. After the promulgation of the new Constitution in 1988, the number of municipalities with their own agricultural technical assistance agencies grew significantly. These municipal-level agencies are typically coordinated by the Municipal Secretariat of Agriculture. According to data provided by ASBRAER (Brazilian Association of State Entities for Technical Support and Rural Extension) in July 2001, the official technical assistance and extension system consisted of almost 23,000 officials, of which more than 11,000 were working as agricultural extensionists, stationed in one of Brazil's 4,167 municipalities.

The national system responsible for agricultural research in Brazil (The Brazilian Agricultural Research Company, or EMBRAPA) engages directly in research but also has responsibilities regarding the coordination of research activities by third parties. Direct research and development activities take place in national- and state-level product-based research centers. Coordinating activities include, among other things, the development and formulation of norms, standards, and research programs. The links with and between universities, state corporations for agricultural research, and private research and development initiatives are encouraged in order to help avoid the duplication of research efforts. EMBRAPA's conventional product and productivity-oriented structure began to change as of the beginning of the 1990s. At present, EMBRAPA acknowledges the relevance and pertinence of such topics as sustainable development, agro ecology, interdisciplinary approaches, and food security. The role of municipalities in agricultural research is limited.

Federal and state governments intervene in rural areas by means of a diverse range of programs that are relevant for the agricultural sector and independent from the municipality. At the time of our fieldwork (2002) relevant and important federal programs included Banco da Terra, PRONAF Custeio e Investimento, PRONAF Infraestrutura, PROGER, the Fundo Nacional do Meio Ambiente, the Compañía Nacional de Abastecimento, and the Programa Nacional de Reforma Agrária. State governments may implement programs of their own. For example, in Paraná, programs like Paraná 12 Meses and Paraná Ambiental operate in rural areas independently from the local governments.

The Empirical Design of the Analysis

This section provides details regarding the data collection and the operationalization of both the dependent and the independent variables that are used in the statistical model underlying the analysis presented in this chapter.

Data Collection

The data was gathered between January and June 2002 (southern states) and in October 2003 (northeastern states). One hundred municipalities were randomly selected from a universe that included all those municipalities that, according to the last census (1995),[5] had less than 20,000 inhabitants and where more than half of the population lived outside of the municipal capital. Fifty municipalities were selected in the southern states of Rio Grande do Sul (24), Santa Catarina (15), and Paraná (11). Another fifty municipalities were selected in the northeastern states of Alagoas (3), Bahia (9), Ceará (4), Maranhão (6), Paraíba (8), Pernambuco (4), Piauí (7), Rio Grande do Norte (6), and Sergipe (3).[6] The number of selected municipalities per state is proportional to the total number of rural municipalities per state. Map 4.1 shows the geographical distribution of the 100 municipal territories in our sample.

The mayors of all one hundred municipalities were interviewed using a standardized semistructured survey instrument. Furthermore, in these same municipalities the research teams contracted by the Food and Agriculture Organization of the United Nations[7] (FAO) interviewed the representatives of two randomly selected CBOs working in the small-scale agricultural sector. Consequently, the analysis presented in this chapter is the product of conversations with a total of three hundred people who played key roles in the agricultural services provision and production

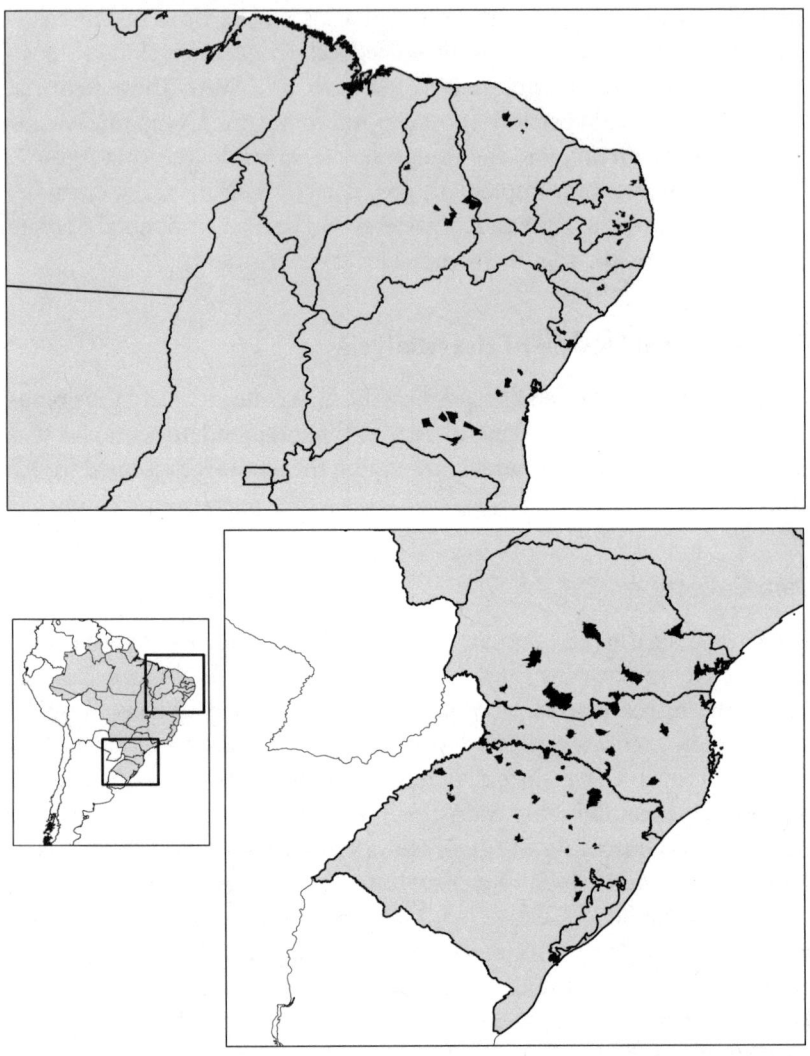

Map 4.1 Sampled municipalities in Brazil ($n = 100$). (Map by Frank van Laerhoven)

process in one hundred rural municipalities in twelve Brazilian states. The questions included in the questionnaire refer to the frequency and characteristics of the interaction among citizens and local, federal, and state government representatives working in the agricultural sector. Also, a range of data on the general characteristics of the respondents and their municipality was recorded.

Dependent Variables

For the operationalization of the two hypotheses that guide the analysis, we particularly examined the variation observed in four different, but complementary, dependent variables. These represent different indicators of local-government involvement and performance in rural development activities. Figure 4.1 depicts the variation among rural municipalities for all four dependent variables.

The motivation of the local government to invest time, effort, and resources in activities targeting small-scale agriculture is quantified by two indicators. First, we examined variation in the assignment of human resources to the support of the municipal agricultural sector; does the municipality have agricultural extension workers on its payroll (Model 1)? Second, we explored deviation in the reported willingness of local government to collaborate with CBOs active in the agricultural sector in the coproduction of certain public services (Model 2).

Also, from the survey results two indicators were derived that capture part of the variation in the quality of local public services' performance, the subject of our second hypothesis. First, variation in the reported response of local governments to CBO requests for support was used as an indicator. Did CBO representatives report to have received satisfactory assistance from the local government when they asked for it (Model 3)? Second, an indicator was used that recorded whether or not, according to the CBO representative, local governments have managed to solve a problem that a CBO confronted (Model 4).

As a first step, we sought to explain the observed variation in the local authorities' willingness or motivation to invest time, effort, and resources in the support of small-scale agriculture. In a majority of the selected municipalities (89 percent), a significant percentage (60 percent) of the population depended on agriculture. Although more than 70 percent of the municipalities had contracted personnel specifically dedicated to the agricultural sector, there is no statistically significant

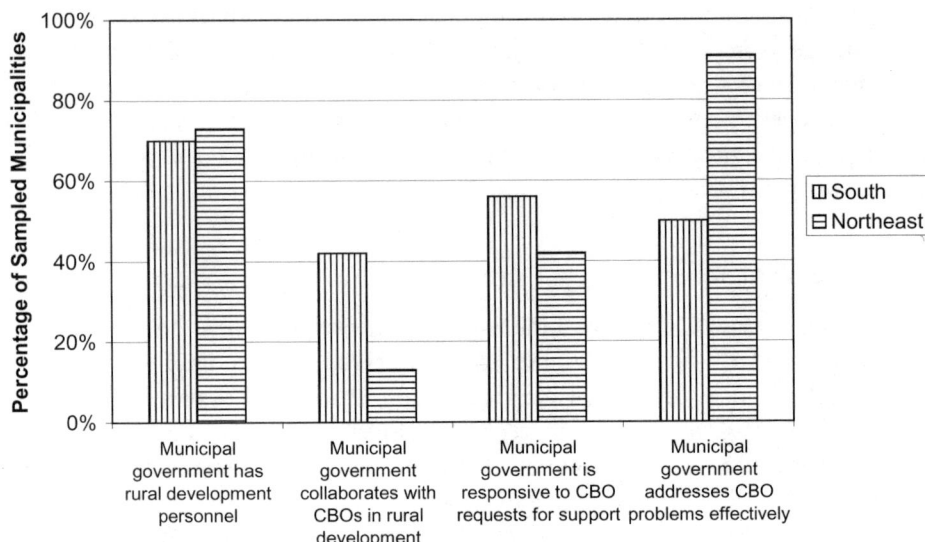

Figure 4.1 Variation in local-government involvement and performance in rural-development activities in rural Brazil ($n = 100$) (FAO Municipal Survey 2002).

congruence between the population's dependency on the agricultural sector and the probability of finding municipal personnel specialized in this area.

In addition, we explored deviation in the reported willingness of local government to collaborate with CBOs active in the agricultural sector in the coproduction of certain public services. In 28 percent of the municipalities in the sample, at least one of the two CBOs interviewed reported to have jointly undertaken activities with the municipality. But again, the probability of finding proof of cooperation between local authorities and CBOs was not significantly correlated with the relevance of the agricultural sector in the municipality.

As a second step, we sought to understand the possible causes of the variation observed in the quality of municipal services. As indicated above, we have identified two specific indicators that we argue capture different aspects related to the competence of these public services.

First, if a CBO stated that it requested support from the local authorities to solve a particular problem, the organization was asked whether or not it was satisfied with the response to that request. In seventy-six of the one hundred municipalities included in the sample, at least one of the two CBOs interviewed mentioned having requested support from the municipality (forty northeastern municipalities and thirty-six southern municipalities). Of those CBOs asking for municipal assistance, 64 percent reported to be satisfied with the response they received.

Second, if CBO representatives reported that their organization encountered certain obstacles, they were asked whether or not, in their opinion, the local authorities did everything they could to solve those problems. In 71 percent of the selected municipalities, at least one of the two CBOs interviewed stated its satisfaction with the support received from the municipal government to solve a problem it considered to be of particular relevance. Although the number of CBOs that requested support without obtaining an adequate response from the local administration is higher in the northeast, it can be observed that those same northeastern CBOs have, in general, a higher level of appreciation for the municipality's problem-solving capacity than their counterparts in the south. In both cases, a t-test reveals that the differences are statistically significant ($p < 0.05$ and $p < 0.01$, respectively). The descriptive statistics of all four dependent variables are presented in table 4.1.

Independent Variables

Table 4.2 shows the descriptive statistics of the independent variables used in the regression analyses. The independent variables are related to the institutional mediation argument outlined in the first chapter of the book. The variables that are hypothesized to have an impact on the local government's motivation to support small-scale agriculture and the quality of local public services are divided into two categories. First, the analysis includes a series of variables that represent the general characteristics that may be relevant: (1) the percentage of the population that depends on agriculture, (2) the number and average size of the farms in a municipality, (3) the human development index, (4) the number of problems that CBOs report to encounter, (5) distance to the state capital, and, (6) some personal characteristics of the mayor.

Second, the models include a series of variables related to the interaction between the local government and CBOs, and between the local government and the state and federal governments, respectively. The

Table 4.1
Description of the statistical models

Hypothesis	Model	Dependent variables	Description	N	Mean	Standard deviation	Minimum	Maximum
The local government is motivated to support small-scale farmers	1	The municipality has a staff of professional agronomists	Binary variable	100	0.730	0.446	0	1
	2	At least one CBO has participated in a joint activity with the municipality	Binary variable	96	0.281	0.452	0	1
The local government produces quality services for small-scale farmers	3	Local government support is requested by CBO, positive response	Binary variable	76	0.645	0.482	0	1
	4	Local government has satisfactorily addressed the CBO's problems	Binary variable	98	0.714	0.454	0	1

following variables represent the central part of the institutional mediation model (the so-called action arena): (1) the number of CBOs in the municipality, according to the mayor, (2) the organizational level of the CBOs, according to the mayor, (3) the existence of a participatory forum (CMDR), (4) the frequency with which CBOs request support from the local government, (5) the importance of field visits as means of interaction between authorities and CBOs, (6) the frequency of the local government's interaction with federal programs, and, (7) the frequency of meetings between local government and state programs' representatives.

Empirical Results

Table 4.3 shows the results of the four different logit regression models. The first observation regards the small N reported for the models. The one hundred initial cases that the models are based on are trimmed down even further due to the cumulative effect of unit nonresponses. Long (1997) argues that the use of a sample smaller than one hundred in maximum likelihood estimation leads to nonrobust results. Small samples lower the precision of the estimates and introduce bias into the maximum likelihood logit estimator. Determining sample size is often a trade-off between precision of the results and budgetary constraints. In the case presented in this chapter, arguments related to the costs of data gathering were particularly important. In an attempt to deal with the imprecision of the regression results due to the small sample size, we will consistently provide the width of the confidence intervals for the coefficients we discuss. Whenever necessary and possible, we will put our claims regarding the results in perspective of the acknowledged imprecision.

What Motivates Municipal Governments?

Why are some municipalities seemingly more motivated than others to design, adapt, and implement policies in support of the (small-scale) agricultural sector? More specifically, why is the importance of the agricultural sector reflected in the composition of the municipal roster in some municipalities but not in others? And, why do some municipalities collaborate with CBOs in the coproduction of certain services while no evidence of cooperation between CBOs and local authorities is found in others?

Table 4.2
Description of the independent variables

Independent variable	Description	N	Mean	Standard deviation	Minimum	Maximum
Action arena: Institutional mediation						
Interaction between local government and community-based organizations (CBOs)						
Number of CBOs (according to mayor) (logged)	Count	99	21.717	19.012	2	100
Municipality has a participatory policy forum (CMDR)	Binary (yes/no)	98	0.704	0.459	0	1
CBO requests local government support (0 = no, .5 = 1 CBO, 1 = both CBOs)	Ordinal (0–1)	97	0.586	0.373	0	1
CBOs are well-organized (according to mayor)	Binary (yes/no)	100	0.520	0.502	0	1
CBOs and local authorities interact through field visits (1 = no, 2 = rarely, 3 = yes)	Ordinal (1–3)	98	1.561	0.643	1	3
Interaction between local government and federal/state government						
Local government interacts with how many central government agencies?	Count (0–6)	100	1.940	1.523	0	6
Local government interacts with state government	Count meetings per year	100	4.390	7.120	0	48

Exogenous variables

		N	Mean	SD	Min	Max
General Characteristics						
Proportion of municipal population that depends on agriculture (according to mayor)	Percentage	100	76.090	16.101	8	100
Farms per capita	Continuous	100	0.138	0.057	0.005	0.276
Average farm size	Continuous (ha)	100	28.57	28.443	2.347	144
Municipal human development index	Index (0–1)	93	0.677	0.095	0.506	0.832
Municipality is located in the northeast	Dummy	100	0.500		0	1
Number of problem areas identified by CBOs	Count (0–5)	100	3.010	1.017	0	5
Distance to state capital	Continuous (km)	100	262	178	35	731
Characteristics of mayor						
Number of years the current mayor has resided in the municipality	Continuous (years)	91	28.956	14.969	1	63
Number of years the current mayor holds the mayorship	Continuous (years)	95	4.380	1.751	1	11
Education level of the current mayor	Ordinal (1–6)	100	3.610	1.463	1	6

Table 4.3
Logit regression results

Variable	Model 1	Model 2	Model 3	Model 4
Action arena: Institutional mediation				
Interaction between local government and community-based organizations (CBOs)				
Number of CBOs (according to mayor)	1.559**	−0.303	1.782**	−0.181
	(0.620)	(0.427)	(0.874)	(0.488)
CBOs are well-organized (according to mayor)	0.423	1.194*	3.640**	1.458*
	(0.814)	(0.694)	(1.453)	(0.845)
Municipality has a participatory policy forum (CMDR)	1.091	0.440	−0.733	0.765
	(0.853)	(0.775)	(1.180)	(0.907)
CBO requests local government support	0.374	1.246	—	0.940
	(1.037)	(1.008)		(1.129)
CBOs and local authorities interact through field visits	−1.020	0.320	1.796*	−0.441
	(0.586)	(0.482)	(0.930)	(0.633)
CBOs and local government collaborate in the coproduction of services	—	—	—	1.957**
				(0.990)
Interaction between local government and state/central government				
Local government interacts with how many central government agencies?	0.185	−0.479**	−0.162	0.351
	(0.123)	(0.242)	(0.367)	(0.274)
Local government interacts with state government (annual meetings)	−0.091	−.0560	−0.136	−0.184
	(0.263)	(0.089)	(0.114)	(0.133)
Exogenous variables				
General characteristics				
Proportion of municipal population that depends on agriculture (mayor's opinion)	0.007	0.008	−0.071**	−0.068*
	(0.026)	(0.027)	(0.030)	(0.039)
Farms per capita	−9.176	−1.868	17.151	3.903
	(8.120)	(7.504)	(14.144)	(8.813)
Average farm size	−0.637	−0.312	1.451*	−0.193
	(0.571)	(0.475)	(0.727)	(0.632)
Municipal human development index	0.829	−4.451	−6.473	−5.346
	(10.084)	(10.057)	(15.410)	(10.466)
Municipality is located in the northeast (as opposed to the south)	−1.734	−2.132	−1.513	4.527*
	(2.031)	(2.114)	(3.358)	(2.716)
Number of problem areas identified by CBOs	0.559	−0.641*	−0.124	0.542
	(0.347)	(0.3421)	(0.690)	(0.470)
Distance to state capital	−0.006**	—	—	—
	(0.003)			

Table 4.3
Continued

Variable	Model 1	Model 2	Model 3	Model 4
Characteristics of mayor				
Number of years the current mayor has resided in the municipality	0.008 (0.033)	0.015 (0.029)	0.037 (0.042)	−0.045 (0.039)
Number of years the mayor holds the mayorship	0.332 (0.303)	0.268 (0.247)	0.203 (0.316)	−0.843** (0.381)
Education level of the mayor (1–6)	−0.007 (0.236)	0.109 (0.239)	−0.690 (0.424)	−0.304 (0.276)
General statistics				
Constant	−1.519 (8.654)	0.984 (7.226)	−1.980 (15.723)	12.064 (9.914)
Log likelihood	−29.974	−34.356	−21.864	−26.705
N	77	76	60	74
Pseudo r^2	0.320	0.275	0.404	0.407
Prob > chi^2	0.0420	0.053	0.013	0.004

Notes:
Model 1: Municipal agricultural personnel
Model 2: Coproduction of public services
Model 3: Local government responsiveness
Model 4: CBO problems satisfactorily dealt with by local government
Regression coefficient, with standard error in parentheses:
* $p < 0.10$
** $p < 0.05$

Municipal Agricultural Personnel. The first model explains 32.0 percent of the observed variance in the presence of municipal officials working on agriculture (pseudo r^2). The model predicts that when there are more CBOs operating in a municipality (according to the mayor's estimate), the probability of finding municipal personnel attending the agricultural sector increases. Taking a 95 percent confidence interval into account, it turns out that the outcome is particularly robust for the higher values of this particular independent variable.

The variable that captures whether or not CBOs and local authorities interact by means of field visits also refers to an institutional arrangement that could influence the form and intensity of political pressure perceived by local decision makers. Although this variable is correlated with the probability of finding municipal staff working in the agricultural sector, the direction of sign of the regression coefficient is counterintuitive; it seems that the higher the frequency of interaction between CBOs and local authorities through field visits, the lower the likelihood of finding municipal agronomists. The likelihood of finding municipal agricultural officials rises to 92 percent when the number of meetings between CBOs and municipality through field visits is at its lowest. When this frequency is at its highest, the probability drops to 60 percent.[8] A speculative explanation for this somewhat puzzling result is that having bureaucrats dealing with farmers leads to a decrease of contacts of political decision makers with farmers.

Finally, the distance to the state capital seems to matter. The smaller the distance to the closest administrative hub, the higher the probability of finding agricultural experts on the municipality's payroll. It is more problematic to make the reverse claim (the larger the distance, the lower the probability), since for municipalities located relatively far away from the state capital, the confidence interval around the predicted probability of finding personnel specialized in agriculture ($y = 1$) turns out to be fairly wide. The finding makes intuitive sense. Isolated municipalities may (for example, because of lack of access to markets, and the scarcity of economic opportunities) be more likely to have relatively fewer resources to hire specialized personnel. Or, municipalities closer to the capital may be more attractive to prospecting bureaucrats.

Coproduction of Public Services. Model 2 explains 27.5 percent of the variance in the dependent variable. Approaching the subject of local-government motivation from the particular angle of the cooperation between CBOs and local governments proves to be clarifying too. There are three variables with statistically significant regression coefficients. However, what is surprising in some cases is the direction of signs of the coefficients.

Our analysis shows that the role played by the organized civil society is extremely relevant. When CBOs have an acknowledged low level of organization, one is less likely to encounter forms of local government—CBO collaboration in the coproduction of certain public services. When the mayor's appreciation of the level of organization of the CBOs is at its lowest, the likelihood of finding some form of coproduction is 14 percent. When his/her appreciation of CBO organization is at its highest, the probability of finding forms of collaboration rises to 36 percent. The greater the mayor's confidence in the organizational levels of the CBOs, the greater the probability that he/she may effectively cooperate with them in the production of local agricultural services.

We argue this to be congruent with our hypothesis: poorly organized citizen organization will be less effective in pressuring local authorities to get involved in solving their problems. Also, local government may be less interested to team up with CBOs that, according to them, have sub-par levels of organization, since they anticipate the outcome of collaboration to be negative.

When the interaction between the local government and the federal government reaches its lowest value (while all other variables are held constant at their mean), the probability of finding evidence of coproduction (i.e., cooperation between local government and one CBO) is 45 percent. This percentage unexpectedly drops to 4 percent when the interaction between the federal and the local government is at its highest value. In other words, it is less likely for the CBOs to cooperate with municipal officials in the production of certain public services when the level of intimacy between city hall and the capital is higher.[9]

A possible explanation for this finding is that a pronounced presence of the central government in the municipality may "crowd out" the local government. It is possible that local authorities feel less responsible for responding to the demands of their constituents when central-government agencies take care of certain issues. It is also possible that when representatives of the federal government are present at the local level, they do not want to relinquish control to their local counterparts. Another explanation is that CBOs may perceive the federal authorities as more capable of responding to their demands and, consequently, bypass the municipality when seeking support. Finally, a more intimate contact with the federal government could result in a more expedient access for local governments to additional resources. If that is the case, the cooperation with CBOs in the production of services might prove to be less necessary, since coproduction can be motivated by the potential of cost reductions.

A final statistically significant (noninstitutional) variable that explains variance in observed evidence of coproduction is the number of problems encountered by CBOs. When the number of problems identified by CBOs is at its lowest value, the probability of finding evidence of coproduction is 67 percent. Surprisingly, this percentage drops to 8 percent when the number of problems faced by CBOs reaches its highest value. In other words, the higher the number of problems CBOs face, the lower the likelihood of finding evidence of cooperation between CBOs and the municipality in the production of services.[10] It seems that the greater the pertinence of solving problems in a collective manner, the least likely it will be that collective action between agricultural producers and municipal officials will actually occur.

Although the models provide information on the general association among variables, they do not expound further on the causal mechanism that underlies this relation. Could a good working relationship with the local government result in fewer complaints from CBOs regarding the problems they perceive? Would the CBOs, once they are involved in coproduction activities, cease to perceive so many insurmountable problems just because they are receiving support? Could their definition of "problems" change by their mere participation in coproduction activities? Once again, the results of this analysis call for a more detailed look at these intriguing questions.

What Determines Quality in Agricultural Services?

Why are some municipalities seemingly more able than others to design, adapt, and implement policies in support of the (small-scale) agricultural sector that are perceived by their beneficiaries as adequate and of reasonable quality? More specifically, why are some municipalities responsive to the requests expressed by local agricultural producer organizations while others are not? Why do some local governments possess a greater problem-solving capacity than others?

Local Government Responsiveness. In twenty-four of the one hundred municipalities included in the sample, both CBOs interviewed mentioned that they had never requested support from the municipal government (ten in the northeastern region and fourteen in the southern region). These cases were not included in this part of the analysis. Model 3 explains 40.4 percent of the variance observed in the CBOs' appreciation of the response given by the local government to their requests for assistance.

When the level of interaction between CBOs and municipal representatives—specifically by means of field visits—shifts from its lowest to its highest value, the probability of observing a positive municipal response to a request expressed by a CBO rises from 67 percent to 99 percent. We would argue that a hands-on, pragmatic relation between local authorities and CBOs is beneficial to the municipality's ability to respond adequately to farmers' demands.

Also, the higher the number of CBOs present in a municipality (according to the mayor's estimation), the higher the probability of obtaining a positive municipal response to a request for assistance. This finding confirms the trend that emerged in the previous segment of the analysis. When the total number of CBOs shifts from its lowest to its highest value in this sample, the probability of observing a positive municipal response to CBO requests dramatically rises from 14 percent to 99 percent. High levels of farmer organization seem to send a strong message to local authorities.

The mayor's perception of the organizational level of the CBOs present in his/her municipality also has an impact on the level of local governments' responsiveness. When the perception of the organizational level of the CBOs shifts from its lowest to its highest value, the probability of observing a positive response to a request rises from 47 percent to 97 percent.

Besides these institutional variables, two variables representing structural characteristics are statistically significant. When the percentage of the population that, according to the mayor, depends on agriculture is at its lowest, the probability that the CBOs will be satisfied with the municipal response to their request for assistance is 100 percent. However, when this percentage is at its highest (i.e., many people depend on agricultural activities for their livelihoods), the probability that the CBOs will be satisfied with the municipal response to their request for assistance drops considerably, to 56 percent.

The direction of the sign of the coefficient is intuitively unexpected. One would expect that when agricultural producers constitute a large part of the local electorate, the elected local officials would be more inclined to address the demands of this segment of the population. The finding could mean that the presence of a relatively high number of farmers results in a higher number of requests that, due to the lack of resources, cannot all be addressed. In this case, the likelihood of interviewing a CBO unsatisfied with the municipal response is higher.

Another unexpected result is that when the average size of the farms in a given municipality is at its lowest value, the probability of finding a positive response to a request is 21 percent. When this size is at its highest (i.e., when the farms are larger on average), the probability of a positive municipal response remarkably rises to 99 percent. It is possible that the presence of large-size farms in a given municipality could be related to the relative importance of "agricultura patronal" in that locality. These corporate farms may have more political leverage. They can be argued to have easier and more effective access to the local political agenda and the decision-making process regarding the municipal public expenditure.[11] If this is actually true, this finding may be related to the phenomenon of elite-capture.

Local Governments' Problem-Solving Capacity. Model 4 has an explicative power of 40.7 percent. The significance of an organized civil society, consistent throughout this study, is again confirmed by this part of the analysis. When the mayor perceives that the organizational level of the CBOs is at its lowest value, the probability of finding CBOs satisfied with the municipal capacity to solve their problems is 75 percent. This percentage increases to 93 percent when, according to the mayor, the CBOs are at their maximum level of organization.[12]

Furthermore, it seems that the cooperation between organized small-scale farmers and local authorities effectively and significantly contributes to the good performance of the agricultural services: when there is no evidence of a CBO involvement in the coproduction of certain services, the probability of finding CBOs satisfied with the municipal capacity to solve their problems is 79 percent. This probability rises to 96 percent when the CBOs are somehow involved in the coproduction of services that are relevant to them.

In addition to these institutional variables, there are some variables representing exogenous characteristics that significantly contribute to the explicative power of this particular model. When the mayor is in office for the minimum number of years, the probability that the CBOs will be satisfied with the municipal problem-solving capacity is 99 percent. When the mayor is in office for the maximum number of years, this probability drops dramatically to 3 percent.[13]

One would expect that with time a local government's experience, and thus its ability to perform well, would gradually increase. This does not, however, seem to be the case. What could this unexpected impact of the number of years served by the mayor on the CBOs' appreciation of the municipality's role as problem solver mean? A possible explanation could be that a new mayor starts his or her term enthusiastically, but this enthusiasm wears off as time passes. Or, CBOs may be willing to give a new mayor the benefit of doubt at the beginning of his or her term. A more cynical explanation for this phenomenon would be that as time passes, local interests manage to gradually encapsulate the local government's political agenda. If this is true, this would be another piece of evidence in favor of the elite-capture argument.

When the proportion of the population that, according to the mayor, depends on agriculture shifts from its lowest to its highest value, the likelihood of finding CBOs satisfied with the municipality's problem-solving capacity drops from almost 100 percent to 58 percent. Although the result is counterintuitive, it is consistent with the results of Model 3. A possible explanation is that the greater the number of farmers, the greater the number of problems to be solved. Given the limited resources of the municipality, it may be impossible for the local authorities to solve all problems that small-scale farmers encounter. Consequently, the probability of finding a CBO that is unsatisfied with the municipality's problem-solving capacity is greater.

Model 4 is the only model that reveals a significant difference between the southern and northeastern regions of Brazil. When a municipality is located in the south, the likelihood of finding CBOs satisfied with the response given by the municipality to one or more of their problems is 47 percent. This probability for the municipalities in the sample located in the northeast is 99 percent. This is intriguing, and deserves a more detailed assessment, given that the northeast of Brazil scores consistently low on a number of important socioeconomic indicators.

Conclusions

Brazil has implemented a series of decentralization reforms that are among the most far-reaching in the region. Local governments have a relatively high level of autonomy to decide on the allocation of public resources, and also in the area of rural development and support to the local small-scale farming sector. In addition to that, the reforms specifically promote the emergence of institutional arrangements that allow the insertion of local interest groups into the municipal policy-making process. Participatory policy platforms are an integral part of local governance. Nevertheless, governance outcomes still vary among rural municipalities. Not all local governments hire personnel dedicated to the agricultural sector, despite reported high percentages of the population depending on small-scale farming. Furthermore, they are not always inclined to collaborate with CBOs to support them in the joint solution of particular problems, even when doing so would potentially lead to better results. Not all municipalities are equally responsive to farmers' requests for support. And finally, some local governments seem to be better able to solve problems experienced by small-scale farmers than others.

The actual impact of the decentralization reforms is better understood when focusing on the incentive structures to which local politicians respond. Also, it proves helpful to be aware of contextual particularities related to biophysical and socioeconomic parameters. It is not the mere mechanical implementation of the decentralization reforms that guarantees good performance of local agricultural services. The decentralization reforms' impact is locally mitigated by institutional arrangements that direct form and intensity of interaction between policy actors operating in various, partially overlapping, polycentric policy arenas. When studying local governance, understanding this institutional mediation is essential.

One of the more consistent findings of this study relates to the crucial role of the organized civil society. The political pressure exerted by local-producer organizations contributes consistently and significantly to the success of decentralization reforms. This analysis reveals that the presence of many consensus-building structures among local farmers that are additionally highly organized not only seems to motivate the mayor to take action on their behalf, but also contributes to an effective increase in the quality of locally produced services.

A sensitive issue is the role of the federal government in the decentralization process. There is evidence that coproduction—i.e., the participation of the beneficiaries themselves in the production of agricultural services—contributes to the enhancement of the performance of these services (Model 4). There is also evidence, however, that when the relationship between the municipality and the capital is intimate, it is less likely to observe cooperation between local authorities and CBOs. In Brazil, the central government applies a strong decentralist rhetoric. This rhetoric has been translated into a series of innovative reforms. Nonetheless, a range of federal programs is still operating at the local level. In practice, these programs turn out to "compete" with local governments in matters related to the support of small-scale agriculture. There seems to be evidence of a "crowding out" effect that tends to downplay the relevance of the local government's role as an actor in the decision-making processes regarding such policies.

However, the dilemma regarding the relationship between the central and local government is more complex. We have speculated that some unexpected regression results could be attributed to the vulnerability of local governments to elite capture. When the farms in a given municipality are larger, the probability of a positive local-government response to the demands expressed by the farmers increases. Also, when a mayor is in office longer, the probability of CBOs appreciating the local government for its problem-solving capacity decreases. Elite capture is a risk acknowledged in the literature on decentralization policies (Platteau 2004; Schönwälder 1997). In addition, Peterson (1995) suggests that the lower government echelons are more interested in development policies and tend to ignore distributive policies.

Within the confines of the available data, we can get a hint regarding what can be expected to determine the presence of a certain number of central-government programs in a municipality. To dig deeper into this question, we ran a Poisson regression model to analyze the effects of a series of plausible independent variables (distance from the state capital, the municipal human development index, the local government's interaction with the state government, and average farm size) on the number of central-government programs with which the mayor reports to interact regularly. Although the explanatory power of this Poisson regression model is limited, it provides several important hints about the factors that help determine the number of programs. The only independent variable that turns out to have a statistically significant impact on the number of central-government programs is average farm size within the municipal territory. What is interesting is the negative sign of this variable's regression coefficient, meaning that as the average farm size increases, more federal government programs seem to be present in municipalities with smaller farms. This finding seems to suggest that whereas local governments may be inclined to give in to rent-seeking pressures by bigger farmers—larger average farms are associated with a more responsive local government in Model 3—central-government programs may be more genuinely seeking to support those who need it the most

The policy implications of this analysis can only be modest given the many uncertainties surrounding the quantitative part. On the one hand, it seems wise to add CBO support to decentralization reforms. Policy makers should try to guarantee that the anticipated beneficiaries of greater autonomy for local governments have the incentives to organize and put the pressure on. In the absence of an organized civil society vigorously knocking on the doors of town hall, a local government may be inclined to not let go of its newly acquired powers. Elite capture is around the corner in a polity that traditionally was (and may as well still be) managed by local strongmen. On the other hand, central government has to strike the balance between its presence mitigating elite capture, and leading to a crowding-out effect at the same time. This may be the hardest challenge for those pursuing an improvement in governance through decentralization reforms.

5
Chile
A Free-Market Model of Decentralization

With Paul Lewin

Whereas municipalities in Brazil are supported by a mandate that provides them with a fair amount of autonomy regarding policy making and implementation in the agricultural sector, their Chilean counterparts can, but are not formally expected to, play a role in this area. The Chilean approach to agricultural and rural development includes a number of mechanisms that aim at the creation of quasi markets, for example by means of so-called competitive funding (Umali-Deininger 1997). Contrary to Brazil, where the municipal authorities are expected to take the lead in organizing stakeholders to access central-government support, in Chile the initiative lies with the farmers. The local government may partner with beneficiaries in their attempts to access resources to finance their projects, but this is not specifically encouraged. In this chapter, we analyze to what extent these differences influence the way that local-level institutions affect rural-development outcomes from the perspective of small-scale farmers.

We noted in chapter 3 that municipalities in Chile do not have a legal obligation or specific budget support from the central government to implement activities or programs in support of rural development. Programs and resources for this sector are concentrated in the ministries and agencies of the central government. In fact, the current law does not even compel ministries or agencies that engage in rural-development activities to coordinate these activities with the municipality. Given this legal and political framework, any action performed by the municipalities to deliver rural-development services to their inhabitants is voluntary in nature and must be self-funded. This might lead one to predict that Chilean municipalities do not offer agricultural services. However, many of them, especially rural municipalities, assume a certain degree of responsibility for the generation of these services. The goal of this chapter is to gain a better understanding of why this might be the case.

Some examples of the public services related to rural development that municipal governments provide include technical and administrative assistance in the formulation of small farmer-owned projects to be submitted to central-government funding sources; technical field assistance to small- and mid-sized farms; technical training courses for farmers; support for the establishment of farmers markets; promotion of the formation of producers' cooperatives; and provision of places for community-based organization meetings, among others. Given the voluntary nature of municipal services for rural development, it seems natural that there would be a great deal of variation among municipalities when it comes to the existence and quality of the rural development-related public services. The following two examples of municipal production of rural-development services illustrate this variation.

When the field team visited the municipality of Antuco in the Eighth Administrative Region, we observed strong interactions between the municipality and community-based organizations. The activities of small-scale farmers were commonly supported by the public services organized by the municipal authorities. These services support small farmers in rural-development project formulation and submission to national programs and competitive technical-assistance funds administered by the central government agencies. This municipality's effort has positively influenced farmers' opinions about the role of the municipal authority in rural development. They recognized the importance of the help provided for their productivity, profitability, and performance level as an organization or cooperative. Also, the farmers we spoke to believed that if the municipality had more money, the support of their activities would be greater. Because of the good relationships between the CBOs and the municipality, several joint projects are underway. Although most of the resources come from nonmunicipal sources, most notably the national programs for rural development and the competitive technical-assistance funds, the degree of success among farmers actually gaining access to these funds may be attributed to the robust relationship between local farmer groups and their municipal-government officials.

On the other hand, this positive experience contrasts with the realities found in the municipality of Licaten in the Seventh Administrative Region. Here, we observed that the interactions between farmers and local authorities were practically nonexistent. The community-based organizations have neither influence nor voice in the policy-making process in the community. Also, the farmers we talked to expressed a lack of interest and overall fatigue in trying to get the "bureaucratic municipality" to assist them with their problems in the agricultural sector. They said they preferred traveling to the regional capital if they wanted to make their voice heard, even if such efforts had not yielded many positive results in the past. Disappointingly, no matter to whom they turned, they had had little success in drumming up any governmental support at all.

Because local governments in Chile are under no obligation to provide public service in agriculture and rural development, the situation in Licaten comes as little surprise. It is more surprising that the municipal authorities in Antuco have decided to go beyond the call of duty. The rest of this chapter will be dedicated to trying to sort out the forces behind such mixed outcomes.

The unexpected existence of public services for rural development raises the question as to why local politicians would voluntarily invest their scarce resources into these programs when they are not required to do so by law. According to the community-based organizations, almost 80 percent of the sampled municipalities had professional agricultural engineers, more than 60 percent acknowledged the municipal governments' relevance in rural development, and more than 60 percent reported the presence of agricultural-management improvement activities.

Even though the municipalities do not have a legal obligation to provide public services related to agriculture and rural development, many of them do in fact provide them. Moreover, several municipalities not only provide an array of such services, but also obtain high ratings from the local users regarding the quality of these services. According to the results of the fieldwork performed for this study, the representatives of the community-based organizations in the vast majority of the Chilean municipalities maintain that the conditions to solve problems in the agricultural sector have improved during the last five years. In addition, most Chilean municipal governments are perceived by the same community-based organizations as relevant actors in dealing with agricultural issues. In summary, although the central-government policy does not actively promote the role played by municipal governments in the field of agricultural governance, local producers and their organizations do acknowledge their relevance and value their performance within the sector.

Such variation cannot be explained by the formal arrangements between the central government and the local governments. The contention of this chapter, which will be corroborated through an empirical analysis, is that the effectiveness of the local institutional arrangements, both formal and informal, explains (1) why some municipalities decide to provide services and (2) why some municipalities obtain better results than others.

What Motivates the Chilean Municipal Governments?

Prior research has found that the municipal action toward a specific sector is driven by the relative force of (1) the effective commitment of the central government, (2) the potential for financial gain, and (3) the demand of the constituency and specific stakeholder groups. The inference is that these same incentive sources are at work in the Chilean municipal environment.

The Existence of a Central-Government Commitment

When the agencies of the ministries or state services in which the agricultural-sector development programs and resources are concentrated coordinate their activities with the local government, the outcome that can be expected is an interaction that inspires the municipalities to take action within the sector.

In the Bolivian forestry sector, Andersson (2003) reached the conclusion that the greater the communication between the municipal authorities and the central-government representatives, the greater the probability of observing a delivery of municipal services to that sector. In addition, Gibson and Lehoucq (2003), in Guatemala, demonstrated that when the interaction between the mayor and the central government in certain productive sectors is greater, these sectors are given higher priority than others. Therefore, similar outcomes may be potentially expected in the Chilean public sector, even in the absence of a municipal legal obligation to deliver said services.

The Existence of Financial Gains for the Municipality

As suggested by Larson (2002) and Pacheco and Kaimowitz (1998), the existence of potential financial gains for the municipality can have an effect on the probability of a municipal intervention in the agricultural sector. The logic behind this reasoning is that municipal administrations with a low economic base of agricultural resources are less likely to have the required critical mass to deliver at least the minimum amount of agricultural and rural-development services for these to be profitable.

One can expect, however, that this characteristic would play a lesser role in the municipal incentive structures within the Chilean context, because municipalities in Chile are not allowed to raise their own funds from this sector. The revenues derived from such sectors are rather of an indirect nature.

The Existence of Political Gains for the Mayor

As suggested by Andersson (2002), when the municipal population is more dependent on farming, a greater provision of municipal services to the sector can be expected. Consequently, we use the number of farms within the municipality as an indirect measure of the number of agriculture-dependent families. Given that the mayor is elected by popular vote, and the fact that each farmer and his or her family represent essential votes, more farmers would simply mean a greater incentive to generate local public services related to rural development.

Why Some Municipalities Are Able to Produce Higher-Quality Services Than Others

Prior research has highlighted the significance of taking local-level institutions into account to explain the variations in terms of the quality of several public goods and services (Oakerson 1999; Ostrom 1996a; Gibson et al. 2000; Ostrom et al. 2002). Evidence provided by empirical studies related to the local governance of natural resources suggests that local institutions tend to screen, adapt, and sometimes ignore the instructions ensuing from nationally implemented public policy (e.g., see Agrawal and Ostrom 2001; Wade 1989; Baland and Platteau 1996). Consequently, in order to explain which conditions support a more efficient local management of agricultural services, we need to consider the local institutions that influence the creation of such services. A distinction is made among institutions regarding the (1) coprovision and (2) coproduction of services.

Institutions for the Coprovision of Services

A public-service provision unit is the authority that takes collective decisions regarding the type of service to be provided, how it will be funded, the type of quality control to be implemented, how the service production will be organized, and how much the consumer will be charged for the service (Musgrave 1959; Oakerson 1999). When these collective decisions are taken based on the broad participation of the population to be benefited by the projected services, then the institution is called an institution for coprovision (Andersson and van Laerhoven 2007). The significance of popular participation in public decision-making processes has been well established in empirical literature on decentralization (Blair 2000; Fiszbein 1997; Ribot 2002; Wyckoff-Baird et al. 2000). In the Chilean municipal context, the assumption is that the existence of coprovision institutions for agricultural public services increases the probability of providing high-quality services within the territory.

Institutions for the Coproduction of Services

A service production unit is the entity in charge of implementing the service defined by the provision unit. The production unit transforms the inputs received from the provision unit (or from the coprovision unit) into a product (Oakerson 1999). Prior research has shown that one of the main ingredients to achieve an efficient and effective production is to incorporate the local knowledge on the area's biophysical and socioeconomic conditions to the production of the service (Hayek 1948; Ostrom et al. 1994). When the consumers of services take part in the production of the services, the institution is then called a service coproduction institution. Several studies have submitted evidence of the coproduction positive influence on the quality of public services (Ostrom 1996a; J. Jacobs 1961). It is therefore assumed that the existence of municipal institutions for the coproduction of rural development services in Chile is associated with a higher service-quality level.

Noninstitutional Causal Factors

Other variables that can also influence the generation of municipal services and their quality are: the number of years that the mayor has resided in the municipality, the mayor's education level, the mayor's political affiliation, the wealth of the municipality, the number of farms, the region the municipality belongs to, the community's Human Development Index, field presence of municipal technical staff, the existence of degraded soils, and the number of community-based organizations and their level of organization. Each of these variables and their potential influence are described herein below.

Years that the mayor has resided in the municipality: The number of years that the mayor has lived in the municipality endows him or her with greater knowledge regarding the territorial and population needs.

Mayor's education level: The higher the level of education of the mayor, the easier it should be for him or her to obtain competitive resources from public-development funds to implement productive agricultural projects.

Mayor's political affiliation: This variable seeks to measure the influence that the mayor's political party could have on the actions taken in the agricultural arena. If the mayor is affiliated to one of the ruling parties, it is possible that the regional prefect or the regional directors of the Agricultural Ministry's departments could favor him or her with some additional funds obtained through competitive funds.

Wealth of the municipality: Larson (2002) showed that in the Nicaraguan experience, the three most successful municipalities in the provision of forestry services were, at the same time, the wealthiest.

Number of farms: When the municipality has a larger number of farms, it can be expected that its population would be more closely involved in the governance and use of this resource. Consequently, it can be expected that a large number of farms would correlate to a greater delivery of municipal services to the sector.

Region: The geographical area determines the productive strategy, the concentration of land, and the characteristics of the producers. In the case of Chile, both the climatic and the producers' characteristics vary from north to south. The central-northern part of the country is characterized by irrigated, labor intensive, and export-oriented farming. On the other hand, farming in the southern part of the country uses less technology, is more extensive, less labor intensive, and more domestic market–oriented. Given the above, it can be expected that the delivery of municipal services in rural development would acquire greater significance in the southern part of the country than in the central-northern part, where the agricultural production has been mainly undertaken by agricultural companies.

Human development index (HDI):[1] It can be expected that the municipalities with a higher HDI would show better results. A higher HDI involves lower poverty levels and higher education and service levels.

This entails the availability of more resources to invest in activities other than those that are mandatory in order to satisfy the basic needs of the municipal inhabitants.

Field presence: An effective coproduction of public services for the rural populations demands the field presence of government authorities. A greater field presence of the authorities facilitates their assessment of the local conditions and the development of locally adequate solutions.

Existence of degraded soils: The demand for public services is usually higher in those municipalities where a high percentage of the local producers are working in areas of high soil degradation.

Number of community-based organizations active in the agricultural sector: It is expected that the pressure exerted by the constituency upon the municipal administration to deliver rural-development and agricultural services would be stronger in those municipalities with a higher number of community-based organizations involved in the agricultural sector.

Capability of community-based organizations: If community-based organizations are well organized, it is more likely that they will lobby efficiently before the municipal government, and that they might attract the attention of municipal, regional, and central authorities for the purpose of solving those problems prioritized by their organizations.

Empirical Analysis

In order to find out which factors explain the motivation of Chilean municipal governments to generate services for the agricultural sector and the conditions enabling the delivery of high-quality services, a survey was conducted in forty rural municipalities located between Regions 3 and 10 of the country. The selection of those forty rural municipalities was made at random using two basic criteria to define their rural character. These criteria are: (1) total population of less than 20,000 inhabitants and (2) rurality index greater than 50 percent. Map 5.1 shows the geographical location of our forty sampled municipal territories. The representativeness of the sample was verified after its selection. Several characteristics of the sample were compared against the total municipal population regarding averages and variances of a series of variables.[2] Applying the F- and t-tests (assuming unequal variances), no significant differences were found (95 percent confidence level) between the sample and the total population of the small rural municipalities.

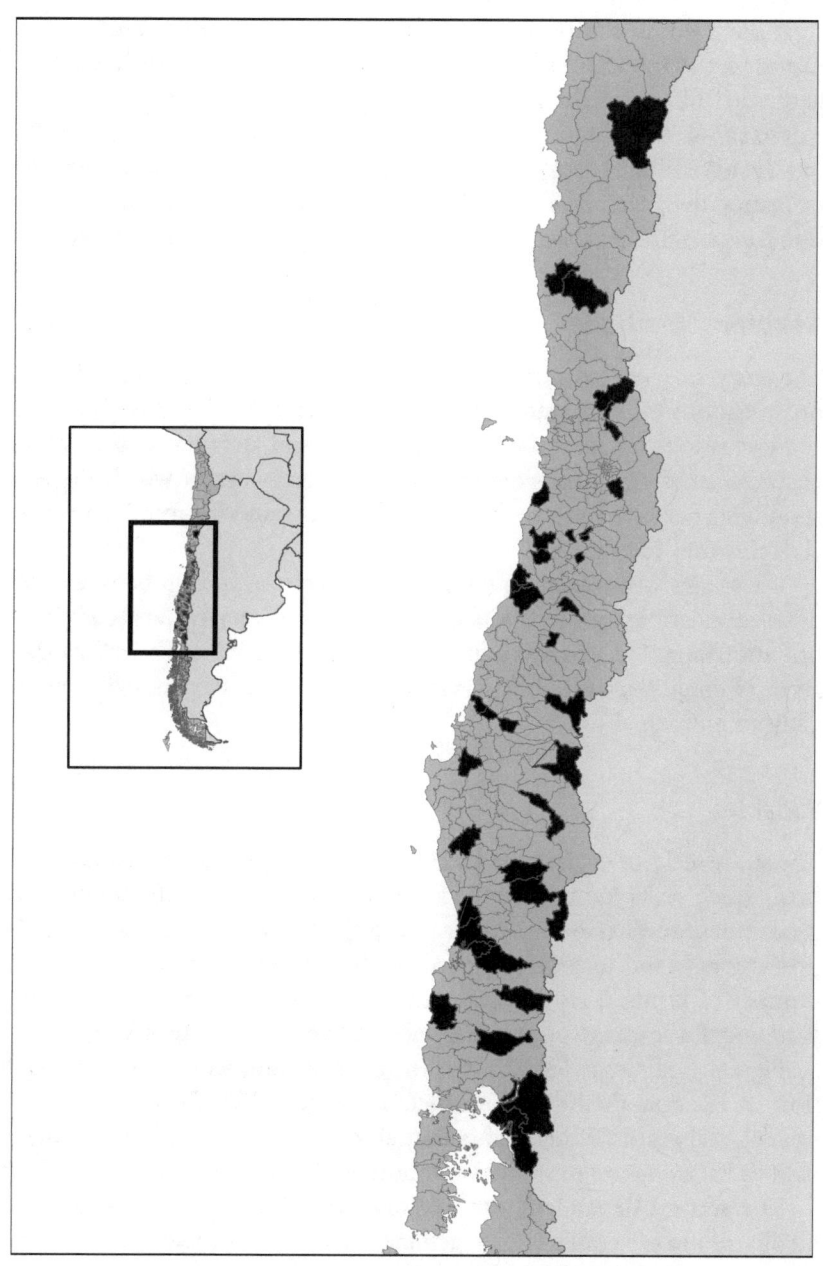

Map 5.1 Sampled municipalities in Chile (*n* = 40). (Map by Paul Lewin)

A survey was conducted in the selected municipalities among the mayors and three community-based organization representatives active in the agricultural sector of each municipality. The objective of this survey was to capture the characteristics and perceptions of local actors regarding the agricultural sector, their interests, their political and economic priorities, their technical capabilities and, most significantly, the institutional arrangements that constitute the municipal governance system.

Analytical Methods

The answers given by municipal authorities (A) and community-based organizations (CBOs) were entered into a database. The analysis of the surveys' results involved the homogenization and systematization of the answers, taking into consideration the different ways in which the respondents perceive the governmental authorities and the municipal officials that they identify.

We use statistical techniques to analyze the relationship between the different possible causal factors and indicators of varying levels of mayors' motivation to produce rural development services, as well as the levels of quality of the public services for rural development delivered in Chilean municipalities.[3]

Variables

The study seeks to explain the variance of three dependent variables. The first, which seeks to measure the level of commitment of the municipal government toward the agricultural sector, was defined as the number of professionals and technicians hired by the municipality divided by the number of farms. This division was made in order to more efficiently compare the coverage of public services delivered by the municipality.

Figure 5.1 shows a descriptive statistic of the municipalities' distribution in relation to the professionals hired to fulfill the needs of the agricultural sector. It highlights that almost 80 percent of the municipalities have one or more hired agronomist or technician.

The second dependent variable describes the trend related to the quality of the agricultural management during the last five years in each municipality. The variable called "agricultural management improvement" derives from a question posed to the community-based organiza-

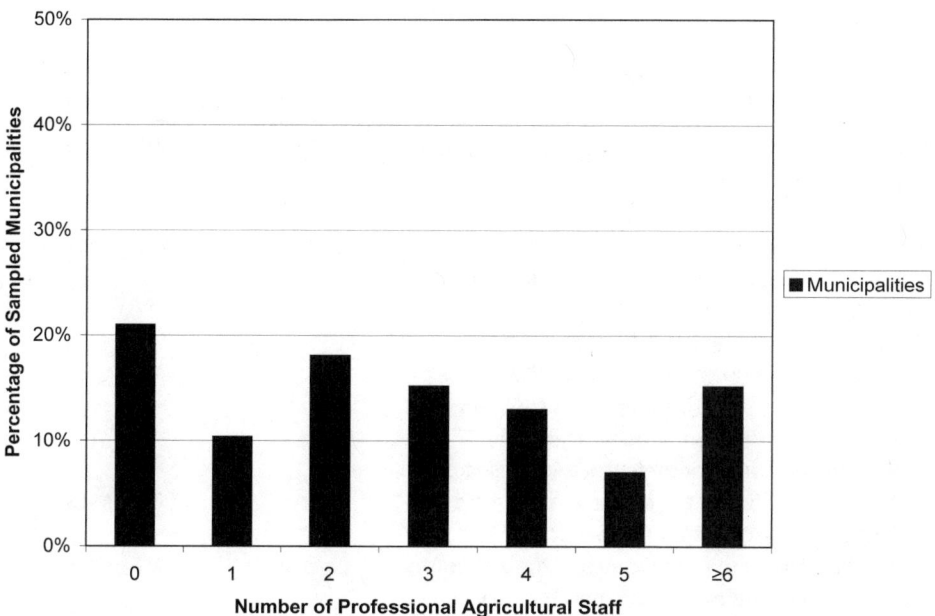

Figure 5.1 Percentage of municipalities as per number of hired agronomists and technicians (FAO Municipal Survey 2002).

tion representatives that were interviewed. The question was: "In what way have the conditions to solve problems in the agricultural sector changed during the last five years?" If at least two of the three representatives responded that the conditions had improved, a value of one was assigned, and a value of zero if the response was negative.

In the third model, the dependent variable used describes the municipal government's relevance in the agricultural sector. As the previous variable, this variable was generated by the survey addressed to the representatives of CBOs. The question posed was whether or not the organization had requested municipal government intervention in the agricultural sector during the last twelve months. In the municipalities where at least two of the three representatives answered in the affirmative, a value of one was assigned, and a value of zero was assigned to the remainder of the municipalities.

Based on the empirical works that were previously discussed in

Table 5.1
Description of variables used in the analysis

Variable description	Comment	Source
Number of agricultural professionals and technicians hired for each 100 farms	Professionals per 100 farms	FAO survey, 1997 Census
At least two community-based organization representatives responded that the conditions to solve problems in the agricultural sector have improved during the last five years	Binary	FAO survey
At least two community-based organization representatives have requested municipal support for the agricultural sector, pointing out the municipal government's relevance in the sector	Binary	FAO survey
Meetings held between the mayor and the regional directors of agricultural public services	Binary	FAO survey
Mayor's opinion on the significance of the agricultural sector's contribution to municipal revenues	Ordinal	FAO survey
Periodicity of the meetings between the mayor and the agricultural CBOs	Number	FAO survey
The mayor's affiliation with ruling party	Binary	SUBDERE
The mayor has completed high school	Binary	FAO survey
The mayor has a university degree	Binary	FAO survey
Years that the mayor has resided in the municipality	Number	FAO survey
Municipal budgetary availability per inhabitant	Budget/capita	SNIM[1]
The municipality belongs to a region farther south of Region 7	Binary	SNIM
Municipal human development index	Ongoing	SNIM
Existence of a participatory platform within the municipality	Binary	FAO survey
Existence of activities jointly performed by community-based organizations and the municipal government	Binary	FAO survey
Number of days per month in which the municipal staff works in the field	Ongoing	FAO survey
Percentage of degraded soils in the municipal territory	Percentage	FAO survey
Number of community-based organizations in the municipality	Ongoing	FAO survey
Organizational capabilities of community-based organizations according to the mayor	Binary	FAO survey

[1] National System of Municipal Indicators

Table 5.2
Descriptive statistic of variables

Variable	CBOs	Average	Standard deviation	Minimum	Maximum
Professionals per farm	39	0.283	0.252	0.000	1.090
Management improvement during the last five years	39	0.641	0.486	0	1
Municipal government relevance	39	0.641	0.486	0	1
Regional directors meetings	39	0.564	0.502	0.000	1.000
Economic significance of agriculture	39	2.333	0.772	1.000	3.000
Periodicity of meetings between mayor and CBOs	39	1.211	1.035	0.000	3.000
Political affiliation of the mayor	39	0.462	0.505	0.000	1.000
The mayor has completed high school	39	0.154	0.366	0.000	1.000
The mayor has a university degree	39	0.410	0.498	0.000	1.000
Existence of degraded soils	39	40.897	22.379	5	90
Years that the mayor has resided in the municipality	39	35.564	18.380	2.000	64.000
HDI of the municipality	39	96.364	52.090	42.920	243.220
Municipal budget per inhabitant	39	0.667	0.478	0.000	1.000
The municipality is farther south than Region 7	39	0.539	0.505	0.000	1.000
Coproduction institutions	39	0.615	0.493	0	1
Coprovision institutions	39	0.333	0.478	0	1
Field presence	39	1.846	0.670	1	3
Number of community-based organizations	39	95.897	67.964	15	293
Community-based organizations' capability	39	0.487	0.506	0	1

this section, the assumption is that any of the independent variables before mentioned could have a bearing on the motivation of the municipal governments and on the quality of the services delivered. Table 5.1 describes the independent variables, and table 5.2 summarizes the main descriptive statistics for each variable. One observation was dropped from the statistical analysis because the data from this municipality were incomplete.

Results

The first model, using the number of agronomists per farm as the dependent variable, was evaluated using the Ordinary Least Square (OLS) method. To estimate the second and third models, which use binary dependent variables, binary logit estimators were used. The results obtained for each model are shown in table 5.3.

The results obtained in the first model show that the four variables that explain the presence of agronomists in the municipal governments are (1) the mayor's high-school education, (2) the mayor's college education, (3) the years that the mayor has resided in the municipality, and (4) the municipal budget per inhabitant.

In this sense, the results provided by the model to explain the municipal performance regarding the delivery of services in rural Chile differ from the results obtained in other countries of the region. However, the other two models used to examine the conditions that have a bearing on the probability of attaining a higher agricultural management within the municipality show similar results to those obtained in other countries.

Discussion of Results

While the municipalities in Chile are under no legal obligation to produce agricultural services, many rural municipalities have a staff of hired agricultural specialists. As per the research carried out in other countries of the region, the municipal performance in a specific sector seems to be driven by the relative strength of three sources of incentives: (1) the effective support to and supervision of the local government by the central government and its agencies, (2) the potential for financial gain, and (3) the demand of the electorate and specific stakeholder groups. In the case of Chile, however, municipal actions regarding the production of rural-development services seem to depend to a greater extent on other variables.

This study found that the central government failed to exert an effective pressure in order to motivate municipalities to produce agricultural services. Although Chilean law does not compel ministries or state services that perform agricultural activities to coordinate said activities with the municipality, it was expected that in the measure that the mayors were involved in a greater interaction and coordination with the directors of the Ministry of Agriculture's decentralized agencies, the municipalities

Table 5.3
Econometric analysis results

Independent variables	Agronomists per farm[a]	Management improvement[a]	Municipal relevance[a]
Regional directors, meetings	0.049	0.012	0.019
	(0.068)	(0.187)	(0.222)
Economic significance of agriculture	0.021	−0.01	0.020
	(0.051)	(0.122)	(0.036)
Periodicity of meetings between mayor and CBOs	0.064	—	—
	(0.051)		
Political affiliation of the mayor	0.05	0.122	0.101
	(0.078)	(0.088)	(0.091)
Time mayor has completed high school[b]	0.222	0.996	−1.216
	(0.079)**	(0.764)	(0.818)
The mayor has a university degree[b]	0.213	0.996	−1.216
	(0.081)**	(0.764)	(0.818)
Years that the mayor has resided in the municipality	0.005	0.068	0.086
	(0.002)**	(0.045)	(0.269)
HDI of the municipality	0.001	0.027	−0.018
	(0.001)*	(0.012)**	(0.011)
Municipal budget per inhabitant	0.002	0.006	0.003
	(0.001)**	(0.013)	(0.015)
The municipality is farther south than Region 7	0.126	—	—
	(0.092)		
Hired agronomists	—	0.091	0.098
		(0.179)	(0.355)
Presence of degraded soils	—	0.102	−0.760
		(0.037)***	(0.881)
Coproduction institutions	—	−1.453	3.695
		(1.342)	(2.166)**
Coprovision institutions	—	−0.896	4.425
		(1.527)	(2.097)**
Field presence	—	1.764	−1.049
		(1.042)*	(1.087)
Number of community-based organizations	—	—	0.050
			(0.023)**
Community-based organizations' capability	—	—	−2.004
			(1.737)
Constant	−0.715	−17.493	7.742
	(0.246)**	(8.61)**	(5.881)
Number of observations	39	39	39
Prob > F	0.0063	0.0105	0.0012
R-square	0.4876	0.4529	0.5718

Note: Factors with standard errors in parentheses:
* $p < 0.10$
** $p < 0.05$
*** $p < 0.01$
[a]Model 1 uses least squares estimators, while Models 2 and 3 use binary logit.
[b]For Models 2 and 3, only one variable is included to describe the mayor's education level: a continuous variable that measures the mayor's years of schooling.

would feel compelled to take action in the agricultural sector, as per the findings of Andersson (2001, 2003), Gibson and Lehoucq (2003), Fiszbein (1997), and Pacheco (2000) in other countries. We did not find this to be the case in Chile. This result may be explained by the fact that the municipal mandate in rural development is to a greater extent voluntary in Chile compared to many other Latin American countries.

In addition, the econometric regression results show that the potential of financial gains for the municipalities exerts no influence over the delivery of municipal agricultural services, as suggested by Larson (2002) in the study related to Nicaragua, and by Pacheco and Kaimowitz (1998) in the study related to Bolivia. The foregoing is not surprising in the Chilean case, as the law prevents municipalities from obtaining their own funds from this sector. The main sources of revenue administered by the Chilean municipalities are: land taxes, business licenses, and vehicle circulation permits. It would be advisable, however, to perform additional research to further corroborate this outcome, as the conducted survey did not measure the existence of potential secondary gains (associated to rural nonagricultural employment) that could have a greater impact on the agricultural development of the community.

The demands of the constituency and specific stakeholder groups were also a nonsignificant factor in the model developed. In this sense, the results obtained differ from those found in other countries by Ribot (1999a, 1999b, 2001), Andersson (2003), and Gibson and Lehoucq (2003), who propose that the political pressure from these groups is one of the main institutional incentives compelling the municipalities to take action in support of a specific sector. Contrary to evidence gathered in other countries, this result could be because, even though stakeholder groups may be present in the community, the degree of organization and interaction among them could be less than optimum as to exert an effective pressure on the local government. Ortega (2005), in the case of Brazil, found that though a certain degree of organization exists in the municipalities, a minimum degree of interaction is required among stakeholder groups, and between such groups and the local government, in order for their demands to be effective and materialize into action. In the case of Chile, additional research is necessary to determine why the stakeholder groups in the communities that were studied are not exerting an effective pressure on the municipalities. If none of these local institutional variables seems to systematically influence the likelihood of observing the delivery of agricultural services by professional municipal officers, what factors do?

The years that the mayor has resided in the municipality proved to be a significant variable in the delivery of municipal agricultural services. This implies that the mayor's awareness of the challenges faced by the municipality and its inhabitants plays a major role when deciding on the delivery of agricultural services. In addition, it can be expected that the longer the mayor has lived in the municipality, the closer his or her involvement and relationship with his or her neighbors. In this sense, the pressure exerted by the constituency may exist in an informal manner, because it is easier for the neighbors to approach the mayor to discuss their needs and problems in nonofficial situations. In general, one characteristic of the rural municipalities is that everybody knows everybody else and is aware of each other's problems. Nonetheless, this assumption must be reviewed and tested through further studies since, with the information available for this study, the foregoing is merely a hypothesis.

The years of education of the mayor also proved to be a significant factor in the delivery of municipal agricultural services. By law, all mayors must have completed at least eight years of schooling (complete basic education). However, in those municipalities whose mayors have completed additional years of schooling, the probabilities of the municipality delivering rural-development services increase. The fact that mayors with more years of schooling produce more services can be explained by several reasons. One of them is that the higher the level of education of the mayor, the easier it is for him or her to obtain competitive resources from public development funds to implement productive agricultural projects. Another reason is that he or she is better equipped to appraise the economic and social implications of the sector's development for his or her community.

As per the results obtained in the econometric regression, the availability of financial resources for the delivery of municipal rural development services is significant and, therefore, the wealthiest municipalities tend to offer a larger amount of these services. This result is consistent with the results obtained by Larson (2002) in Nicaragua, where the most successful municipalities in the delivery of services are also the wealthiest.

At the 90 percent confidence level, the level of human development as measured by the human development index (HDI) seems to have a positive effect on the probability of providing more municipal agricultural services. This result implies that the less needy a given municipality is, the more services it is likely to have available for its citizens. Since multivariate regression detects correlation only, we have to speculate about the causal direction between the two variables. It might be that the HDI is higher because there are more services. Or, it may be that a relatively high HDI—an index that includes a measure for education, too—points toward the superior organizational skills of local-policy actors.

The results of the first model analysis suggest that the institutional arrangements among local actors exert no significant impact on the municipal government's motivation to produce and deliver agricultural services. Nonetheless, it is important to consider that the dependent variable used may not be the most suitable as a proxy of the municipal government's commitment with the agricultural sector. The mayors could have included in the reported number of municipal officials working in the agricultural sector the staff financed by the central government (INDAP), who only occupy office space in the municipality. This could have generated a distortion in the results obtained by this study and would explain why the Chilean case shows results that differ from the results obtained in other countries studied. Due to the characteristics of the conducted survey, however, this was the variable that seemed the best suited for estimating the municipal government's commitment.

The analysis of the remaining two models reveals the significance of the local institutional arrangements in the creation of an institutional environment that favors the solution of agricultural challenges and that fosters the perception that the municipal government is a relevant actor in the agricultural sector.

In the second model, three variables seem to have a significant impact on the probability of observing an agricultural management improvement at the municipal level. Two of these variables—the HDI and the existence of degraded soils—are not institutional, but a third one—the municipal government's field presence—is. The institutional variable—the one associated with the municipal authorities' field presence—proves to have the greatest impact on the probability of observing a trend of favorable opinions regarding the sector's governance. Holding all other variables constant at their mean values, if municipal agents would spend one day per month extra in the field, the probability of observing a positive trend would increase by 31 percent.

Regarding the noninstitutional, statistically significant control variables, when the percentage of farmers working on degraded soils is at its lowest point, it is very unlikely (7.6 percent) to observe a trend of favorable opinions regarding the sector's governance and, conversely, when at its highest point, it is very likely (99.8 percent) to observe favorable opinions regarding agricultural governance. Apparently, Chilean municipalities do a particularly well-appreciated job supporting farmers facing problems related to soil degradation.

The results of the third model—using the relevance of the municipal government in the agricultural sector as the dependent variable—also show(more prominently so than the second model discussed above) the significance of local institutions, whether formal or informal, in achieving a suitable municipal governance in the sector. Factors that seem to have a bearing on the probability that community-based organizations may consider the municipal government as a relevant actor within the sector are (1) the presence of institutions for the coprovision of services, (2) the presence of institutions for the coproduction of services, and (3) the number of community-based organizations within the municipality. In other words, the local institutions that organize the interactions among actors at the municipal level exert a significant impact on the municipal relevance in the agricultural sector.

Of the three variables that exert a major effect, the coprovision and coproduction institutions have a very strong, positive impact on the probability that the municipality may be perceived as a relevant actor. For example, the creation of a participatory municipal forum—a coprovision institution—increases said probability from 64.5 percent to 95.0 percent, holding all other independent variables at their mean values. The impact of the coproduction institutions' existence is even greater in municipalities lacking said institutions, where the probability that CBOs may consider the municipality to be relevant for the sector is only 19 percent, but when this value rises to its maximum, the same probability increases to 97.8 percent, ceteris paribus. Finally, those municipalities with more community-based organizations in the agricultural sector seem to show a higher probability that the farmers would request municipal government interventions in the agricultural sector. An increase of one CBO per municipality is equivalent to a 0.5 percent increase in the likelihood of observing high municipal government relevance in the sector.

Both the second and the third model produced results that are coherent with the theoretical propositions related to the significance of the presence of formal and informal institutions at the local level to provide a framework for the farmers' participation in the decision-making processes regarding the provision and production of agricultural services. It seems that the municipalities that have created coprovision and coproduction institutions are better equipped to provide viable answers to the challenges faced by the rural sector.

Conclusions

The study allows us to conclude that the institutional arrangements for collective action among the actors of the municipal-governance system are not the only factors explaining the variation in municipal performance in the agricultural sector. On the contrary, to explain the variation in the appointment of technical staff to the agricultural sector, the institutional factors are not the main determinants. Rather, the likelihood of delivery of these services is associated with the availability of municipal resources, the mayor's level of education, and his or her knowledge of the area and its inhabitants, a factor that differs from the results obtained in other countries. As for the probability of observing signs of a higher quality in the public services delivered, the local institutional arrangements seem to have a remarkable positive influence, just as in the other three countries included in this study.

The results obtained in Chile are remarkable because they show that the mere presence of municipal consensus-building forums is insufficient in itself to foster a fair and democratic municipal system of governance. Moreover, these results demonstrate that most of the decisions related to the public investments for rural development and the promotion of agriculture and rural development in general are still made in the central government in the capital city. The design, implementation, monitoring, and assessment of development funds, promotional instruments, and social-policy programs are not usually the responsibility of local governments. To date, municipal governance is still primarily concentrated in areas related to health, education, infrastructure, and public safety. The Chilean municipalities that do produce rural-development services do so by their own initiatives and using their own resources.

The Chilean case presents an imbalance between the central government's objective of a macro-level policy and the realities that prevail at the local level. Thus, the local governments' potential to ensure effective creation and implementation of public-service programs related to rural development, and the mobilization of inclusive citizen participation in such programs, lacks an enabling incentive structure. Consequently, such programs are rarely created in rural Chile, where resources are scarce and the needs are many. For local politicians in this context, it makes more sense to draw on the central-government programs that already exist.

Notwithstanding these limitations, the results also imply that local governments in Chile represent a potential that has not been fully exploited by the country's public policy for rural development. The analysis suggests that Chilean municipal governments could play a more significant role in the agricultural sector in the future, as most of them are already performing activities of a significant scope and magnitude, but they could achieve even more with greater authority and support.

Given the foregoing, it seems particularly important to explicitly address the role of rural municipalities and mechanisms of cooperation between local authorities and farmers when thinking about a reform of the agricultural services' provision system. The municipalities might play their most constructive role if allowed to act as intermediaries between local farmers and central-government institutions, consolidating and submitting to the latter the demands related to the provision of services or support for contracting the services required by the local farmers. In addition, the reform might involve a policy-making process that stresses institutions for downward accountability and transparency so that the right public services are delivered, in an efficient manner, and to those farmers who need them the most.

We believe that the outcome of our research is significant because it provides information on the links between collective action and the supply and quality of the rural-development services produced at the local level. In Chile, the current knowledge about the operation and effects of the consensus-building mechanisms between the agricultural producers and the municipality is very limited and is essentially built on theoretical ideas that have not been put to the test in the real world. In this sense, this study performs one of the first empirical tests of the conditions that are believed to influence the existence and quality of these public services. However, many questions are left unanswered by this study. One of these questions is under what conditions the central government would be prepared to transfer more resources, rights, and responsibilities to local governments for the creation of rural-development programs. And if the central government decides to devolve such powers, what specific division of roles between the center, the municipality, the farmers, and other parts of civil society would make the most sense for the Chilean public economy? These are questions that are gaining relevance in Chile, and public policy for rural development would benefit from more systematic research on these.

One way for Chilean government officials and other individuals interested in answering the question of what would happen if the Chilean government did decide to decentralize more of the decision-making powers related to rural development to municipal governments would be to study the countries in the region that have already started such experiments. One country that would be of particular relevance to study for reformist Chileans would be Mexico, because this is a country that recently decided to step up its efforts to involve local governments more in rural-development activities. In the next chapter, we analyze how local governments and community-based organizations in Mexico have responded to this reform process.

6
Mexico
A Case of Limited Decentralization

With Fabián González and Juan José Ochoa

One important difference between Mexico and the other three countries included in this study (Brazil, Peru, and Chile) is the local-government mandate. In the case of Mexico, the municipalities' formal influence on agricultural matters is almost nonexistent, and they have only recently gained legal jurisdiction in rural-development matters. All this is reflected by the lack of financial resources as well as by the overwhelming influence enjoyed by state and federal governments. In Brazil, the municipal government enjoys greater decision-making authority over these services through the Municipal Councils; in Chile, the services are more free-market oriented; while in Peru, the centralized structure does not officially recognize the role of local governments in delivering services for rural development.

Mexico's insertion in international markets during the 1980s, and the search for efficiency in public administration pursuant to international changes, gave rise to a series of decentralization reforms that are shaping public policies in Mexico to this day. Within the context of the reactivation of the decentralization process, President Ernesto Zedillo's administration launched a broad "Program for a New Federalism" during the six-year period between 1995 and 2000. This renewed federalism meant the exercise of the state sovereignty and municipal freedom, strengthening the powers of both these local governments. This process was acknowledged within the 1995–2000 National Development Plan,[1] which also set forth the main spheres of governmental action where processes of federalization were to be fostered, i.e., health and social security, the promotion of agriculture, rural development, and the protection of natural resources and the environment. This new federalism program sought to generate the institutional conditions needed to address pressing local issues and take advantage of the capabilities ensuing from the region's diversity, particularly in natural resources, to become an instrument for the redistribution of resources and opportunities.

Despite the inclusion of rural-development goals in the reforms, and the significant resources that were actually transferred to municipalities, most of local-government efforts have concentrated on the operation of traditional services and urban-infrastructure programs. Until recently, not much progress had been made regarding the decentralized governance of rural-development activities in Mexico. During the course of our fieldwork in 2002, it became evident that relatively few municipalities had created their own rural-development programs to support the productive activities of the rural poor, but we also observed an enormous variation in the degree of importance placed on rural development by different municipal governments. In this chapter, we seek to explain what factors help explain such variation.

Agricultural-service activities in Mexico are governed principally by federal and state governments, while the municipalities are left—for the time being—with the exclusive mandate of managing, implementing, and monitoring selected project activities within these programs. Even under such institutional constraints, we propose that the municipal governments play a crucial role in the creation of institutional arrangements that can bring about public policies for improved agricultural productivity in the rural areas. To illustrate the important role played by municipal governments, we provide two examples from different parts of Mexico.

One of the municipal governments that we visited during our fieldwork is the municipality of Comala in the state of Colima. Here, we observed strong interaction between the municipal officials and rural smallholders. The intense activity of coffee growers in the sierra has been constantly backed by the municipal authorities, regardless of their political party, mainly due to the strength of the coffee growers' CBO itself and because, for several administrative periods, the municipalities in power cleverly have taken advantage of this strength to negotiate resources or support the farmers' negotiations. This has exerted a positive influence in the farmers' opinion of the municipality and has greatly facilitated the local governance of the agricultural sector, as it encourages other farmers to improve their respective organizations.

This positive experience is in stark contrast with the realities found in the municipality of Cuautitlán de García Barragán, in the state of Jalisco. Here, we observed that the interactions between farmers and local authorities were essentially nonexistent. In the community of Cuzalapa, different interests of forest users and farmers oppose a natural-resources conservation policy in a biosphere reserve managed by the federal government, since by decree the forest utilization should have ceased. This situation led the federal authorities and the local residents to part ways, since the latter strongly preferred to resume forest utilization. However, the strong presence of the federal government opposing this utilization, and the meager participation of the local government in the process, prevented institutional resources from being allocated to support other types of productive activities that could have benefited these farmers.

These two examples illustrate that the work performed by municipal governments can have a high impact on the rural poor, since their decisions are often of high local relevance as they may involve quick solutions of disputes between citizens, public construction works, and the delivery of services, as well as the monitoring and enforcement of the municipal ordinances and other regulations.

Background

More than 25 percent of Mexico's total population resides in rural areas. In terms of agricultural production, rural localities face many challenges. The general lack of infrastructure and financial resources, weak governmental organizations, and few extension and training programs all limit the prospects for future improvements in terms of rural development.

The rural population[2] resides in about 190,000 different communities —Mexican municipalities usually consist of multiple communities— generating great population dispersion and a huge obstacle to centralized provision of basic services and infrastructure, hence increasing the economic management cost of the production units.

In addition, the labor structure of the agricultural sector reveals that more than 50 percent of its working population is composed of individuals with no land of their own, participating in a seasonal labor market that offers few or no social security benefits as well as scarce training and development opportunities. For example, SAGARPA (2001) calculated that the average added value per employee in the agriculture sector is four times less than in other economic sectors. In addition, they found that the specific weight of the agricultural income in the farmers' total income is inversely proportional to the size of the production unit: for farmers with less than two hectares, the agricultural income accounts for as much as 70 percent of the total income.

Furthermore, the Mexican countryside is characterized by the prevalence of smallholdings,[3] a low level of technological support (90 percent of all farmers lack proper access to it), and a population pyramid with large cohorts under fifteen and over fifty. The situation is particularly dire in the country's indigenous communities,[4] where 75 percent of its inhabitants are living in conditions of extreme poverty.

Between 1993 and 1999, the average productivity per hectare increased by 5 percent, while the relative prices of the agricultural sector decreased by 25 percent. This situation contrasts with the food-manufacturing sector, which not only increased productivity but also, during the same period, experienced a price increase that was 3 percent above the general level of actual prices of the economy. This income generation advantage presented by the transformation of agricultural products has not been fully capitalized by the small-scale agricultural farmers due to their scarce incorporation into the processed-food markets (SAGARPA 2001).

Given the dire situation in rural Mexico, a fundamental challenge faced by scholars, practitioners, and political actors alike is to find ways to strengthen the local authorities in the rural municipalities of Mexico so as to not only empower them but also to provide them with the means and incentives to undertake the new competencies assigned to them by the decentralization process. The purpose of this chapter is to contribute to this challenge by analyzing factors that are likely to be associated with superior municipal-service performance in the rural societies of Mexico.

Municipal Governance of Rural Development in Mexico

As per the last wave of reforms in Mexico, the relevance of the municipal government has increased significantly. With the introduction of the 2002 Law on Sustainable Rural Development, municipal officials have ever-increasing responsibilities, powers, and resources at their disposal. However, many of the amendments to other laws and policies have remained stagnant, without producing actual and practical changes on the ground. This section reviews the literature that seeks to explain why the changes have failed to materialize.

Enrique Cabrero (2000, 4) claims that one reason why major differences exist between the formal mandate and the actual situation in the field has to do with the history of the political regime in Mexico. He maintains that one of the core issues of the current decentralization process of the public sector in the country is "the absence of management instruments to incorporate a comprehensive vision of local development so that the municipality can be perceived as a development promotion agent and as part of a regional project, with a diversity of actors and resources that are both complementary and competitive among the regions of the country. The vision of the municipality as an isolated entity that should be self-sufficient and unique has generated policies that are inefficient and projects that are weak."

On the other hand, Victoria Rodríguez (1998) points out that the decentralized reforms of the mid-1980s were brought about more as a response to a need for democratic legitimization than as an integral and coordinated effort to improve the performance of the public administration. Decentralization placed the presidential centralism's hegemony at risk (even more so at a time when the opposition began gaining ground in state[5] and local governments). Nonetheless, the then ruling party—the Institutional Revolutionary Party (Partido Revolucionario Institucional, or PRI)[6]—considered it to be necessary in order to maintain—or, regain —its legitimacy.

Decentralization has therefore not taken place in the way that the formal laws and regulations would suggest. In its territorial review on Mexico, the OECD (2003) points out that the transfer of responsibilities to the state and municipal entities has failed to be followed by the transfer of resources, audit capability, and institutional and staff training necessary to exercise the new competencies. The report concludes that the factors that determine whether the states and municipalities are able to perform as expected are related to the extent to which municipal governments have sufficient financial resources, capacities, and efficient administrations.[7]

The current situation implies a largely underutilized exploitation of the decentralization advantages: thanks to the greater autonomy acquired through the decentralization process, the progressive and successful sectors and territories are better positioned to make adequate decisions that would in turn be more effective responses to perceived problems and needs. However, in more underdeveloped regions, the OECD report continues, the decentralization process might actually lead to further development retardation: here, economic difficulties would be worsened by the decentralization process, since they would be less capable than before of receiving assistance and support from the central government (OECD 2001, 18–19). Lack of financial support and qualified human resources are routinely brought forward when discussing sub-par municipal performance. Although we do not deny the importance of these factors, by emphasizing the relevance of institutions for collective action—institutions that facilitate coprovision and coproduction of

96 Chapter 6

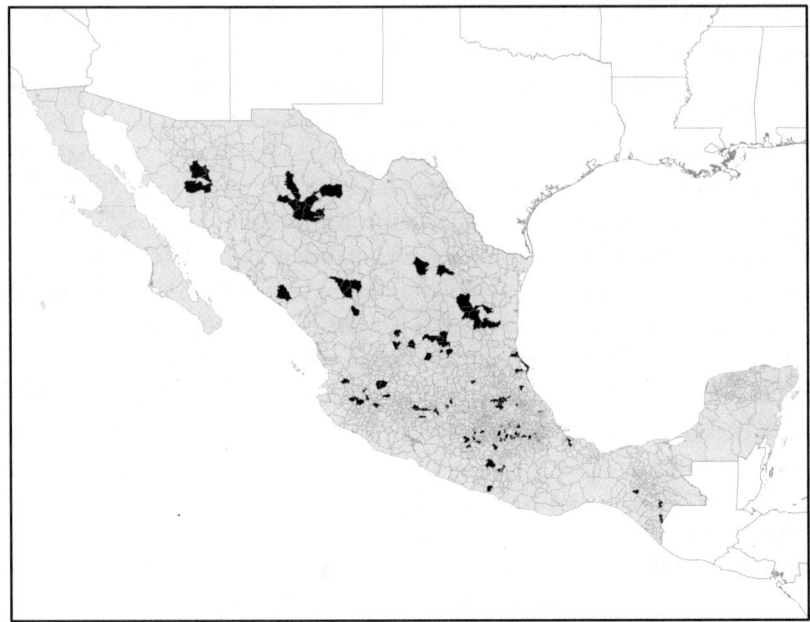

Map 6.1 Sampled municipalities in Mexico (*n* = 150). (Map by Krister Andersson)

public services—in this book, we broaden the scope of local-governance analyses beyond the usual suspects.

Variation in Municipal Performance in the Mexican Agricultural Sector

Because the performance of new rural-development initiatives in Mexico increasingly depends on the effectiveness of municipal governments, it is important to study and monitor how these local administrations handle their new responsibilities in the agricultural sector. This section presents the results obtained from a survey among respondents in a representative sample of 147 rural municipalities in twenty-one Mexican states.[8] Map 6.1 shows the geographical distribution of these municipalities throughout the Mexican territory. Three individuals associated with municipal services for the agricultural sector were interviewed in each of the 150 municipalities: the mayor and two community-based organization leaders of the municipality.

The results of the survey confirm the significance of the agricultural vocation for the citizens of rural municipalities. In 89 percent of the municipalities visited, the majority (60 percent) of the population makes its living from the agricultural activities. However, this significance is not always mirrored in the mayors' political priorities. A bit more than half of the rural Mexican municipalities do not have technical staff working in the agricultural area. Nonetheless and despite this lack of technicians, according to the mayors, almost 60 percent of the municipalities jointly perform activities with the CBOs in the agricultural sector.

Similarly, a bit more than half of the community-based organizations' leaders interviewed (51 percent) consider that the main problem of the municipalities is the lack of economic resources. Twenty-six percent considered that the main problem is the lack of support provided by federal and state governments to the municipalities. Mayors largely shared this view.

One often-expressed justification for decentralization is the local governments' capacity to be aware of and respond to the farmers' demands. This taken-for-granted argument is somewhat challenged by our respondents. The survey asked community-based organizations whether or not the municipal agricultural services effectively responded to the local needs. Figure 6.1 shows that community-based organizations have different opinions regarding the quality of existing services.

To assess the farmers' perception regarding possible changes in the quality of the agricultural services provided in the municipality since 1996, we asked the community-based organizations' representatives to compare the quality of the current services with those provided five years ago, before the recent decentralization initiatives in the agricultural sector. The responses presented in figure 6.1 show that a little more that half of all respondents consider that the services have not improved.

These indicators show that municipal performance in rural Mexico is very mixed. This observation is in fact very consistent with our findings in Brazil, Peru, and Chile. In the next section, we explore the factors that might explain why some municipalities perform better than others in the agricultural sector. Our analysis particularly explores the role played by the local-level institutional arrangements in the organization of work in the agricultural sector and in rural development.

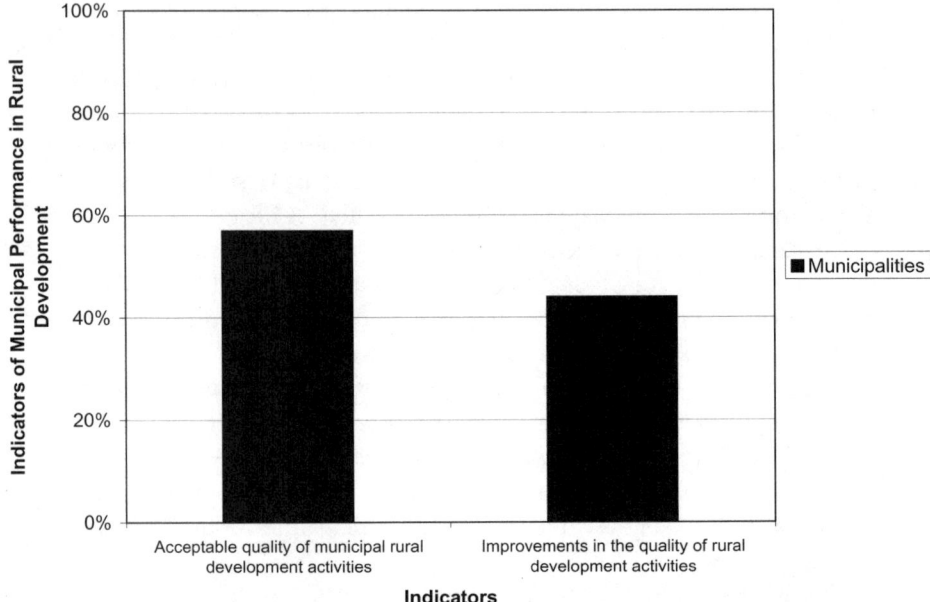

Figure 6.1 Indicators of Service Quality among Mexican Municipalities (FAO Municipal Survey 2002).

Empirical Analysis

The empirical analysis explores the role of formal and informal institutions created by actors involved in the provision and production of agricultural services in the selected Mexican municipalities. The analysis aims at increasing our knowledge regarding the impact of institutions for collective action on the local government's potential to promote local development in rural areas. Through the systematic analysis of the conditions and characteristics of the 147 municipalities, we test the following hypothesis:

The level of performance of public services in their attempt to alleviate poverty, halt environmental degradation, and promote productivity increases in the agricultural sector is associated with the character of the institutional arrangements for collective action at the municipal level.

We test the validity of this hypothesis by examining a series of more specific subhypotheses. According to the first subhypothesis, the municipal government will be motivated to provide agricultural services in its territory as long as it is in the mayors' political or economic interest to do so. In this context, we propose that there are at least three sources of institutional incentives that would motivate the mayor to give political priority to the management of agricultural services: (1) the mayor's perception regarding the pressure exerted by the central government, measured by the periodicity of agriculture-related meetings between both parties; (2) the pressure exerted by CBOs on the mayor, measured by the periodicity of agriculture-related meetings between CBOs and the mayor; and (3) the existence or nonexistence of a municipal forum or council where actors meet to plan joint activities.

The second subhypothesis suggests that the quality of agricultural public services is associated with the local institutional capacity to effectively communicate and cooperate with actors working in the agricultural sector within the municipal territory. In other words, we propose that the probability of providing high-quality services increases when the municipal administration promotes communication and cooperation arrangements with local actors.

We further propose that there are two local institutional arrangements that have a bearing on the production of high-quality agricultural services: (1) the existence of activities that are jointly planned and implemented by the municipal government and the CBO, and (2) the political stability in the municipality, measured by the time served by the current mayor. Table 6.1 shows the descriptive statistics of each variable considered in the analysis.

The statistical analysis explores the influence of these institutional variables on the municipal performance in the agricultural sector through a systematic comparison of the experiences obtained in the 147 selected municipalities. This comparison controls for the potential influence of other variables not directly related to the local institutional arrangements but that could also influence the quality of municipal services. For instance, the personal attributes of the mayor (i.e., education level, whether or not he/she is a native of the area, etc.) and several structural characteristics (size of the municipality, population density, municipal budget, etc.) are frequently cited as alternative explanations for variable municipal performance in the decentralization literature (e.g., see Fiszbein 1997; Larson 2002; Blair 2000; Nygren 2005). The incorporation of

Table 6.1
Description of variables

Variables	Description	Minimum	Maximum	Mean	Standard Deviation
Municipal technicians	Binary variable showing whether the municipality has its own agricultural staff (1 = yes, 0 = no)	0	1	0.503	0.502
Coproduction of services	Binary variable that shows whether agricultural services are produced in cooperation between local government and CBOs (1 = yes, 0 = no)	0	1	0.517	0.501
Farmers' response	Binary variable that specifies whether or not the municipal administration has positively responded to the requests for intervention voiced by local farmers	0	1	0.531	0.501
Improvements in agricultural management during the last five years	Binary variable describing the perception of community-based organizations regarding the trend of municipal agricultural management (1 = improvements since 1996, 0 = lack of improvements since 1996)	0	1	0.441	0.498
Demand of the central government	Periodicity of monthly meetings between central and municipal government representatives	2	12	6.545	3.514
Demand of CBOs	Periodicity of monthly meetings between municipal government and community-based organization representatives	1	10	5.308	2.866
Coproduction institutions	Binary variable describing whether or not there is a municipal system to plan and implement joint activities between the local government and community-based organizations	0	2	0.860	0.827

Variable	Description			
Existence of a municipal forum	Binary variable describing whether or not there is a municipal forum for participatory planning	0	2	0.545	0.757
Political stability	The number of mayors that have ruled since 1996	0	3	1.622	0.637
Property sizes	The average size (in hectares) of the agricultural properties in each municipality	0.061	129.772	6.695	15.567
Population density	Number of people per km² in each municipality (2000 census)	0.004	14.850	0.953	1.986
Agricultural population	Ratio of people engaged in agricultural activities as a primary economic activity (2000 agricultural census)	10.068	118.678	48.923	20.411
Southwestern region	Binary variable that describes whether or not the municipality is located in the southwestern region	0	1	0.664	0.474
Soil degradation	Perception of the mayor as to the ratio of agricultural properties with degraded soils	0	100	50.378	21.814
Transfer of funds	The significance of the funds provided by the federal government for agriculture	0	5	3.007	2.105
Human development index	Index that includes measurements on illiteracy levels, infant mortality and Gross Domestic Product per capita (UNDP 2000)	0.429	0.784	0.682	0.066
Municipal income per capita	Municipal budget per individual residing in the municipality (2000 national census)	33.785	1541.735	216.624	193.959
Permanency	Years that the mayor has resided in the locality	0	64	39.175	11.937
Education	Level of mayor's formal education	0	6	3.580	1.813
Gender	Mayor's gender (0 = male, 1 = female)	0	1	0.028	0.165

Note: For each variable, *N* equals 147.

these variables in the statistical analysis allows us to isolate the influence of institutional variables from alternative explanations to the observed outcome variance.

Results

The empirical analysis seeks to shed new light on two major questions related to the performance of the decentralized governance of rural-development services in Mexico: First, what motivates mayors to intervene in the agricultural sector? Second, what institutional factors have a bearing on the provision and production of good-quality agricultural services?

What Motivates Mayors?

We performed a quantitative analysis to explain why some municipalities are more motivated than others to provide agricultural services and to cooperate with community-based organizations. We used statistical methods of logit regression in the two models. Table 6.2 shows the results of the analysis.

The variables considered in the first regression model explain 47 percent of the variance in the number of municipalities that have contracted professional staff in the agricultural sector. Controlling for the potential influences of structural characteristics of the agricultural sector and the personal attributes of the mayor, it is clear that the existence of several incentives positively affects the likelihood that a municipality will contract a professional agronomist. Specifically, three institutional variables explain why some municipalities are more motivated than others: the demands from the central government ($p < 0.10$), from the electorate ($p < 0.10$), and of the institution for municipal participatory planning ($p < 0.10$). In addition, it is clear that those municipalities with a higher ratio of farmers working in degraded soils are the ones most motivated to invest in hiring municipal technical staff. All other things equal, the existence of consensus-building forums and the existence of other institutions that encourage and facilitate the frequent interaction between representatives of the authorities and community-based organizations are key factors to explain the varying degrees of motivation for local authorities to intervene in agricultural activities.

The second step in our quantitative analysis is to examine the factors

Table 6.2
Binary logit results

Variables	Model 1: Agricultural staff	Model 2: Coproduction of services	Model 3: Political response to farmers	Model 4: Agricultural management improvements
Institutional arrangements				
Central government's demand	0.080*	−0.042	−0.104	0.130**
	(0.049)	(0.073)	(0.070)	(0.062)
Demand from CBOs	0.169*	0.272***	0.474***	0.187
	(0.095)	(0.087)	(0.170)	(0.158)
Coproduction institutions	0.255	NA	0.617**	0.735***
	(0.290)		(0.281)	(0.258)
Existence of a municipal forum	0.558*	0.819***	−0.082	0.084
	(0.315)	(0.284)	(0.316)	(0.282)
Political stability	−0.535	−0.363	−0.178	−0.373
	(0.416)	(0.346)	(0.375)	(0.340)
Structural Characteristics				
Size of agricultural properties	0.021	−0.007	−0.079**	0.014
	(0.019)	(0.016)	(0.038)	(0.015)
Population density	−0.051	0.194	0.090	0.042
	(0.114)	(0.149)	(0.125)	(0.102)
Percentage of agricultural population	−0.058***	−0.001	0.004	−0.007
	(0.014)	(0.011)	(0.012)	(0.011)
Southwestern region	0.217	−1.077*	2.421***	0.343
	(0.597)	(0.582)	(0.654)	(0.578)
Soil degradation	0.032***	0.025**	−0.004	0.019**
	(0.012)	(0.011)	(0.011)	(0.010)
Central government transfer	0.012	0.238**	0.050	−0.021
	(0.108)	(0.104)	(0.103)	(0.093)
Human development index	−3.874	2.656	0.136	−0.067
	(3.670)	(3.159)	(3.293)	(3.008)
Municipal resources	0.001	−0.001	−0.001	0.001
	(0.001)	(0.641)	(0.001)	(0.001)
Attributes of the mayor				
Mayor's years of residence	0.024	0.035*	0.000	−0.002
	(0.020)	(0.019)	(0.018)	(0.016)
Mayor's level of formal education	−0.200	0.103	0.256**	−0.144
	(0.130)	(0.115)	(0.120)	(0.108)
Mayor's gender	−0.129	2.335	24.656	−0.319
	(1.336)	(1.611)	(1.496)	(1.263)
Constant	2.203	−5.766**	−2.979	−1.620
	(3.118)	(2.935)	(2.885)	(2.589)
Observations	147	147	147	147
r² (Nagelkerke)	0.47	0.38	0.41	0.25

Note: Regression coefficient, with standard error in parentheses:
* $p < 0.10$
** $p < 0.05$
*** $p < 0.001$

having a bearing on the municipal decision to collaborate or not with community-based organizations in the production of agricultural services (coproduction). Our analysis shows the particular significance of five key factors. Two institutional variables stand out. First, the existence of a municipal forum where the different actors meet to plan the municipal agricultural activities has a positive and highly significant effect ($p < 0.01$) on the probability of materializing such cooperation, when all other variables are held constant. The intensity of the community-based organizations' demands also exerts a positive and significant influence ($p < 0.05$) on the probability of the emergence of such cooperation.

The influence of these two factors is consistent with our logic regarding the motivation of local politicians. Nonetheless, the role played by the central government in relation to such cooperation is surprising. As per the analysis, the cooperation between the municipality and CBOs increases when the mayor receives significant funds from the central government to develop the agricultural sector. This outcome could be related to the existence of federal programs such as Alianza para el Campo and PROCAMPO in the sense that a municipality that receives funds from these sources would be more inclined to cooperate with a farmer organization to carry out activities jointly. It is therefore possible that cooperation is more viable when the municipal authorities have access to these funds.

Our analysis shows that those administrations located in areas where a high percentage of farmers suffer from degraded soils have a higher probability of developing cooperation opportunities between the municipal authority and the community-based organizations. However, given the fact that the question regarding soil degradation was asked to the mayor, properly, the outcome suggests that the probability of coproduction of agricultural services increases when the mayor perceives the problem to be more severe.

Federal and state agricultural-support programs increasingly demand more control mechanisms regarding the use of the resources transferred to municipalities and farmers. Federal policies are increasingly aimed at overcoming paternalism and subsidiary schemes, at the promotion of accountability mechanisms, at local ownership, and the empowerment of farmers. The governmental strategy in Mexico, at least officially, promotes the idea that municipalities should be increasingly transformed into actors who facilitate a process in which farmers come together to agree on development priorities and resources. As a consequence, many municipalities increasingly become involved in the agricultural sector's development processes, using a diversity of existing forums such as the Municipal Councils for Agricultural Development, the Committee for Municipal Development Planning (COPLADEMUN), and now, with the 2002 Law on Sustainable Rural Development, through the corresponding municipal committees.

The operational mechanism of all these forums is similar in nature. They are led by the mayor, and all social actors involved in the matter participate in the discussions regarding existing problems and possible solutions. The agenda-setting powers of the mayors and other municipal officials are likely to affect the role of these institutions, and at the margin one can expect the performance of the forums to depend at least in part on the personal commitment of the mayor as well as the response given by the state and federal authorities to the demands generated by these forums. This said, however, it is clear from the results of our analysis that the forums display an independent effect on the municipal government's commitment to rural development.

What Institutional Factors Have a Bearing on the Quality of Agricultural Services?

The second subhypothesis of the study suggests that the quality of public agricultural services is associated with the local institutions' effectiveness in facilitating communication and information exchange between actors involved in the municipal governance of public services. Two indicators of the quality of public services were used in the empirical analysis: (1) the degree of municipal responsiveness to the farmer organizations' demands for intervention in the agricultural sector and (2) the community-based organizations' perception regarding potential improvements in the quality of public-service administration during the last five years. It is worthwhile to point out that the analysis under this subhypothesis is not limited to public services exclusively produced by the municipal government. On the contrary, the analysis takes into consideration the potential role of the municipal government in the provision and production of services that often involve actors at higher levels of governance, such as, for instance, at regional, state, and national levels.

Figure 6.1 shows the diversity in the community-based organizations' perceptions of the quality of agricultural services. Herein below, through the statistical analysis, we explore the possible causes of these differences.

The regression regarding the municipality's responsiveness to the requests of farmer organizations (table 6.2, Model 3) reveals that the independent variables considered explain 41 percent of the variance. The same variables explain 25 percent of the variance in the perception of changes in the quality of the agricultural services (table 6.2, Model 4). The results of the regression suggest that the responsiveness toward farmer organizations is determined by a combination of the following independent variables:

- The level of formal education of the mayor (a mayor with a higher level of education has a greater probability of being responsive to the demands of community-based organizations).
- The region where the municipality is located (it is more likely that a municipality located in the country's southwestern region responds positively to farmers than municipalities in other parts of the country).
- The average size of agricultural properties in the municipality (it is less likely that the administration of a municipality with large-sized properties will consider the farmers' demands than municipalities with smaller-sized properties).
- The existence of coproduction arrangements between the municipality and the local communities (more such arrangements generate greater attention to the problems of small-scale farmers).
- The strength of the organized demand from local farmers (a stronger demand generates an increase in the probability of responding positively to farmers' demands).

As per our analysis, factors explaining the differences in perceptions regarding the improvement of the quality of agricultural services during the last five years are, by degree of influence, the community-based organizations' demands ($p < 0.01$), the central government's demand ($p < 0.05$), and the severity of degradation of farm lands in the municipality ($p < 0.05$). These three variables have a positive effect that is statistically significant.

The positive effect of the community-based organizations' demand on the perceived amelioration of local-government performance is statistically significant in both models 3 and 4. This result highlights the relevance of the institutions for downward accountability.

The analysis also speaks to the potential role of municipal governments in facilitating the delivery of public services that may not be formally mandated to them. Note that the indicator related to the quality of services refers to agricultural services in general, and not only to services delivered by the municipality. However, the clear influence on the municipality-related variables, such as the demands received by the mayor from the community-based organizations and the central government, suggests that the municipal government's decisions have a distinct effect on the quality of public services for the agricultural sector. In spite of a limited mandate for the sector, it is clear that the Mexican municipal governments can play a significant role in facilitating the production of high-quality agricultural services.

One of the major limitations of the federal government is its limited capacity to serve the end users; except for the education and health sector, in which—although full coverage is not yet provided—the services in these areas are provided through an infrastructure that compels efforts to be coordinated with state and municipal governments. Following this logic, the municipal response to the demands voiced by farmer organizations, and the perception of CBOs regarding public-service administration improvements, are directly related to, first, the federal government's potential to generate mechanisms that incorporate local actors in both the governance of resources for those programs and in their operation, and second, the capacity of municipal authorities and farmer organizations to assume the responsibilities involved.

Discussion of Findings

Our results indicate that there is a statistically significant relationship between the quality of agricultural services and the development of viable local institutions for inclusive and participatory planning and implementation of public services. It is important, however, to point out that these "viable institutions" can display many different organizational schemes. For the southwestern component of our study, although social participation is a necessary condition for collective action at the municipal level, it is not in itself a guarantee of good agricultural services. Therefore, the fact that a good number of municipalities in the south-southeastern region of Mexico fulfill certain conditions regarding social organization, citizen participation, and the presence of suitable rural development consensus-building entities, the lack of economic resources of these municipalities prevents them from providing an adequate response to the farmers' demands.

One of the results of our interviews with CBOs is the perception that a large portion of the governmental resources allocated to rural-development support programs, especially those targeting the most marginalized population groups, is used on projects generated at the central level and that these projects seldom coincide with the interests and capabilities of the intended beneficiaries. In fact, the culture of community planning is an aspect that has progressed slowly and, due to the structure of the central-government programs and to an inflexible annual budget cycle, the institutions that are involved in their management are forced to promote externally designed projects among farmers. In their eagerness to get hold of these resources, farmers agree to a participatory process that no longer has any real meaning. Looking at these issues in more depth, we find that, in effect, the greater the level of actual coordination between community-based organizations and municipalities, the greater the degree of farmer satisfaction with the delivered services.

The results obtained in Mexico lead us to believe that all levels of government need to be involved to improve the services to the agricultural sector. The local government can play a decisive role in accomplishing this goal. In this sense, the local government is well positioned within the framework of entities acknowledged by the farmers to coordinate the different programs, projects, or support activities implemented for their benefit.

Our analysis informs us of the actual working conditions in the agricultural sector from the perspective of the actors themselves. It sheds light on their expectations, concerns, and problems, and on the manner in which they consider those problems should be solved. The analysis further shows that the work performed by municipal governments can have a high impact on the population, since their decisions, as inconsequential as they sometimes may seem, frequently have an immediate impact on the lives of the citizens: these are decisions of high local relevance as they may involve quick solutions of disputes between citizens, public construction works, and the delivery of services, as well as the monitoring and enforcement of the municipal ordinances and other regulations.

Conclusions

The study concludes that the agricultural public services are affected by the performance of the local governments. As the process of decentralization progresses, the influence of local governments is likely to increase. Local-government decisions and actions, despite the rather limited de jure mandate of these organizations, are in fact essential to explain the variation in the performance of public services. Without an active local government that is acquainted with the local actors, and aware of their problems and needs, the probability of achieving an effective delivery of agricultural services diminishes.

In general terms, "taking action" in the agricultural sector is hindered, on the one hand, by the lack of infrastructure and budgetary resources and, on the other, by a culture of municipal performance that views the provision of human, material, and economic resources for agricultural development as a concern of the state and federal levels of government, and that does not and should not involve the municipality.

The existence of local institutional arrangements that foster collective action among municipal actors—including CBOs, municipal officials, and officials from central and state governments—is therefore necessary. But to create such arrangements is in and of itself a collective dilemma. Actors need to be motivated to invest the necessary time and effort to create such institutions. Our analysis shows that by studying several sources of incentives, it is possible to accurately predict the level of motivation among local politicians to make these public investments. The results further show a positive relationship between the existence of incentives and the municipal involvement in agricultural services.

We also show, however, that these incentives are rather weak or even altogether absent in many municipalities. This raises an important question for public policy in Mexico. What can be done to make these incentives strong and general enough to mobilize a large number of local governments to become more active in the rural-development initiatives?

One might consider that some mechanisms have a more direct influence than others on this binding condition, such as the physical presence of the federal and/or state institutions' technical staff in the municipal government, or the transfer of economic resources in support of programs, provided the municipality is involved in their distribution and implementation.

Even though the municipality may lack the supervision or physical presence of federal and/or state extension workers and technicians, this does not mean that the town councils are not in contact with representatives of federal and/or state programs. Mayors meet more frequently with federal representatives of social and productive development programs.

Thus, more than half of the mayors interviewed stated that they had met with personnel involved in areas of education, health, and nutrition (Education, Health and Food Program, or PROGRESA) and in contrast, only one-third mentioned contacts with personnel of Alianza para el Campo, mostly when summoned by state or federal institutions.

We can conclude that there is no central government mechanism that compels the municipal government to participate in the agricultural sector, mainly because the objective and implementation of productive development and agricultural-extension programs is decided on at supramunicipal levels by the federal and the state government, where municipal presence is null or marginal.

It seems that the potential financial gains from increased engagement in rural development do not represent a significant incentive for the municipal delivery of public agricultural services. This is because the current structures for the distribution of resources—that deal not only with the resources corresponding to transfers to the municipal administration, but also with the resources available to the state and federal programs for the promotion of rural development—do not allow for a clear municipal intervention in the decision-making processes to determine where the resources should be directed.

It can therefore be assumed that the mayors' motivation derives from the capacity of the citizens or community-based organizations to demand agricultural services. In this context, the Law on Sustainable Rural Development provides a significant advancement opportunity, but they should tread lightly on this path, since there are numerous organizations and communities exerting strong leadership among their members, and such a law could prove to be inadequate for the progress already achieved in those areas.

The previous considerations do not invalidate the hypothesis that positively associates motivation and the provision of agricultural services. When referring to the total universe of the sample, these considerations portray the general situation of the municipalities, helping us understand why the percentage of communities acting in the field of agricultural promotion is so low; therefore, they also help us find other elements—other than those considered in the working hypotheses—that might prove useful in strengthening the local government as an agricultural-development promoter.

Another argument of the study reinforces the need to create effective institutions to transfer information as a prerequisite to the provision of high-quality services. At first glance, the possibility of a widespread existence of quality services may not seem feasible without the corresponding expansion of information-exchange systems, but in order to broaden municipal involvement in the agricultural development and to improve the existing quality of services, the information systems need to be purposefully driven forward through institutions trusted by the farmers. It is impossible to hold any government official accountable without timely and reliable information about government activities. Likewise, it is impossible for the entrusted public officials to respond effectively to citizen demands without good information about the varying local circumstances.

For farmers to be well informed, other factors unrelated to the performance of the municipality are required. The social organization itself can be a significant source of information, as well as regional councils of a mixed nature and the promoters of federal and state programs. All of these are vehicles of information dissemination to the public.

The experience of the Mexican NGO Instituto Maya shows us that the rendering of accounts in open meetings is customary, particularly among indigenous communities ruled and governed by tradition and customs (Bartra and Paz 2002). In these populations, the mayors, as well as agrarian authorities, are appointed by direct vote in a communal meeting; and the indigenous town council is primarily accountable to this group. The Oaxacan legislation—the most advanced in the matter—acknowledges the indigenous municipalities and their forms of government.

Nevertheless, and despite great efforts to democratize the country, some town councils of rural municipalities use the municipal authority for their own benefit or for the benefit of the group that elected them, which in Mexico often leads to the nonexistence of a municipal culture of accountability and of a social counterpart that could motivate such culture.

On the other hand, social participation on its own is not enough to achieve quality agricultural services. Although the results of studies in the north-central and south-southeastern regions of Mexico show a positive correlation among communities where performance is higher—measured in terms of the variable related to quality of agricultural services—said participation has been insufficient in terms of achieving better performance or higher quality in the provision of these services. We attribute this to the lack of budgetary resources and governance capacity to drive their proposals forward in the regional and municipal development planning structure. The strong centralist bias present in productive development programs and in rural public expenditure planning is another possible contributing factor. In small and remote municipalities in areas of extreme poverty and with predominantly indigenous populations, the municipal administrations have limited material resources at their disposal to attract farmers to participate in activities that are perceived as meaningful by the farmers themselves, if they know that whatever solution is agreed upon the municipal government has neither the resources nor the technical capacity to implement it. In this sense, the more organizations that can participate in these deliberations, the higher the likelihood that solutions can actually be implemented.

Finally, the results of the study show a relationship between the local authorities' institutional arrangements for collective action and the management and provision of better agricultural services. They also make it clear that municipal involvement could be decisive in achieving a different economic development trend, aimed at fighting poverty and fostering the best use of the natural resources and habitat.

In the case of Jalisco, the creation of the Law on State and Municipal Planning is one example that includes a forum on municipal planning that must sanction and prioritize the allocation of state-budgetary resources to specific projects in local communities and municipalities. The allocation of resources, in the greatest degree possible, implies the involvement of the organized society through a strategy of participatory planning at the level of each community, and of the representatives of the sectors that constitute the civil society. If these types of mechanisms are strengthened, we would be on the right path to achieve the effective participation of the actors involved in the subject matter of promoting economic, agricultural, and environmental development.

7
Peru
The Pre-Decentralization Baseline Case

Miguel Jaramillo Baanante

Compared to the other countries in this study, Peru represents a much more centralized regime. As such, Peru represents a baseline case with which we will compare the rural development experiences from the more decentralized countries. This chapter provides an in-depth look at Peru's local governments and their involvement in rural development and agricultural services.

So far in this book, we have seen that municipal governments in Brazil have a mandate to take the lead in the organization of local public policies. In Chile, the beneficiaries of public policy are the intended protagonist. There, an alternative institutional arrangement prevails that has farmers, individually or organized, with or without the help of the municipality, applying for competitive funding for their projects. The Mexican model, as we saw in the previous chapter, is a hybrid that leaves room for both municipal and farmer initiative but these are often hindered by a paternalist, interventionist state. In Peru, we encountered a situation in which municipal and farmer initiatives were often hampered by the rigid, centralized structure. At the time of our fieldwork, the institutional set-up of public services for agricultural and rural development was such that the initiative rested almost completely with the central government agencies. Under such a centralized structure, one would expect to see top-down, unidirectional, and nonresponsive policies that encourage clientelism and corruption. This is not what we found in many of the one hundred municipal governments that we visited. As this chapter will show, the reality is much more complex than that.

Introduction

The Andean Cordillera cuts across the Peruvian territory generating—due to variations in elevation, climate, and topography—significant ecological diversity and different ecosystems, offering unique and diverse conditions for the development of agricultural activities. The most accepted classification differentiates eight natural regions (Pulgar Vidal 1986). These regions run parallel to the Pacific coastline, ascending from the coast, passing through the Andean highlands, and sloping down into the Amazonian rain forest.

Its high level of ecological heterogeneity and diversity makes Peru one of the ten megadiverse countries in the world due to the variety of ecosystems, species, and genetic resources. Such diversity is accompanied by cultural heterogeneity, which is, in turn, associated with technologies and production systems to exploit diverse and sometimes fragile environments, such as those nestled in some inter-Andean valleys of Peru. These resources, properly used, could be a source of income for rural households, most of which live below the poverty line. That this is not the case has to do with different issues, and this study focuses on one of these major factors: the lack of adequate agricultural services to the rural poor. The objective is to evaluate the role of institutional arrangements at the local level in the delivery of agricultural services and their potential influence on the quality of such services. Through this analytical process, we expect to be able to identify conditions that might trigger improvements in the availability and quality of these services.

Two examples of situations we encountered during our fieldwork can illustrate the role that municipal governments can play in the provision of services for the agricultural sector, its potentialities as well as its pitfalls. One actually involves a number of rural municipalities from the San Martin region, in the northern Amazonian territory, associated under the San Martin Municipalities Association (AMRESAM, by its Spanish acronym). One of its activities has been to promote better information services for agricultural producers in the region. Along this line, the association signed an agreement with the Agriculture Ministry Information Office in order to provide market information to the network of rural municipalities in the region. Thus, thanks to this institutional arrangement, producers have had access to valuable information on input and product prices, which has allowed them to make better-informed business decisions.

The other example has a different twist, showing the pitfalls that municipalities may encounter in their efforts to promote agricultural development. A number of municipalities in the Peruvian Highlands managed to establish a working relation with a central government–run program called PRONAMACHS. This program financed a professional specialized in soil and forest management hired by the municipality. His role was to provide technical advice to peasant communities in the municipality. However, this experience did not last long because the final demise of President Alberto Fujimori's administration brought drastic changes in the program, eventually ending it altogether. The different outcomes in the two examples raise questions about the underlying causes of such variation, and what factors might sway the local government to play a more active and constructive role in rural-development activities.

Despite Peru's centralized approach to agricultural and rural policy, the central conclusion—very much congruent with our findings in the other countries—of the Peruvian part of the analysis presented in this book is that collective action at the district level plays an important role in both the provision of agricultural public services and their perceived quality. Specifically, the existence of a consensus-building forum in a district is significantly associated with the existence of agricultural services and the positive perception of their quality. Although the municipal government does not provide services directly, it plays a political brokerage role vis-à-vis central-government agencies specialized in the provision of agricultural services. Thus, policies oriented to improving access and use of agricultural services among rural producers should take this into account when designing interventions.

The chapter is organized as follows. After this introduction, a background section gives a brief description of the recent performance of the Peruvian agricultural sector as well as of the institutional elements associated with the agricultural sector. The third section discusses the municipal mandate and the agricultural sector, participation mechanisms at the local level, and the current state of the decentralization process. Methodological aspects are discussed in section four. Sections five and six present and discuss the results of the analysis. The chapter concludes in section seven with recommendations for future research and policy efforts.

Background: The Peruvian Agricultural Sector

During most of the last three decades of the past century, the performance of Peruvian agriculture was dismal. After the 1969 agrarian reform, agricultural GDP grew at an annual rate of less than 1 percent throughout the 1970s and 1980s, accumulating a 30 percent drop in the sectoral product per capita. These numbers reflect a massive drop

Table 7.1
Annual average national and agricultural GDP and population growth rate, 1951–1999

Period 1/	GDP		Population
	National	Agricultural	
1951–60	5.4%	2.2%	2.7%
1961–70	5.1	3.4	2.9
1971–80	3.7	−0.1	2.8
1981–90	−1.8	1.0	2.2
1991–99	4.9	6.0	1.7
2000–2005	4.0	3.6	1.5

Source: BCRP, INEI. Developed by GRADE.

in investment, in turn associated with an institutional framework unfriendly to private initiative as well as price policies oriented to benefit urban consumers or industries, often at the cost of agricultural producers. Terrorist violence and general economic crisis in the eighties further impoverished the rural sector. By the end of the eighties, agricultural exports were at about the same level as that of two decades earlier.

This trend has been reversed during the last decade or so. Between 1991 and 1999, the agricultural GDP increased at an annual average rate of 6 percent, above the rate for the economy as a whole (see table 7.1). The sector's traditional exports had doubled by 1997 while nontraditional exports almost tripled. Since then, total exports have more than doubled again, thanks almost exclusively to nontraditional products (Jaramillo 1999).

While recent overall growth has been considerable, whether in terms of production or exports, the distribution has been quite uneven. Small producers and the Andean communities have not yet attained a significant participation in the development process of the sector. The coastal region, with less than one-fifth of the total agricultural producers, generates more than half of the agricultural GDP; this situation is just the opposite in the highlands, where most producers reside and low productivity dominates.

Although significant resources have been invested in upgrading rural infrastructure, particularly roads, there is clearly a deficit of public infrastructure and services for rural areas. While a consistent and aggressive policy to overcome this deficit has yet to be introduced, large hopes are put in political reforms aimed at improving the state's efficiency and closeness to citizens' needs, particularly those in remote and rural areas, through decentralization. Seen in this light, the decentralization reform represents an effort to improve the efficiency in the delivery of public services to those Peruvians who have historically tended to get the least in both volume and quality. Among them, rural producers are prominent. The fieldwork for this study, however, was conducted in 2002, before the decentralization reforms for the agricultural sector were implemented. Thus, the Peruvian case represents a baseline case when compared to the decentralization processes in the other countries—Brazil, Chile, and Mexico—included in our study.

Agricultural Policies in the 1990s

During the 1990s, significant achievements were attained in Peru in matters related to macroeconomic management: inflation was controlled, fiscal accounts balanced, external trade liberalized, and private investment promoted.[1] Although these first-generation reforms produced economic stability and GDP growth during the 1993–97 period, they failed to generate the timely policies required to bring down barriers hindering the growth of specific economic sectors, which in turn, could have generated a greater employment expansion.

In this context, the agricultural sector was not one where reforms proceeded swiftly. This is the case, for example, with water rights. Although this was a big topic of public discussion, not much was advanced in implementing a system of water rights that could eliminate the inefficiencies in the use of such a scarce resource. In relation to land markets, the disorderly manner in which the land-division process was implemented during the agrarian reform of the late 1960s, and the process of land subdivision it triggered afterward, produced a fragmentation of land property. As a result, there was a loss of scale economies associated with the potential for mechanization, sanitation processes, procurement of inputs, maintenance of irrigation and drainage systems, and investment in research and development. In addition, transaction costs in the land market increased.

While the right of tenancy and productive use of the land were fundamental categories within the agrarian-reform framework, the current legal framework has given back preeminence to property rights. A large titling program was implemented to formalize property. The development of land markets moves only slowly, however, in a context where the lack of dynamic rural-labor markets provides a disincentive for poor landowners to sell their land despite its low profitability.

Concerning the credit market, the expectation was that commercial banks would meet the needs of the so-called modern or high-investment agriculture. Consequently, specific financial entities—Cajas Rurales—were created to satisfy the small-scale commercial farming needs previously catered by the liquidated state-owned Banco Agrario. However, these mechanisms have provided limited coverage despite a significant growth throughout the decade (Alvarado and Ugaz 1998; Trivelli 2001). Revolving funds were established to address the needs of the subsistence agriculture (household farms and peasant communities).

The Forest Law passed in June 1997 provides the institutional framework for the sustainable exploitation of forest resources. As per the basic criterion set forth therein, the state maintains the tenancy or domain over natural resources, and the concession becomes one of the options to grant individuals a right of use, contingent to approval of a mandatory management plan. Another criterion is the mandatory drafting of an ecologic-economic zoning plan for the use of natural resources, thus enabling the application of spatial planning principles to determine utilization, preservation, and conservation zones, oriented to prevent environmental problems and other sources of conflict.

Important agricultural policies were implemented through special programs. These include the National Agrarian Health Service (Servicio Nacional de Sanidad Agropecuaria, or SENASA), the Export Promotion Commission (Oficina de Promoción de las Exportaciones, or PROMPEX), the National Program of Watershed Management and Soil Conservation (Programa Nacional de Manejo de Cuencas Hidrográficas y Conservación de Suelos, or PRONAMACHS), the Special Land Titling and Cadastral Project (Proyecto Especial de Titulación de Tierras, or PETT), and the Subsectorial Program of Irrigation (Programa Subsectorial de Irrigaciones, or PSI). Some of them applied a technically based management, such as the case of SENASA, which played a significant role in promoting plant health, and PROMPEX, which achieved significant progress in establishing strategic alliances with the private sector to promote export activities, despite its limited operational budget. Others, such as PRONAMACHS, were used as a political control mechanism, particularly after the 1995 re-election of President Fujimori.

In relation to agricultural services, Peru has a large number of extension programs that involve the state, NGOs, and private entities. By the mid-1990s, the expenditure in extension services was estimated at $38 million per year, representing about 0.8 percent of the agricultural GDP, well below the average in developing countries. It is estimated that technical assistance reached some 250,000 farmers, most of them through public programs focused on the highlands region (Jaramillo 2003). Although public services still cover about one-third of production units in the coastal region, the presence of private service providers is significantly larger than in the other regions: more than double that in the highlands and more than triple that in the rain forest Amazonic region.

Public Organizations in the Agricultural Sector

According to law, the objective of the Ministry of Agriculture is to promote the sustainable development of the agricultural sector within the context of a market economy. For the purposes of this law, the sphere of the agricultural sector is quite ample, comprising land used for agricultural purposes, grasslands, forests, and uncultivated, farmable land; the waters, banks, and basins of rivers, lakes, and forest resources; flora and fauna; crops, stockbreeding, silviculture, use of forest and woodland resources; agricultural technology services, agricultural health and safety, natural-resources conservation and governance; the agro industry, agro exports, and marketing of products and inputs. The Ministry of Agriculture's responsibilities include "the formulation, coordination and assessment of national sector-related policies in matters of preservation and conservation of natural resources, as well as the establishment of conditions allowing the free participation of agricultural agents and private investment promotion." The different organizations within the Ministry are shown in figure 7.1.

During the 1990s, the Ministry of Agriculture proceeded to separate its normative and regulatory tasks. Also, executive tasks related to research, health, and natural-resources governance were transferred to the so-called decentralized public organizations (OPDs). At the same time, as noted above, special projects were used for the delivery of services and the attainment of specific objectives, seeking to channel resources with a sufficient level of autonomy and efficiency, within the context of substantial downsizing, as part of a general public-administration reform.

The regional and subregional agrarian departments were created by

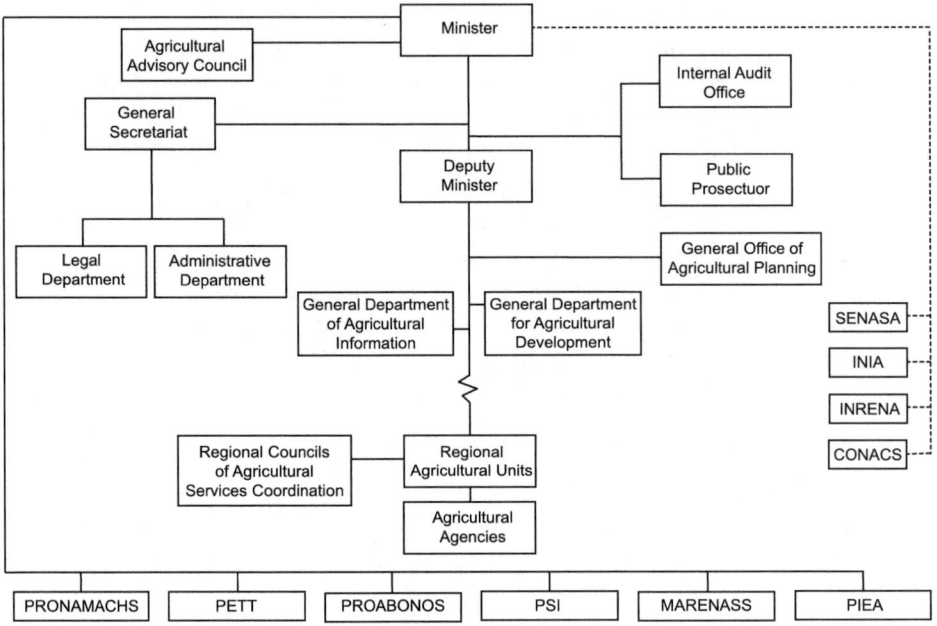

Figure 7.1 Organic structure of the Ministry of Agriculture (FAO Municipal Survey 2002).

law as deconcentrated bodies that assume the roles and responsibilities of the Ministry of Agriculture at the regional level. Also, agricultural agencies and centers are available at the local level. The agricultural agencies and the regional departments, respectively, constitute the first- and second-level authorities in matters related to administrative procedures.

Agricultural agencies and centers have many weaknesses and face problems that limit their operational capacity due to a thwarted decentralization process and lack of budgetary allocations. Their problems are associated with institutional rules: administrative dependence on both regional authorities and the Ministry of Agriculture, restrictions to tailor policies to the local context, and deficient inter- and intra-agency communication and coordination, but also with low investment in human resources, ineffective administrative styles, and poor equipment and resources.

In sum, during the 1990s, a comprehensive reform of the state was not achieved. Specifically, decentralization was not advanced. Evidence of this is the scarcity of resources and responsibilities allocated to the agricultural regional departments and local agencies. Although an attempt was made to downsize the state's structure at the beginning of the 1990s, subsequently, instead of transferring the first-tier services to competent private-sector organizations or agencies, the state retained its control over them through the creation of special projects. Also, instead of focusing on its normative tasks and the generation of policies, strategies, and instruments, the Ministry of Agriculture turned to operational activities. In this context, the projects and programs themselves became the development policy. This "project-mongering" resulted in the lack of a comprehensive and coordinated approach, as well as in heterogeneous performance among the different implementing agencies, which often applied different approaches to their activities, with limited coordination among themselves. The political use of these projects and programs became increasingly an issue in the latter part of the decade.

The Municipal Mandate and the Agricultural Sector

The Organic Law of Municipalities (LOM), No. 23853, dated 1984, prescribes that municipalities, both rural and urban, are bodies of the local government with economic and administrative autonomy, accountable for the integral development of the territory under their jurisdiction and of its inhabitants (Title I, Chapter II). The 1993 Constitution prescribes two levels of municipal government: provincial and district, and declares that both have political, economic, and administrative autonomy in matters under their jurisdiction. In addition, it invests municipalities with responsibilities such as the organization, regulation, and administration of local public services under their jurisdiction, as well as with the development and regulation of activities and/or services in matters of education, health, housing, sanitation, environment, sustainability of natural resources, collective transportation system, circulation and traffic, tourism, conservation of archaeological monuments, and history, culture, recreation, and sports, according to law (Art. 195).

In practice, however, the broad mandate and autonomy awarded by the regulations fail to materialize. On the one hand, the jurisdictional scope between the provincial and district level has not been clearly divided and, on the other, district governments have not been given the necessary instruments to fulfill all the duties and powers vested in them by the law.

The main role of the municipality is to plan, implement, and promote

—through the pertinent bodies—an array of actions aimed at providing citizens with the proper environment to satisfy their vital needs for housing, health, inputs, education, recreation, transportation, and communications (LOM, Title III, Chapter I, Art. 62). To achieve this goal, all provincial municipalities should design, implement, and oversee comprehensive development plans, territorial development plans, and urban expansion plans (Art. 70).

Regarding the promotion of rural development—subject matter of this study—the law provides primarily for three specific municipal roles:

1. Territorial development, housing, and collective security, as per Article 65 (Title III, Chapter I). This municipal duty comprises the following tasks: land-use planning differentiated by lands for urban use and for agricultural use, and within the latter, providing for future agricultural expansion areas; conservation of local fauna and flora; and the national development and recovery of the natural resources found within their jurisdiction. It also entails the promotion or implementation of irrigation and communication projects that facilitate the development of local activities, among them, agriculture.
2. In matters related to the supply and marketing of products, municipalities should support the development of agricultural activity—especially where rural territory predominates—through development of infrastructure, including marketplaces, livestock slaughterhouses, and roads, as well as by organizing fairs to encourage direct sale by agricultural producers, also fostering the consumption of local goods. Through this type of infrastructure, the municipalities can and should exert a certain degree of control over the products' prices, quality, and sanitation (Article 68).
3. In matters related to environmental health, the municipalities should, according to Article 66, disseminate environmental and health-education programs, as well as foster reforestation and epidemic-control campaigns.

Formal Participation and Cooperation Mechanisms between Community and Municipality

In accordance with Article 79 of LOM, five main community participation mechanisms exist in the municipality: legally held municipal elections; neighborhood associations (Juntas de Vecinos) and Communal Committees—in charge of overseeing the proper delivery of public services to beneficiaries and the timely implementation of communal works; the exercise of the right of petition; community polls; and the information that the municipalities should provide to the community. There is also a sixth mechanism, town meetings, that applies only to municipalities with a constituency of less than 3,000 voters.

In practice, however, municipal experiences involving the active participation of the community are rather scarce, an issue that is related to the electoral rules applicable to the election of municipal authorities. In effect, electoral rules significantly strengthen the mayor's authority. First, while in the case of national elections the constituency can vote for a presidential slate and, separately, for a congressional slate, at the municipal level the voter has only one vote, making the candidates on the slate quite politically dependent on the figure of the candidate for mayor. Second, the winning candidate is the one who obtains more votes, no matter what the total percentage. Up until the municipal elections in 1998, the runoff election was applicable only when the winner's percentage was less than 20 percent. Third, the law provides that the mayor obtain half plus one of the council's seats, while the opposition seats are assigned according to the method of proportional representation.

These rules produce very peculiar outcomes, even contradicting the will of the constituency. A study by Eyzaguirre (2001) provides examples: in the 1998 elections in the district of Tibaya, Arequipa, the winning slate obtained 52 percent of valid votes and three of the five seats available in the council; in the district of Yanahuara, the winning slate obtained 35 percent, but a greater majority in the council: four out of five available seats; in the district of La Joya, the winning slate obtained 1,986 votes and four seats, the runner-up obtained 1,741 votes and one seat, and the third slate, in spite of obtaining 1,573 votes, was awarded no seats.

These regulations, which disturb the municipal government scheme of checks and balances, were designed to vest the mayor with the power of administration free of political obstacles, thus facilitating a more efficient administration. However, the ensuing negative consequence is that the mayor does not feel the need to seek a political coalition or the support of the population through information and accountability. The mayor's prominent role in the municipal government is a phenomenon present in many municipalities of the country. The opposition's participation, always represented by a minority in the council, is dependent upon the will of the mayor.

The power of the mayor can also be perceived in the lack of oversight. Evidently, a council largely conformed by members of the same political party as the mayor is not interested in examining the actions of the latter when faced with a deficient performance or eventual allegations of corruption. The representatives of the opposition who try to investigate instances of corruption have to battle against the difficulty to obtain the internal information required to prove the case. The council can declare the seat of the mayor vacant, though this decision is ultimately revised in the last instance by the National Electoral Jury through lengthy proceedings. For a community far away from Lima, seeing the process through could be quite difficult. Thus, despite being so close to the population, local governments generally display very weak signs of accountability, particularly in larger jurisdictions.

The above factors have led to a search for mechanisms—other than those that are electoral—to encourage greater participation of the community in local affairs. Accordingly, since 2002, the Ministry of Economy and Finance is promoting the drafting of participatory budgets at the local level, based on District Development Plans prepared with the participation of the community. This is a first experience of aperture and transparency that is gaining momentum but is not a legal obligation for the mayor. In fact, there are known cases of mayors who do not participate in consensus-building forums, alleging that these have been politicized by the opposition. However, there are also many mayors who actively promote the community's participation through different mechanisms, such as consensus-building roundtables or forums. The data gathered by our survey, for instance, identifies consensus-building forums in approximately 20 percent of the districts.

In sum, the regulations contain generic mandates regarding the municipalities' role in local development, with the exception of those regarding spatial planning, a matter in which it does have a specific and exclusive mandate, although not very well defined between the provincial and district level. In theory, each of the almost two thousand district municipalities should comply with all duties set forth in the LOM. In practice, municipalities fail to do so due to lack of resources and management capabilities. As of 2003, other central-government entities, as well as regional-level entities, fulfill the duties assigned to them by other laws. Both authorities and citizens acknowledged this. Thus, municipal authorities "do what they can" instead of "doing what they should." The ambiguity in the legal attribution of responsibilities does not contribute to facilitating the citizens' control over the authorities' administration.

The Situation of the Decentralization Process at the Moment of the Study

In June 2002, the Congress of the Republic approved the Law on the Basis of Decentralization, which sets forth the purpose, principles, objectives, and general criteria of the decentralization process; establishes the authority of the three levels of government; determines the assets and resources of regional and local governments; and regulates government relations at their different levels. The municipal competencies related to economic development and local-level consensus-building included within this regulation are:

- To draft and approve the local development plan agreed on with the community.
- To approve and facilitate the mechanisms for participation, consensus-building, and oversight of the municipal administration by the community.

Presently, the Congress of the Republic is discussing a new Organic Law of Municipalities that, like the previous one, assigns a broad range of duties, as well as very limited resources, to the municipalities.

These observations suggest that even though their legal mandate is broad, the agriculture-related role of local governments in Peru is quite limited. The lack of financial resources, technical capacity, and formal accountability regarding the drafting and implementation of political responses in the sector imply that it is highly unlikely that the local Peruvian government would be actively involved in the provision of agricultural services. However, as this study documents, some local governments in the rural environment have a significant role in the provision of agricultural services to their communities. However, this role is not associated with direct-service provision, but instead with their political brokerage capacities vis-à-vis specialized agencies in the central government. Further, this role is enhanced by collective action. Thus, we find greater satisfaction with the provision of agricultural services in those municipalities where participation has been institutionalized through a consensus-building forum (*foro de concertación*). The following analysis tries to identify factors associated with municipal involvement in agricultural-service provision and its consequences.

Empirical Analysis: Data and Methods

The core data for the analysis were collected through a questionnaire survey targeted at: (1) municipal mayors of rural districts and (2) representatives of the two main community-based organizations of the same districts. Although fieldwork was performed independently for the coastal, highlands, and rain-forest areas, very similar questionnaires were used, and these were administered just a few months apart in each region.[2] The questionnaire was essentially the same as those used in the other countries. A few changes were introduced in order to adapt the language to local parlance.

Data from the survey was supplemented with those from other sources in order to generate an expanded database. The results below focus on those variables significantly correlated with our outcome variables, plus a few others useful for the discussion.

Sampling and Fieldwork

The study's sample framework included all the rural districts of Peru, defined by the following characteristics: (1) district population of less than 20,000 inhabitants and (2) percentage of rural population greater than 50 percent. The districts included in the sample were selected through a nonstratified random sampling. A number of reserve districts were also considered. The selected sample included fifty coastal municipalities, forty-seven highlands municipalities, and three Amazonian municipalities. Map 7.1 presents the geographical distribution of these municipal territories. Tests for the difference of mean and variance confirm that there are no significant differences between the sample and the universe regarding two critical variables: percentage of rural population ("rurality") and a population density index. We can therefore be fairly confident that this is a representative sample of rural municipalities in Peru.

A total of 298 individuals were interviewed for the survey in one hundred districts, out of the three hundred planned. Two mayors could not be located and interviewed. In each district, the questionnaire was responded to by the mayor or by his/her representative, and by repre-

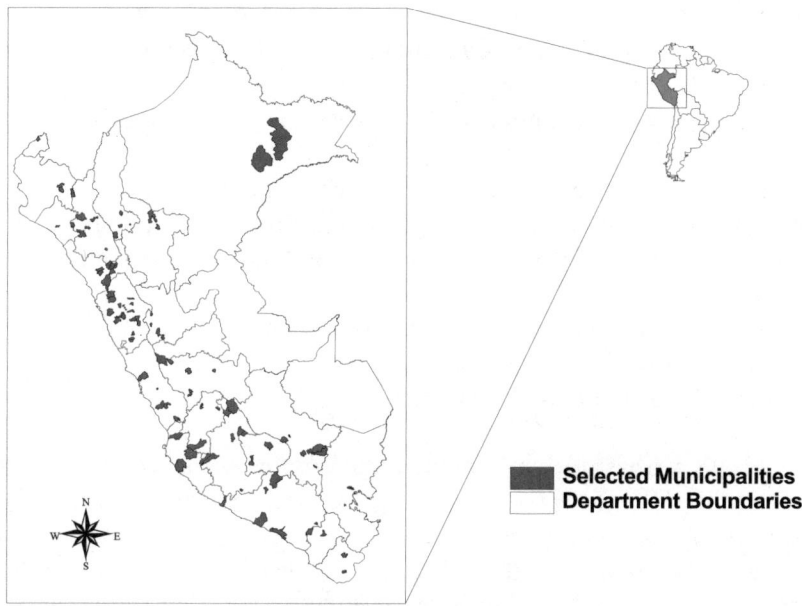

Map 7.1 Sampled municipalities in Peru ($n = 100$). (Map by Krister Andersson)

sentatives of two community-based organizations linked to the agricultural sector. One was the chairman of the Commission of Water Users (Comisión de Regantes) and/or representative of some local producers' association, and the other was the chairman of the Peasants' Community (Comunidad Campesina).

Analytical Methods

Quantitative techniques were used to analyze the data collected. Specifically, probabilistic models (probit) were estimated in order to test the hypotheses. Our outcome variables were: (1) the existence of agricultural public services and (2) the perception of the users regarding the quality of those services.

The model can be enunciated as follows:

$$S_i = \alpha + \beta M_i + \gamma A_i + \delta P_i + \zeta D_i + \theta Ac_i + e_i$$

where,

- S_i is a dichotomous variable that equals 1 when there is at least one agricultural public service / satisfaction with the services provided in the district i, and 0 otherwise;
- M_i is a vector of the municipal organization characteristics in district i;
- A_i is a vector of the characteristics of the mayor in district i;
- P_i is a vector of the political environment characteristics in district i;
- D_i is a vector of demographic and socioeconomic characteristics of district i;
- Ac_i is the instrumental variable that captures the collective-action characteristics in district i; and
- e_i is the error term of the equation.

Ideally, with enough information, the hypothesis could be put to test for each of the different types of agricultural services for which the survey inquired. For most services, however, not enough observations are available to perform the exercise, as in most districts these services are nonexistent. In fact, the model could be applied only in the case of technical assistance services. Given this fact, an additional variable was generated to establish whether at least one service was provided in the district. An additional problem is that the highlands questionnaire did not collect information on whether or not services are provided. Instead, a direct question was formulated regarding service satisfaction, making it impossible to determine if dissatisfaction is due to the inadequacy of the services or to the fact that they do not exist in the district. For this reason, only the sample for the coastal area has been used in this part of the analysis.

The perception of service quality is measured on the basis of answers to the question regarding service satisfaction. Specifically, a dichotomous variable was generated, taking the value of one when at least one problem of the district's agricultural sector is satisfactorily addressed by the public services in the opinion of at least two of the interviewees per district. In this case, we have been able to use the nationally representative sample.

One issue that needs to be dealt with is the potential endogeneity problem with the collective-action variable. The characteristics of collective action in a district cannot be assumed exogenous to the socioeconomic or political-district features. In effect, some of the characteristics of the municipal organization, community-based organizations, the mayor, the political scene, and other socioeconomic features of the district may be correlated with the characteristics of collective action in the district, while at the same time they influence the provision of services and the perception of their quality. Thus, the more or less active participation of the population in public affairs, as well as the specific characteristics of this participation, do not constitute another attribute of the community or district, but are rather conditioned by other related characteristics at the district level. Consequently, in order to identify the impact of collective action on dependent variables, we need an instrumental variable that can capture this effect but is not correlated with other characteristics of the district.

The expanded database referred to above allowed us to identify such instrumental variables. We choose to use the "existence of a consensus-building forum" as the instrument for collective action. In order to test the hypothesis of endogeneity, i.e., the possibility that our exogenous variables determine our dependent variables and the collective-action variable, the usual tests were implemented. These tests allow us to reject such hypothesis.

Results and Discussion

As discussed above, Peru had shown little progress in matters of decentralization at the time of gathering the information for this study. Therefore, it is not surprising that most of the mayors interviewed (88 percent) responded to the question related to the situation of these reforms by saying that these are unknown of in their respective districts. Consequently, in contrast to the analyses of the other countries presented in this book, the idea behind this study is not to assess the impact of these reforms on the provision of agricultural services, but rather to focus on the role played by institutional arrangements for collective action at the local level in driving the provision of acceptable-quality services, as perceived by the representatives of the agricultural sector's organizations.

Hypothesis 1

The first hypothesis to be tested is that local institutions for collective action in the rural districts generate positive incentives to motivate local politicians to take action in the agricultural sector.

The first two columns in table 7.2 show the model where the presence

Table 7.2
Determinants of the existence of at least one agricultural service/technical assistance service

Determinant	At least one agricultural service		Technical-assistance service	
	Coefficient	t	Coefficient	t
Mayor's age (edad_alc)	−0.0117	(1.9961)**	—	—
Mayor's schooling level (inst_alc)	−0.2635	(2.1562)**	0	−0.7618
Municipal planning forum (Foro)	0.3258	(1.9417)*	0.0714	(1.8959)*
Agriculture Ministry's importance to mayor (Minag)	0.1622	(1.9693)**	0.0009	(2.5976)***
Transfers to local from central government (ingresos_GC)	0.0634	−1.3858	—	—
Percentage of votes for mayor (porc_votos)	0.6384	(2.1124)**	0	(2.0766)**
Municipal coordination with CTAR (reun_munctar)	−0.3734	(2.0631)**	−0.1347	(2.2295)**
Percentage of local residents in the main CBO (porc_socios)	0.1186	−1.0389	0	(1.8229)*
Altitude (altitude)	−0.0001	(1.7873)*	—	—
Population under poverty line (fgt0)	−0.0189	−0.056	0	−0.6804
Severity of poverty in municipality (fgt2)	0.8022	−0.9922	0	(2.1407)**
Observations	50		50	
LR chi2(11)	25.18		28.6	
Prob > chi2	0.0086		0.0004	
Pseudo R2	0.5032		0.7063	
Log likelihood	−12.42898		−5.946829	

Note: Absolute value of t-statistics is in parentheses
Significance of the statistic:
* at 90%
** at 95%
*** at 99%

($y = 1$) or absence ($y = 0$) of any type of service is the dependent/outcome variable. Our instrumental variable for relatively strong collective action, i.e., "forum," is positively associated to the provision of services, increasing the probability of having some kind of agricultural service by about one-third. The connection between collective action at the district level and the provision of agricultural services is thus quite clear. The other indicator of collective action, the percentage of local residents in the organization who are the main participants in the local collective action institutions (porc—socios), does not seem to have a significant impact on the probability of having some kind of service provision.

As for the municipal organization characteristics, when the Ministry of Agriculture is one of the three major institutions cooperating with the municipality (Minag), the impact is significant. The reason behind this association is that rural municipalities, in general, lack technical capabilities of their own to provide or hire agricultural services. Thus, the association with the Ministry of Agriculture enables the delivery of services. The municipality acts as a political broker that facilitates access to those services.

In contrast, the frequency of meetings with the regional government (reun—munctar) has a strong negative impact on the provision of services, which relates to the fact that the regional government has little to offer to the agricultural sector. On the contrary, this variable could be signaling another kind of municipal priority that competes with the provision of agricultural services but not necessarily with agricultural development. For instance, regional governments focus their investments in infrastructure. If frequency of meetings is an indicator of the mayor's involvement in favor of greater infrastructure investment in the district, this may or may not favor agriculture, but it certainly competes for the mayor's attention to the promotion of more and improved agricultural services. The provision of services does not seem to be affected by the fact that the municipality is highly dependent on the central government for revenue (ingresos—GC) or, in other words, by the lack of collection capacity of the municipality.

Regarding the mayor's characteristics, age has a negative impact on the results. That is to say, the provision of agricultural services is associated with younger mayors. On the other hand, surprisingly, the probability of having provision of services decreases when the mayor has higher education. However, the proportion of mayors with higher education—reaching 60 percent—is suspicious, when among the rural labor force the number barely exceeds 5 percent. Alternatively, the level of education could possibly point toward a lower degree of identification with the local environment, since professional development would tend to distance the mayors from the rural communities. In this context, casual observation during the fieldwork indicates that some mayors do not customarily or permanently reside in their districts.

As for the political environment, the probability of having provision of services is greatly affected by the percentage of votes obtained by the elected mayor (porc_votos): for every five additional percentage points obtained, the probability of providing services increases a little more than 3 percent. This is consistent with the interpretation put forth above of the mayor as a political broker. In this context, the additional effectiveness is associated with the additional political leverage gained by obtaining more votes.

Regarding the district's socioeconomic characteristics, the level of poverty, measured either by incidence (fgt0) or by severity (fgt2), does not seem to play a role in the existence of agricultural public services. The district's physical altitude, measured at the level of its capital, does have a negative impact, a fact that is consistent with other findings related to the provision of public services. For instance, Escobal and Torero (2000) have shown that this variable has an impact on poverty, the pathway being the scarcity of public assets.

The last two columns of table 7.2 show the results obtained from the second formulation of the dependent variable, which relates exclusively to technical-assistance services. Overall, the model corroborates previous findings even when, in this case, the presence of a consensus-building forum has a much lower impact than in the previous model. Also, the poverty severity index acquires statistical significance, but its impact is quite low.

Hypothesis 2

The second hypothesis tested is that the incidence of strong local institutions for collective action in the rural districts is associated with a higher level of performance of the agricultural services.

Table 7.3 presents the results. As can be observed, although the components somewhat differ from those of previous models, a constant result is the significance of the collective action on the degree of satisfaction with agricultural services. The presence of a consensus-building forum increases the probability of observing satisfaction with the agricultural services provided by almost eight percentage points. In addition, the number of organizations in the district interested in agricultural matters is also relevant, though its impact is low.

The variable identifying those districts where agriculture is the main contributor to the municipality's revenues (contrib) is significant in this model. This is an indication that when financial gains are at stake, the

Table 7.3
Determinants of the probability of observing satisfaction with the services provided

Determinant	Coefficient	t
Economic importance of agriculture for municipal revenue (contrib)	0.0805	(2.1839)**
Municipal planning forum (Foro)	0.0783	(2.0333)**
CBOs involved in agriculture (Orgs_agric)	0.0010	(1.7188)*
Located on the coast (costa)	0.0715	(0.9789)
Farming agency present in municipality (agencia)	−0.0222	(1.6152)
Percentage of population living in extreme poverty (pobex)	0.1626	(1.5214)
Percentage of rain-fed lands (porc_secano)	−0.0700	(1.6876)*
Percentage of population with at least one unsatisfied basic need (pobnbi)	0.2162	(1.8293)*
Population under poverty line (fgt0)	0.1341	(1.0191)
Severity of poverty in municipality (fgt2)	−0.3533	(1.138)
Altitude (altitud)	0.0000	(0.7681)
Observations	93	
LR chi2(11)	29.63	
Prob > chi2	0.0018	
Pseudo R2	0.4382	
Log likelihood	−18.989369	

Note: Absolute value of t-statistics in parentheses
Significance of the statistic:
* at 90%
** at 95%
*** at 99%

authorities feel more motivated to adequately address the needs of the agricultural sector.

Some characteristics of the district do seem to matter. Specifically, the percentage of district lands under a rain-fed regime (porc_secano) has a negative impact on the satisfaction with agricultural services. This may indicate that the agricultural services, typically offered in technological packages, are not the most suitable for farms lacking irrigation infrastructure. Variables related to the political environment do not seem to matter.

Finally, the only indicator of the socioeconomic level that is clearly significant is the percentage of the population with at least one unsatisfied basic need (pobnbi). Surprisingly enough, the sign of the variable is positive. A plausible explanation could be that in the most marginal areas of the country, the municipal government is oftentimes the only authority to which the population can turn when seeking assistance.

Conclusions and Policy Discussion

The main result of this study is that the hypothesis that collective action at the district level plays an important role in both the provision of agricultural public services and their quality is substantiated by the empirical analysis.

As for the first hypothesis, in addition to collective action, a relation of cooperation with the Ministry of Agriculture also affects positively the provision of agricultural services. This relates to the role of political broker played by the municipal authority vis-à-vis the central-government bodies. Consistent with this idea is the result related to the significance of the volume of votes by which the mayor was elected; its positive sign is indicative of the greater negotiating capacity (political leverage) gained by a mayor elected by a larger margin. Nonetheless, it should be noted that the mayor can use this leverage to advance priorities different from the provision of agricultural services, as suggested by the negative sign of the frequency of meetings with the regional government, a body that has little or no involvement in matters related to agricultural services.

As for the mayor's characteristics, age matters, and the youngest are the ones most likely to promote the provision of agricultural services. A surprising outcome, however, is the negative sign obtained by the mayor's level of education. As previously mentioned, the strong percentage of mayors with higher education in the sample seems somewhat suspicious, but the anecdotic evidence also suggests that absenteeism may be greater for mayors with a higher education, due to the fact that their professional development horizons are broader.

Regarding other characteristics of the district that could impact the provision of services, the physical altitude of the capital has a significant effect: the greater the altitude, the lower the probability of having access to agricultural public services. Other studies have also verified the impact of this factor on other public services. Finally, the poverty indicators do not seem to play any role.

When instead of considering services in general we focus on technical assistance, the previous results remain with small variations. The effect of our instrumental variable decreases but, on the other hand, the agglutinant power of the most important community-based organizations acquires statistical significance with a positive, although somewhat low, impact. Something similar occurs with the poverty severity index.

As for the second hypothesis, the positive and significant impact of collective action is maintained, and the number of organizations dedicated to farming in the district also has a positive impact, as well as the sector's contribution to municipal revenues. The foregoing suggests that mayors are responsive to financial incentives, generating the possibility of a virtual circle where producers contribute more to the local public expenditure but, at the same time, receive better services. Regarding the farmers' satisfaction, the proportion of rain-fed lands is also a significant factor: the larger the percentage, the lower the satisfaction levels. This could lead us to question how adequate the services are for this type of farmer, who practices a more technologically intensive agriculture made possible by irrigation.

Finally, the evidence presented supports the core hypothesis of the book, namely, that the performance level of public services—in their efforts to alleviate poverty, halt environmental deterioration, and boost the agricultural sector—is associated with the institutional arrangements for collective action at the municipal level.

Implications for Public Policies

The contribution of this study is valuable because knowledge regarding the real-life operation and true impact of collective action in Peru and in most developing countries is very limited. In fact, the current notion about the operation and impact of consensus-building mechanisms on agricultural producers is based on a few case studies that, albeit useful and illustrative, are no substitute for a more systematic research on potential cause-and-effect associations. In this sense, one added value of the study is to put through rigorous testing ideas commonly taken at face value and that, in the case of Latin America, still need to be weighted against reality.

Short of attaining the identification of causal relations, due to the limitations of cross-sectional data, the study clearly shows a relationship between collective action and the performance of agricultural services, controlling for a broad range of socioeconomic characteristics of the districts, their local governments, political environments, and their community-based organizations. In the case of Peru, another added value of the study is that it provides baseline information for the decentralization reform, the implementation of which began just after data were collected. In this direction, a recommendation is to perform a follow-up study, with a revised questionnaire that would enable the identification of changes after decentralization was implemented.

Peruvian municipalities lack an explicit mandate to provide agricultural services, and most of them also have very limited resources and lack the technical capability to provide them. Recent debates have focused on the need for regions and municipalities to have specific mandates in matters of economic development, a key aspect in relation to overcoming poverty and one that the current decentralization process should address. The closeness and greater sensitivity to the local demands should be counterbalanced, however, with the need to preserve economies of scale and specialization gains in the provision of services, taking into consideration the lack of technical capabilities and risks of political capture at the local level.

In this context, the results of this investigation provide important input about the role of municipalities in the provision of agricultural services. They demonstrate that it is possible for local governments to have an active role in the provision of those services: identifying and channeling the demands expressed by producers, breaching the access gap to specialized institutions responsible for addressing those demands. This means that, in an environment where the municipalities lack technical and financial resources to address these issues directly, and the process to generate the capacity to manage or subcontract agricultural services is still quite limited, the role of intermediation with specialized agencies in the central government seems to be the most appropriate.

Institutionalizing this role should also incorporate public consultations through a forum or another community-participation mechanism, as this affects satisfaction with services positively. To promote and strengthen the producer organizations, however, is a role best suited for institutions that are independent from political power, such as NGOs and international cooperation.

There are successful experiences in remote communities in the Peruvian highlands, where promotion units for economic development at the municipal level act as links between the needs and demands for agricultural services and specialized institutions. For this to happen, however, technical capacity at the municipal level needs to be generated so as to effectively perform that role. It does not necessarily have to be very expensive: typically a promoter with the technical and networking capacities to render the services effective can go a long way in activating the agricultural-services market.

This research provides many useful lessons for the ongoing public-policy debate in Peru. First, the results of the study indicate that collective action in rural districts is associated with more and better agricultural services. Since the local government is in closer contact with the community, it should participate in the provision of agricultural public services. Thus, a reform of the system for delivering these services should explicitly incorporate the role of rural municipalities as political brokers with central-government agencies and define consensus-building mechanisms jointly with agricultural producers.

Second, a broad mandate to promote economic development is already in place in rural municipalities. It is not yet clear, however, what it means in specific terms. Clarifying this mandate, however, involves defining the role of local governments on this matter, something that the recent LOM unfortunately does not contribute a lot to. Although legislative reform may be desirable on this respect, it is also time-consuming and uncertain. Alternatively, dissemination of good experiences can lead other local governments to take action in this area.

Third, the efforts to strengthen the role of municipalities in economic development in general, and in the provision of agricultural services in particular, should target primarily the development of local capabilities. Transfer of resources should be a gradual process measured against the attainment of verifiable institutional development goals. The smaller municipalities already show experiences of this kind through a specialized promoter that acts as a link between the demands of the producers and the institutions specialized in agricultural services. In the larger municipalities, the model could work through a small unit that, in addition to the promoter, should include market information and facilitate marketing channels.

Finally, in relation to the research agenda, two additional points are in order. First, collective action in rural districts might be linked to better public services in general. Therefore, the main lesson may be that efforts should be made to promote a greater participation of the population in the decision-making processes related to public policies generally, not just in the agricultural sector. Second, the need to evaluate interventions is crucial. The best way to accomplish this is through randomized designs that will allow us to draw lessons applicable at national or regional levels. Thus, an evaluation strategy should be incorporated into future intervention designs. Even though a culture of evaluation is lacking in the Peruvian public system, the time has come to start creating such a culture.

8
Comparative Analysis of the Institutional Conditions for Effective Rural-Development Services

So far in this book, we have analyzed the factors that influence public-service performance within both decentralized and centralized governance regimes. Despite the differences in public policies related to rural development from one country to the next, we found surprising similarities regarding the factors that explain the internal variation of performance in both regimes. Local institutions seem to matter regardless of the broader regime type.

In this chapter we take the analysis of institutional arrangements one step further by exploring to what extent the local institutions explain the variation in outcomes for observations within and among all four countries. To do so, we combine the observations from the four countries into one large data set with 1,210 observations from 390 different municipalities. The purpose of this analytical approach is twofold. First, it allows us to examine the argument about the importance of local institutions for a larger sample and thus at a more general level. It also allows us to explore the institutional origins of possible differences in patterns among countries. It is our goal to use this comparativist institutional research design to test the idea that decentralization increases the likelihood of achieving high-quality public services.

A first glance at this combined data set makes it clear that local-governance characteristics vary a great deal both within and among the selected countries (see figs. 8.1 and 8.2 for graphical representations of the intercountry comparisons). However, because the individual chapters in this book analyzed one country at a time, we have been unable to see how differences in national policies between countries might influence governance outcomes. We selected these four countries precisely because of the strikingly different approaches these countries' governments have pursued regarding decentralization. We use a comparative analysis to study how local governments, situated in specific national and local contexts, respond to different decentralization policies. In the next two chapters, we will carry out comparative analyses to shed light on the influence of decentralization policies on two different indicators of local-governance performance: the quality of public services delivered and the degree of citizen participation in municipal decision making.

The Importance of Local Institutions in Public Service Delivery

We argue that a robust local-government organization is a necessary but insufficient condition for successful municipal governance. We contend that "good" governance is dependent not only upon the capacity of one organization—such as the municipal government—but also upon the strength of local institutions, both formal and informal, that nurture and support cooperation and accountability among all the actors involved in the municipal-governance system.

More and more, we observe that local-government agencies—but also nongovernmental actors—emphasize the importance of forming partnerships, both horizontally and vertically, both with the private and the public sector, to implement public policies, or more generally, to solve collective-action problems (coproduction). When this occurs, the local polity becomes ever more "networked," so it seems, which eventually may affect policy making (coprovision) itself. Rather than focusing on local "governments," policy analysts increasingly perceive the local polity as a set of interdependent dynamic networks of "governance." (Rhodes 1996; Stoker 1998; Kickert et al. 1997). Policy networks may cover many governance arenas simultaneously, and they operate at many scales of aggregation. Governance does not necessarily require a single center of power, and "the" government need not always claim an exclusive responsibility for resolving policy issues (see, for example, Frisken 2001; A. J. Jacobs 2004; Fuller et al. 2004; Burns 2002; Davies 2003).

Although there is a growing consensus in the literature that it might indeed be helpful to focus on network arrangements to understand important aspects of policy making and implementation, so far, both scholars and practitioners still have a hard time understanding what local-policy networks exactly are, how they affect governance outcomes, and how they can be studied in a meaningful way. This is caused by, among other things, the nestedness of the institutional arrangements, the fluidity of membership and roles over time and space, the different meaning of networks to their different members, and the dynamic mix of formal and informal exchange relations. However, a promising line of scholarly inquiry is emerging that is based on the premise that the degree of success of local-governance systems depends upon the composition of governance networks and their dynamics, both internal and external (see, for example, McGinnis 1999a, 1999b; Agranoff and McGuire 1998; Klijn and Koppenjan 2000; Toonen 1998).

In the first chapter, we quoted Kooiman and van Vliet (1993, 64), who state that "the governance concept points to the creation of a structure or an order which cannot be externally imposed but is the result of the interaction of a multiplicity of governing and each other influencing actors." We agree with them that (1) actors in governance networks are many, and (2) governance structures cannot be externally imposed. Hence, expecting that decentralization reforms will automatically result in public-service performance improvement is naïve. In many public-administration systems, few actors, if any, have enough information, resources, and power to become efficient public-service administrators on their own. Moreover, access to resources and information tend to be characterized by strong asymmetries, and service providers face the ever-present temptation to take personal advantage of these asymmetries. Given these conditions, the automatic emergence of institutions of collective action is unlikely to occur. Mechanisms of accountability have the potential of supporting the creation of institutions of collective action, but both accountability and cooperation among relevant policy actors require institutions that reduce the transaction costs related to communication among participants. We see human communication as the catalyst that enables the transfer of information that is required to assess the performance of other actors and participants in the governance system. Prior research has proven that information asymmetries in the public-administration systems represent significant obstacles to the improvement of the efficiency and the effectiveness of public policy (Moe 1984; Miller 1992; Stiglitz 2000).

Our institutionalist approach suggests that the level of success of public regimes is codetermined by the specific organizational characteristics of the policy network of actors involved in the municipal-governance system. This network of actors, which includes agricultural producer groups, individuals, municipal-government officials and technical personnel, and central-government representatives, to name a few, faces a series of collective-action dilemmas inherently present in any undertaking aimed at creating public goods and services. A conflict often arises between the actors' personal ambitions and the provision and production of the public good. To overcome these dilemmas, the actors can design and implement institutions, defined as the rules-in-use of the game, to govern the individual performance in such a manner as to be compatible with the public-good objective. However, the creation of such institutions constitutes a (second-order) collective-action problem in itself. Institutions to solve the collective-action problems characteristic of the provision and the production of public goods will therefore not emerge automatically.

Several policy analysts believe that one of the most relevant factors in determining the outcome of decentralization reforms is the local actors' ability to generate and disseminate essential information among the reforms. This ability hinges on the emergence of institutions that reduce transaction costs (Ostrom et al. 1993; Ribot 2002; Andersson 2004). In the absence of communication mechanisms, the actors involved in municipal governance will fail to create public goods and services tailored to the specific preferences of citizens and to the unique characteristics of their resources and demands. Moreover, an asymmetric distribution of information thwarts the citizens' attempts to impose accountability on their political representatives.

We argue that there are two types of local institutional arrangements that are fundamental for attaining effective and efficient decentralized governance. Both arrangements promote a decrease in the information and power asymmetries of the municipal public administration by incorporating citizens in the decision-making processes related to two governance areas that we have explained in detail in the first chapter: the provision and the production of public services (Oakerson 1999).

It can be expected that the presence of institutions of coprovision (i.e., the inclusion of nongovernmental actors in the municipal decision making over services) is relevant to attain effective local governance: when a segment of the population perceives a problem that requires some sort of collective action or public addressing, it is essential to have ample opportunity for the exchange of information among all those involved. We anticipate that mechanisms for facilitating coprovision, in which the beneficiaries of a particular service manifest their problems and express what they need in order to solve them, and where local authorities try to align their response with this demand, will increase the quality of the public services.

Likewise, it can be expected that the existence of institutions of coproduction is relevant, too: when the decision has been made to provide a particular public service, the quality of that service often depends on the beneficiaries' active participation in its production. For instance, involving agricultural producers in infrastructure projects not only enhances the probability that the location, size, or degree of technical complexity is in tune with the true requirements of the users, it also increases the probability that implementation costs will be reduced significantly thanks to the use of voluntary labor and the availability of the precise information required for certain production stages.

We expect institutional variables to have a systematic impact on the performance of municipal governance and on the quality of the services delivered. We therefore focus our empirical analysis on institutions for coprovision and coproduction. We also assess the impact of institutions that facilitate the communication between local governments, central-government representatives, and farmer organizations. To control for the influence of alternative independent variables on service performance, our analysis includes a series of noninstitutional variables that other scholars have portrayed as important. Our empirical analysis includes variables that measure the attributes of the political leadership (education, gender, and length of local residence), data on the locality (such as the continuity of political office, number of professional staff, level of funding, and presence in the field), and the characteristics of civil society (number of NGOs, their level of development, etc.). This particular distinction between sets of explanatory variables is based on the Institutional Analysis and Development (IAD) framework, developed by scholars at the Workshop in Political Theory and Policy Analysis at Indiana University. Figure 1.1 in the first chapter of this book depicts a graphic representation of our adaptation of this framework.

A Comparative Analysis of Local-Governance Performance

From the 1,210 individual interviews conducted during the fieldwork stage of this project emerges a picture of great diversity of the decentralization processes in the agricultural sectors of Brazil, Chile, Mexico, and Peru. In Brazil, for instance, all the southern municipalities have their own agricultural technical units and more than 80 percent of them organize consensus-building policy discussion forums where different actors interact in the decision-making process related to the allocation of public resources and the agricultural activities carried out in the municipal territory. Conversely, only 6 percent of the municipalities in Peru have an agricultural technical unit. Most mayors in Chile, Mexico, and Brazil report to have perceived an impact of the recent decentralization reforms, whereas only 9 percent of their Peruvian counterparts have perceived signs of such processes.

One of the main concerns of the technical and financial organizations that support the strengthening of municipal governments in the region is the limited technical capacity of local authorities in the agricultural sector. To a certain extent, the interviews carried out for this study confirm the overall technical deficiency that many local governments face, but at the same time they reveal a great diversity in the availability of human resources qualified in agricultural matters at the municipal level. In Chile, the municipal administrations have hired an agronomist in almost 80 percent of the municipalities, whereas this proportion in Peruvian, Brazilian, and Mexican municipalities is about 20 percent, 42 percent, and 37 percent, respectively.

Noteworthy is the Peruvian case, where most municipalities—although lacking a specific mandate and financial resources for the agricultural sector—carry out joint activities with CBOs in their territory. In fact, the proportion of municipalities and farmer organizations engaging in the coproduction of public services is larger in Peru than in Mexico, where the federal government has vested municipal governments with relatively more powers and financial resources. It seems that community-based organizations in Peru assign greater value to the role of the municipal government in the agricultural sector than the central government itself. Figure 8.1 describes the statistics of the variables used in the analysis.

These observations suggest that variations in local government agriculture-related activities cannot be solely attributed to the formal mandates held by these governments in the agricultural sector. Consequently, the analysis of this chapter will transcend the formal rules of municipal mandates and will seek the key factors determining efficient municipal governance by looking at both formal and informal institutional arrangements. The analysis suggests that these institutional arrangements are significant factors in determining the decisions and actions taken by actors in the municipal-governance system.

The results of interviews with community-based organizations' representatives reveal that most of them are not quite satisfied with the quality of the agricultural services delivered at the local level: in Chile,

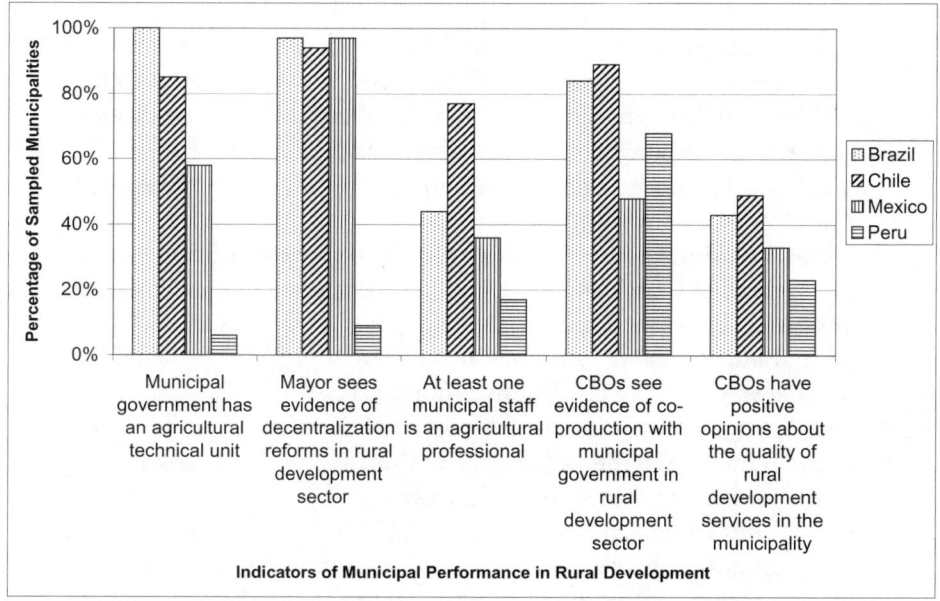

Figure 8.1 Role and performance indicators of the municipal agricultural system (*n* = 1210; FAO Municipal Survey 2002).

where the score given by these organizations to the performance of municipal services was the highest, 50 percent rated the agricultural services' quality as medium or even higher.[1] In Brazil, Mexico, and Peru, farmer organizations were less satisfied with local-government performance. In these countries, 44 percent, 33 percent, and 22 percent of the CBOs, respectively, give their local governments a good approval rating. This observation triggers the core question of this study: Why is the performance of agricultural services in some municipalities better than in others? The study will explore the possible answers to this question by analyzing the results of the 1,210 field interviews performed.

An Empirical Analysis

In this chapter we seek to explain the variance of three dependent variables. The first, which seeks to measure the quality of the agricultural public services available in the municipality, arose from the following question posed to the community-based organizations' representatives: "How would you define the quality of the agricultural public services available in your municipality?" If at least one of the CBOs reported that according to them the quality of municipal agricultural services was adequate, we assigned a 1 to that observation. If none of the CBOs reported to be satisfied with the performance of the municipal agricultural services, a 0 was assigned.

The second dependent variable intends to capture the trend in the development of the quality of agricultural management during the last five years in each municipality. The variable labeled "agricultural management improvement" is derived from a question asked to the mayor: "In what way have the conditions to solve problems in the agricultural sector changed during the last five years?" If the mayor responded that the conditions had improved, a value of 1 was assigned. The observation was coded as 0 if the response was negative.

In the third model, the dependent variable that was used describes the municipal government's relevance in the agricultural sector. This variable was generated based on the response to one of the questions included in the survey targeting the CBO representatives. The question asked was whether or not the organization had requested the municipal government intervention in the agricultural sector during the last twelve months. In the municipalities where at least one of the representatives answered this question affirmatively, a value of 1 was assigned. A value of 0 was assigned to the remainder of the municipalities.

Figure 8.2 displays how the three dependent variables used for our analysis vary per country. From the graph, it can be appreciated how in the Peruvian experience, where decentralization reforms had not yet materialized when the interviews were conducted, very few mayors perceived an improvement in the agricultural-governance conditions during the last five years. Nonetheless, despite significant differences between the four countries in the municipal mandates related to their role in the agricultural sector—a fact reflected by the dependent variable capturing perceived improvement in agricultural management—the actual municipal performance in this area is surprisingly similar in all four countries. This observation alludes to our expectation that it makes sense to broaden our focus of attention and to look beyond formal arrangements of government. A multivariate logit regression analysis was carried out to explain the observed variance in the dependent variables.

Conditions for Rural-Development Services 147

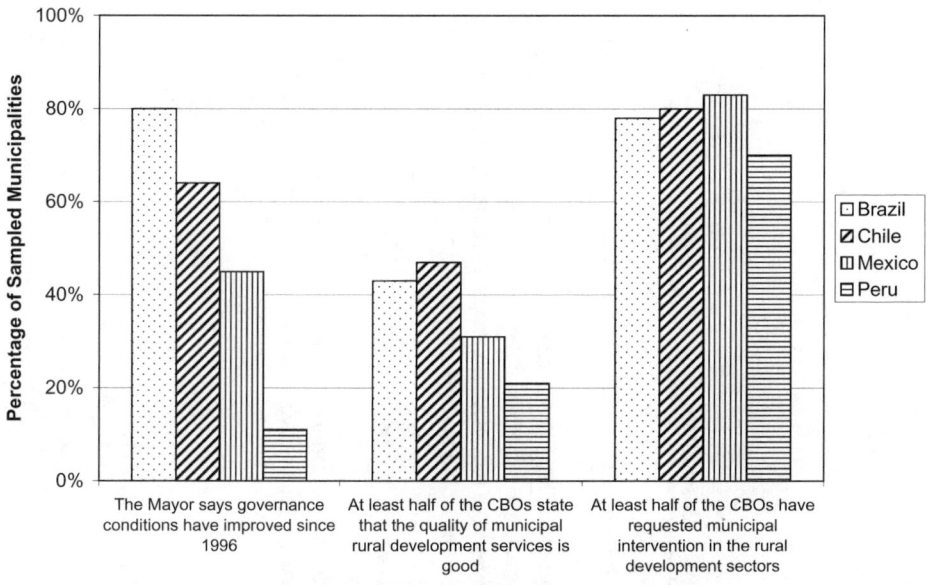

Figure 8.2 Descriptive statistics on the three dependent variables (*n* = 1210; FAO Municipal Survey 2002).

Table 8.1 provides an overview of the characteristics of the independent variables we used in the analysis. This table also explains briefly how the variables were coded. Table 8.2 shows a summary of the main descriptive statistics of the variables used in the analysis.

Results

We used binary logit estimators to assess the three econometric models. The results of these analyses are shown in table 8.3.

To better understand the impact of each independent variable on the three dependent variables, one needs to convert the regression coefficients into the associated changes in probability for different values of the independent variables. Table 8.4 lists how the predicted probability of a positive outcome for the dependent variable ($y = 1$) changes as the independent variable changes from its minimum to its maximum

Table 8.1
Description of variables used in the analysis

Variable	Description
Dependent variables	
Governance improvement (binary: yes = 1, no = 0)	The mayor states that conditions to solve agriculture-related problems have improved during the last five years
Quality of services (binary: yes = 1, no = 0)	At least half of the community-based organizations' representatives state that the quality of the agricultural public services available in the municipality is adequate
Relevance of municipal government (binary: yes = 1, no = 0)	At least half of the CBO representatives have requested municipal support, thus establishing the relevance of the municipal government in the agricultural sector
Independent variables	
Institutions of collective action	
Coprovision (binary: yes = 1, no = 0)	The existence of a participatory platform in the municipality
Coproduction (binary: yes = 1, no = 0)	At least half of the CBOs have undertaken joint activities with the municipal government
Attributes of the mayor	
Gender (binary: female = 1, male = 0)	Represents the mayor's gender
Residence (number of years)	Years of residence of the mayor in the municipality
Education (ordinal 1–12: low = 0, high = 12)	The level of education of the mayor

Attributes of the CBOs

Number (count variable)
: Number of community-based organizations in the municipality, according to the mayor

Capacity (binary: good = 1, bad = 0)
: Organizational capacity of the community-based organizations, according to the mayor

Attributes of the municipality

Central-government funding (ordinal 1–4: low = 1, high = 4)
: Degree of significance of the transfer of funds for municipal agricultural activities made by the central government

Agricultural sector's significance (percentage: 0–100)
: Mayor's opinion as to the significance of the agricultural sector's contribution to municipal revenues

Political continuity (number of years)
: Number of years the mayor has been in office

Agricultural technicians (count variable)
: Number of agronomists working for the municipal government

Field presence (ordinal 1–3: low = 1, high = 3)
: The municipal authorities' relative field presence, measured through the relevance of field visits as a means to interact with CBOs

Source: Based on FAO Municipal Survey (2002)

Table 8.2
Descriptive statistic of the variables

Variables	N	Mean	Standard deviation	Minimum	Maximum
Dependent variables					
Governance improvement	333	0.441	0.497	0	1
Quality of services	306	0.380	0.485	0	1
Municipal government relevance	390	0.795	0.404	0	1
Independent variables					
Coprovision	376	0.396	0.490	0	1
Coproduction	390	0.292	0.455	0	1
Attributes of the mayor					
Gender	390	0.043	0.203	0	1
Residence	390	34.969	14.712	0	80
Education	390	4.606	2.427	1	11
Attributes of the CBOs					
Number	390	29.717	42.765	0	329
Capacity	390	0.603	0.490	0	1
Attributes of the municipality					
Central government's funding	390	1.640	0.607	1	4
Agricultural sector significance	390	78.091	18.448	0	100
Political continuity	393	3.433	1.563	1	12
Agricultural technicians	390	1.873	2.861	0	23
Field presence	333	1.490	0.661	1	3

observed value, holding all other variables constant at their means. Only the independent variables that have a statistically significant impact ($p < 0.10$) are considered in this table. Overall, the statistical analysis confirms our expectation that focusing on the arrangements of local institutions helps to understand why some municipalities perform better than others in the agricultural sector.

Model 1: Governance Improvement

The first model assesses the perceived improvement in the local government's ability to deal with management issues in the agricultural sector. Why did governance conditions improve in some municipalities but not

Table 8.3
Regression results

Independent variables	Governance improvement	Quality of services	Municipal government relevance
Institutions of collective action			
Coprovision	0.675**	0.956***	0.758**
	(0.249)	(0.289)	(0.324)
Coproduction	0.190	0.793***	0.864**
	(0.248)	(0.287)	(0.361)
Attributes of the Mayor			
Gender	0.996*	0.366	1.084
	(0.593)	(0.634)	(1.083)
Residence	0.005	0.020**	0.041***
	(0.008)	(0.010)	(0.011)
Education	−0.003	0.190**	0.153*
	(0.067)	(0.076)	(0.080)
Attributes of the CBOs			
Number	−0.000	0.004	−0.010
	(0.003)	(0.003)	(0.004)
Capacity	0.066	0.593**	−0.403
	(0.250)	(0.280)	(0.325)
Attributes of the municipality			
Central-government funding	0.462***	0.054	0.487**
	(0.161)	(0.206)	(0.243)
Agricultural sector significance	−0.003	−0.004	0.004
	(0.006)	(0.007)	(0.009)
Political continuity	0.083	0.007	−0.345***
	(0.083)	(0.116)	(0.110)
Agricultural technicians	0.074*	0.063	0.014
	(0.045)	(0.054)	(0.073)
Field presence	0.025	0.211	0.678**
	(0.173)	(0.201)	(0.271)
Regime			
Centralized (Peru)	−2.073***	−0.371	−0.839*
	(0.455)	(0.498)	(0.485)
Constant	−1.390*	−3.48***	2.382**
	(.804)	(1.023)	(1.023)
N	384	298	305
Pseudo r^2	0.150	0.130	0.196

Note: Coefficients with standard errors in parentheses:
* $p < 0.10$
** $p < 0.05$
*** $p < 0.01$

Table 8.4
Changing probabilities for predicted outcomes

Independent variables	From (x = minimum)	To (x = maximum)	Difference
Model 1: Governance improvements			
Coprovision	0.336	0.499	0.163
Gender of mayor	0.386	0.630	0.244
Central-government funding	0.245	0.674	0.429
Municipal agricultural personnel	0.363	0.758	0.395
Centralized (Peru)	0.527	0.123	−0.404
Model 2: Quality of public services			
Coprovision	0.284	0.507	0.223
Coproduction	0.298	0.485	0.187
Mayor's residence	0.213	0.568	0.355
Mayor's education	0.220	0.654	0.434
CBO capacity	0.281	0.415	0.134
Model 3: Municipal government relevance			
Coprovision	0.748	0.863	0.115
Coproduction	0.745	0.874	0.129
Mayor's residence	0.493	0.959	0.466
Mayor's education	0.702	0.916	0.214
Central-government funding	0.660	0.931	0.271
Political continuity	0.902	0.171	−0.731
Field presence	0.739	0.917	0.178
Centralized (Peru)	0.831	0.680	−0.151

in others? We asked the mayors of each municipality if, during the last five years, they had perceived an improvement in the overall problem-solving capacity of their municipalities, specifically regarding the agricultural sector. We argue that the variable derived from the answer to this question is an indicator of the overall performance of rural-development governance in a municipality. We assessed the impact of the different local institutional arrangements, the attributes of the mayor, the CBOs, and the municipality, and the geographical location of each municipality on this indicator.

The set of independent variables used in this first econometric model explains about 15 percent of the variance in the observed improvement in the capacity to address the sector's problems as perceived by the community-based organizations. Controlling for the influence of the municipality's characteristics and the mayor's personal attributes, there are five factors that exert statistically significant effects on the probability of observing municipal governance improvement: (1) the existence of a municipal participatory policy discussion forum, (2) a high number of municipal agricultural technicians, (3) significant central-government support, (4) whether the mayor is female, and (5) whether the municipality is located in Peru.

The existence of coprovision institutions, i.e., a forum where municipal organizations can meet to discuss and plan agriculture-related activities, has a positive and highly significant effect. The changes in probabilities included in table 8.4 show that the likelihood of observing an improvement in the agriculture-related problem-solving capacity is about 16 percent higher in those municipalities that do have forums of this kind than in municipalities that do not.

It is also more likely to observe an improvement in agricultural management in those municipalities that have a higher number of agricultural technicians. Municipalities that have the highest number of agricultural personnel are about 40 percent more likely to report that they perceived an improvement in governance capacity compared to those with no agricultural personnel.

Funding from central government to the municipalities for agricultural- and rural-development activities has a positive impact on the probability of finding evidence for improvements in problem-solving capacity in the municipal administration. Mayors who received the highest level of central-government transfers are 43 percent more likely to report that they perceived an improvement in the capacity of the local government to manage activities related to the agricultural sector than their colleagues who reported that they received no such transfers.

Although only seventeen of the 390 municipalities in our sample had a female mayor (4.3 percent), the gender of the mayor has a significant effect on the CBO members' perception of municipal-governance quality. With all other variables held constant at their means, having a female mayor will increase the probability of seeing notable governance improvements by more than 24 percent, from 0.39 to 0.63 (see table 8.4).

Finally, the probability that Peruvian mayors perceived an improvement in municipal management of agricultural affairs during the last five years is about 40 percent lower than for the mayors in the other three countries combined. Peruvian mayors, en masse, report that according to them, things did not get better during the five years preceding the interview. This response contrasts sharply with the situation in Brazil, Chile, and Mexico, where a significant number of municipal executives did notice an improvement.

Model 2: Quality of Municipal Agricultural Services

Why are agricultural services better in some municipalities than in others? The statistical analysis shows that the variation in the CBOs' perception as to the quality of the agricultural public services in their municipalities can be explained by five particular, statistically significant variables: (1) the existence of institutions of coprovision, (2) the existence of institutions of coproduction, (3) the level of education of the mayor, (4) the mayor's residence, and (5) the organizational capacity of CBOs. This outcome is again congruent with our expectation that local institutional arrangements, both formal and informal, that foster collective action are particularly relevant for explaining why public-service outcomes are more successful in some municipalities than in others. If one were to look at formal mandates and associated resources assigned to local governments only, one would expect municipalities in Peru to perform poorly. The Peruvian mayor has virtually no autonomy in the policy process regarding agricultural affairs in his or her jurisdiction, and resources are generally limited. However, the Peruvian municipalities have the same probability of achieving high-quality agricultural services as Brazilian, Chilean, or Mexican municipalities. A focus on institutions of collective action sheds light on this finding that is maybe unexpected from a conventional and superficial policy-analysis perspective. An important lesson derived from this study is that decentralization policies themselves do not automatically produce high-quality public services.

In line with the results of the first model, of all the independent variables, the existence of local institutions of coprovision produces the greatest effect. Holding all other independent variables constant at their means, the marginal effect of having a municipal forum that encourages the farmers' participation in local agricultural policymaking increases the probability of observing high-quality agricultural services by 22 percent compared to those cases where such a forum does not exist.

The impact of institutions of coproduction also proves to be statistically significant. When at least one of the interviewed CBOs reports that they engage in joint projects, together with the local authorities, the probability of observing agricultural services that are graded as being adequate by those who benefit from them increases by an average of 19 percent.

In other words, the main factors that explain the observed variance in the dependent variable in this model (i.e., the quality of the municipal agricultural services) are local institutional arrangements that are not necessarily dependent on whether or not the country in which the municipality is located has decentralized the sector's powers and resources. The result shows the often-untapped potential that municipal governments have to improve the outcome of public policies in the Latin American agricultural sector.

A third influential factor in explaining the probability of observing good-quality services is the mayor's level of education. Municipalities whose mayors have a low level of education are 43 percent less likely to have good-quality services in comparison to municipalities whose mayors have a higher level of formal education. This finding may in general allude to the often-stated importance of human-resource management related to the implementation of decentralization reforms. Another of the mayor's characteristics that turns out to be a significant positive influence on service quality is the number of years that the mayor has resided in the municipality. The longer the mayor has lived in the locality, the more likely the public services are perceived as being of high quality. When all the other variables are held constant at their means, and the residence variable is at the maximum level ($x = 0$ years) the probability of high quality is merely 0.21, but when the mayor has lived in the municipality all his or her life ($x = 80$) the probability increases to almost 0.57, a difference of 36 percent (see table 8.4).

Finally, the organizational level of CBOs according to the mayor's opinion also impacts the quality of the agricultural services offered in each municipality. If the mayor perceives the CBO capacity to be high, the probability of observing good-quality services is 13 percent higher in comparison to municipalities where the mayor's opinion on the CBOs' level of organization is negative.

In this second model, one can observe the advantage of an analytic approach that takes into consideration not only how formal government arrangements affect local-policy actors and their interactions, but also the local, formal, and informal institutions of collective actions. Civil-society groups frequently play a significant role in the public administration in Latin America, and also in rural areas. The emergence of institutions that allow them to participate in local-policy networks can have a significant effect on the quality of municipal governance.

Model 3: Relevance of the Municipal Government

Why do some municipal governments play a more central role in solving problems in the agricultural sector in their jurisdictions than others? The results of the previous two models showed that municipal institutional arrangements and the CBOs' capacity greatly condition the municipal ability to deliver good-quality services. In the context of this finding, it seems legitimate to ask oneself whether or not the CBOs that are active in the agricultural sector perceive local governments as relevant players. If town hall is not considered to be the place to go to have a certain problem addressed, it is hard to imagine how institutions of collective action between local authorities and citizens could actually emerge. Our third model addresses this concern.

Working from a framework that acknowledges only the importance of formal local-government mandates, one would expect that CBOs will perceive the municipality as a more relevant actor in those countries where the central government has granted the municipality more autonomy and substantial discretionary powers to address the concerns expressed by constituents. In our sample, intuitively, one would thus expect that community-based organizations in Brazil, Chile, and Mexico are more inclined to request the intervention of their municipal government than their counterparts in Peru. In our statistical analysis, we do see some evidence of such relationships, but the marginal effect is only 15 percent, and the regression coefficient is significant only at the 0.10 significance level. It would be a stretch to conclude that this barely discernible difference among the countries would be due to decentralization reforms.

Again, the outcomes of the analysis confirm that the official mandate of municipal governments is not the only factor that determines why community-based organizations decide to request municipal government intervention. The variables that turn out to determine the perceived relevance of the municipality in agriculture-related issues are the following: (1) the existence of institutions of coprovision, (2) the existence of institutions of coproduction, (3) the mayor's residence, (4) the mayor's education, (5) central-government funding, (6) the continuity of political office, (7) presence in the field by municipal staff, and (8) whether the municipality is Peruvian.

In municipalities where participatory forums are in place, community-based organizations will request municipal-government intervention in the agricultural sector with a probability of 86 percent. At the absence of such a platform, this probability is 75 percent. Similarly, CBOs in municipalities where there are institutions for coproduction are 13 percent more likely to request municipal intervention in the rural development sector than in municipalities that lack such institutions.

Again, the mayor's personal characteristics seem to make a difference for the likelihood of CBOs approaching the municipality asking for support related to rural-development activities. The more educated the mayor is and the longer he or she has resided in the locality, the more likely the local CBOs are to request an intervention by the local government.

Not surprisingly, municipalities that receive large amounts of funding from central-government agencies to conduct agricultural activities are more likely to be asked by local CBOs to help them out in these sectors. Municipalities with the maximum level of such funding are 27 percent more likely to receive these requests than municipalities with no funding at all. A more surprising finding is the observed negative effect of the continuity of political office on the probability of CBOs asking for municipal interventions. We find that the higher the continuity for political office is, the lower the probability that CBOs view the local government as a relevant actor. The most likely explanation for this finding is that political competition in most of the municipalities, and consequently turnover rates of municipal officials, are very low. A mayor whose political office is not challenged is less likely to pay attention to the demands of rural CBOs. Even if the CBOs have requested municipal support in the past, the longer that such a mayor controls political office, the less frequent the CBOs' requests are likely to be. As soon as the political office changes, however, we may expect a flurry of CBO visits to the local-government offices. Comparing the predicted probabilities for municipalities with the highest and lowest levels of turnover rates, our data shows that CBOs in municipalities with high turnover rates are over 70 percent more likely to request municipal-government assistance related to rural development.

Finally, the more time the municipal-government staff spends in the field, the more likely CBOs are to request municipal-government support. Those municipal governments whose staff have the highest level of field presence are about 18 percent more likely to receive requests for intervention by CBOs than the municipal governments whose staff do not leave their office compound. This result suggests that unless municipal-government staff are rewarded for getting out into the field to work directly with the services to the rural poor, they will be tempted to stay in the office because being out in the field will only generate more unrewarded work for them.

In general, the outcomes highlight the importance of taking both the relationship between actors and the characteristics of the public administration system in terms of mandate, and human and financial resources, into consideration, and not just exclusively focusing the analysis on the capacity of individual organizations such as civil-society organizations or the municipal government.

Conclusions

Since the 1980s, most Latin American countries have experimented with decentralization policies. To begin with, this study demonstrates that in order to analyze these policies, one must acknowledge the huge diversity in the design, implementation, and effects of these reforms. Our study suggests that by focusing on the local institutions, one can stand on solid ground from which to observe how the participants in these institutional arrangements transform the political reform rhetoric into specific actions. Depending on the given context in each particular case, the participants in these local institutions react differently to the introduction of political reforms, construing, filtering, and sometimes blatantly ignoring the government's policy. In this sense, our institutional approach helps to understand the causes that give rise to the diversity observed.

As a result of the decentralization reform, in many countries of the region the role of local governments in the decision-making processes related to the provision and production of public services for the agricultural sector has increased significantly. With the exception of the Peruvian case, most mayors interviewed during the course of our study acknowledged the impact of decentralization reforms.[2]

The impact of the increasingly relevant role of the municipality is also felt in the agricultural sector: many municipalities visited within the context of this study have a technical unit that provides support to the sector. Likewise, with again the exception of Peru, the local authorities of most municipalities have hired at least one agricultural technician who is a part of the regular staff.

It is clear, however, that the expanded mandate of municipal authorities is not always accompanied by corresponding investment in terms of financial and human resources. When the mayors were asked which was the most significant factor preventing them from responding to the most relevant challenges in the agricultural sector, a significant number of them provided an answer related to the perceived lack of budgetary resources and a highly limited staff. Interestingly, the mayors of Brazil and Peru, two countries with very different degrees of decentralization and subsequent levels of autonomy and available assets, seem to feel the same way about the lack of resources.

This study highlights the importance of taking the institutional environment into consideration when seeking to understand municipal governance systems. The results of the study, to a certain point, confirm the validity of the premise that states that increased local-government autonomy regarding decision-making processes and the implementation of agricultural policies generate public services that are more valued by the beneficiaries. However, we provide evidence that the extension of the municipal mandate in itself does not automatically translate into a superior performance of agricultural services. We ascertained that on the one hand, even in Peru, where the municipal mandate is very limited, some municipalities still manage to produce high-quality services. On the other hand, in the other countries in the sample, where local authorities have been vested with a relatively broader mandate, certain municipalities still perform poorly. How can we open the "black box" regarding what "decentralization" means for rural development?

First, we found evidence supporting the validity of the frequently voiced argument that municipalities lack resources, both financial and human, to perform at their best. We found a positive and statistically significant correlation between "improvement of municipal governance" on the one hand, and "central-government funds" as well as "number of technicians" on the other.

However, the most significant contribution of our study, in our opinion, is evidence of the significant impact of local institutions for coprovision and coproduction on all three measures of service quality. Consequently, efforts to support local governments will be more effective if these efforts address not just improvements in financial and human resources, but also the importance of creating spaces and opportunities for frequent interaction among authorities, municipal agents, civil-society organizations, and central-government representatives.

The analysis in this chapter also raises several important questions for future analysis. For instance, if the institutions for coprovision and coproduction are so important, what are the factors that influence their emergence in the first place? What national policies might influence the likelihood of such nontraditional governance arrangements to form in Latin America? These two questions guide the analysis in the next chapter.

9
Does Decentralization Promote Participatory Governance?
A Comparative Analysis

In chapter 8, we found that the institutions for participatory governance at the local level are important determinants of high-performing public agricultural services. In this chapter, we analyze the conditions under which participatory governance is likely to happen in rural municipalities, and whether decentralization reforms increase the likelihood of citizen participation. In other words, we analyze why local politicians in rural areas would decide to open up their decision-making process to citizens. Our analytical approach focuses on the incentive structures of local politicians under both decentralized and centralized regimes. We argue that, regardless of regime type, participatory-governance institutions are more likely to emerge when the goals of these institutions are compatible with the interests of the local executive.

A major finding in the governance literature is that the distribution of governance responsibilities across multiple jurisdictions allows for more flexibility in the provision and production of collective goods than does the centralization of governance within a single jurisdiction (Hooghe and Marks 2003; V. Ostrom et al. 1961). Advocates of strong local governments claim that when local citizens have political authority to organize their own governance institutions, they are more likely to engage in deliberative democracy (Tocqueville [1840] 2003; Habermas 1998; Manin 1987) and to produce public policy that can adjust to local variations in conditions and preferences (Oates 1999; Inman and Rubinfeld 1997). Yet the efforts to create such benefits through decentralization policies presume that local politicians are both accountable to the citizenry and interested in actively seeking citizens' input in decision making. This study raises concerns about such presumptions and seeks to shed light on the conditions that allow local democracies to flourish.

In the field of comparative politics, explanations of why central governments would decide to decentralize emphasize the political-incentive structures of central-government officials. Central government may be swayed to let go of certain powers and resources when there is strong political pressure from powerful elite groups in rural societies (Boone 2003), when local bureaucrats demand increased autonomy in decision making (Eaton 2004), and when the ruling parties of the national government believe that support at subnational levels is more promising than their prospects in national elections (O'Neill 2003). In this chapter, we take the analysis of decentralization incentives one step further by considering *local* politicians' incentives to invite ordinary citizens to participate in the municipal government's day-to-day governance activities and decisions.

In addition to internal political pressure to decentralize, both international-finance organizations and donor governments actively promote decentralization reforms as a strategy to improve public-sector performance and bolster democracy in developing countries (Maro 1990; Ribot 1999a; World Bank 1988). The World Bank, for one, promotes the idea that "decentralization can strengthen democratic participation in government . . . decentralization can improve the quality and coverage of local public services" (Peterson 1997, 1). From this perspective, decentralization represents a quest for deepening democracy and giving citizens a say in the public affairs that most directly affect their own lives (Goldfrank 2002; Agrawal and Ostrom 2001; Evans 1996).

The notion that decentralization facilitates participation is often taken at face value, reflecting the notion that if governments are just brought closer to the people, governments will seek people's input when making decisions. The problem with this view is that it ignores differences in reform strategies, the local settings, and the degree of fit between these two. Consequently, this view also ignores the interests of the local-government officials, to whom resources and responsibilities are devolved through decentralization reforms. In many societies, local-government officials are simply not interested in sharing their political power and control over financial resources with local folks. Because of their traditionally elevated standing in many contexts, local politicians may draw on their political and economic clout to limit the influence of citizens in collective decision making. We argue that it would be a mistake to assume that even democratically elected politicians would spontaneously let go of their control over the political decision-making process. Local political leaders in Latin America—who have traditionally belonged to the political and economic elites—are likely to resist giving up their almost authoritarian leadership positions (Fox 1994, 1996). Simply put, these local strongmen cannot be expected to become facilitators of participatory decision making overnight.[1]

In societies where social, economic, and political inequalities prevail, it is unlikely that local institutions for civic participation will simply emerge as a natural consequence of decentralization reforms. In fact, several recent studies have suggested that exactly the opposite may occur —decentralization may exacerbate existing inequalities through increased opportunities for corruption and elite capture of rents (Bardhan and Mookherjee 2000; Harriss et al. 2005; Platteau 2004; Rile Hayward 2003). The possibility of decentralization both enhancing and hampering participatory local governance begs the question as to when local politicians may be expected to endorse local institutions for participatory decision making in the municipal administration.

The choice to adopt an inclusive decision-making strategy, we argue, depends to a significant degree on the institutional incentives of local politicians. We test this argument with field observations in the rural areas of Brazil, Chile, Mexico, and Peru. We look at how rural local-government representatives in these four countries relate to both central-government officials and smallholder farmers and how these relationships affect the likelihood of involving farmers in the planning, implementation, and monitoring of public services in the agricultural and natural-resource sectors. Drawing on personal interviews in 2002 and 2003 with 1,210 local actors in 390 municipal governments in the four countries, we analyze the conditions under which local governments decide to create governance institutions with varying degrees of citizen participation.[2]

We start by reviewing previous research on the origins, challenges, and potential benefits of participatory governance in local-government administrations. We then develop a theoretical argument and a series of testable hypotheses that emphasize the institutional incentives of local politicians as a major determinant of the creation of participatory municipal-governance institutions. The following section lays out our empirical design, after which we present our findings. In the discussion section, we interpret the apparent different influences of decentralization reforms on local incentive structures. We conclude by exploring the implications of this research for the current public-policy reform process in Latin America and the debate about participatory-governance arrangements more broadly.

Previous Research

Most existing studies on local democracy in developing countries focus on formal mechanisms and institutions for political representation, such as political parties, electoral systems, and voter registration (for example, see Bratton 1999; Cleary 2004; Powell 2000; Langston 2003; Fornos et al. 2004; Greene 2002). A recurring message in these studies is that formal political participation may be strengthened through improved opportunities for communication between state and civil-society representatives. Most of the world's recent decentralization experiences have formally incorporated mechanisms for citizen participation in local governance that go beyond formal election procedures. The literature studying these types of reforms presents a wide array of purported benefits of participatory governance in local governments (for reviews, see Fung and Wright 2001; Ackerman 2004; Goldfrank 2002; Cohen and Rogers 1995).

Existing studies describe how inclusive decision making in decentralized local economies has increased the quality of public services (Andersson 2004; Baiocchi 2001; Ostrom 1996a; World Bank 1996), improved responsiveness and accountability of local government (Ribot 1999a; Goldfrank 2002; Blair 2000; Fiszbein 1997), and even enhanced equitable access to services and productive assets (UNDP 2002; Hardee et al. 2000). One of the major contributions of these studies is that they emphasize the need to distinguish between different *forms* of participation. Goldfrank (2002), for instance, shows how the Montevideo city government's approach to participatory planning had a direct impact on the quality of public services in the city. More specifically, he found that institutions that actively involve the citizenry in decision making, rather than just consulting citizens for their preferences, achieved better results.

Ackerman (2004, 448) takes the same argument one step further. Drawing on successful cases of participatory local governance in Brazil, Mexico, the United States, and India, he argues that "state reformers should move beyond strategies based on exit and voice . . . to establish spaces of full co-governance with society. Instead of sending sections of the state off to society it is often more fruitful to invite society into the inner chambers of the state."

These participation success stories show that it is sometimes possible for governments to design and facilitate the creation of local institutions that enhance democratic deliberation. What these cases do not show, however, is *why* successful experiences of participatory governance emerged in the first place. What is the process by which viable institutional arrangements for inclusive decision making can emerge and flourish, given the adverse socioeconomic and political context in many local polities? The next section reviews the segments of the literature that have ventured an answer to this question.

Potential Determinants of Participatory Governance

By participatory governance, we mean the existence of institutional arrangements that facilitate the participation of ordinary citizens in the public-policy process within the realms of the municipal government. Consistent with the concept of participatory publics developed by Avritzer (2002), we refer to forums organized by the municipal governments that invite the public at-large to take part in deliberation, negotiation, and administrative decision making about public affairs.

There are three predominant schools of thought that have addressed the question as to why local-government officials would choose to invest in participatory governance and give up their exclusive control over the political and financial assets devolved to them through the decentralization reforms. First, the Modernization and political-culture scholars find linkages between increased levels of economic development, improved literacy, the emergence of a politically moderate middle class, and more favorable conditions for more participatory public affairs (e.g., see Fukuyama 1996; Inglehart 1989; Lipset 1959). Their basic argument is that the more affluent and educated members of society are, the more politically aware and interested in politics they will be. Because of citizens' enhanced political interests and awareness, civic engagement in government is more likely to evolve. According to this line of reasoning, the origins of participatory governance are associated with the structure and conditions of society as a whole, rather than in the particular interactions between local-government representatives and citizens.

Another set of explanations comes from a vein in the local governance literature that we might call the New Left. This line of work argues that successful local institutions for participatory governance are associated with a left-oriented party ideology and leadership (see, for example, Baiocchi 2001; Houtzager 2003). Their logic is that Latin American leftist parties tend to be more participatory because of their origin as a reaction against the traditional closed and elitist-oriented political parties. Right-wing parties are seen as protecting the ruling elite's control over governmental allocations and regulation, whereas leftist parties are viewed as seeking to break this power monopoly by increasing citizens' voice in governmental decisions.

Relying on case studies of five governmentally orchestrated participation experiences in the United States, Brazil, and India, Fung and Wright (2001) find patterns of successful institutional design. They propose that successful participatory governance relies on the degree to which governments actually devolve public decision authority to empowered local units, establish formal linkages of accountability between the center and the local units, and create "new state institutions to support and guide these decentered problem solving efforts" (17). When all these conditions hold and participatory governance still fails, they attribute such outcomes to either "lack of capacity, knowledge, internal conflicts, or bad luck" (9). Authors adhering to this literature seek the roots for participatory forms of local government within the town-hall environment: institutions of local democracy depend on the formal policies, attitudes, and actions of central as well as local politicians, and not so much on citizens proactively trying to become a part of the political decision-making process.

The role of local politics in mediating the outcomes of central governments' decentralization policies and in promoting participation is largely absent from the work of the Modernization and New Left scholars and has only recently begun to receive more attention in the decentralization literature. A group of scholars, which we call the Democratic Decentralization scholars, develop this idea. In one of the major studies of this group, Harriss et al. (2005, 6) stress the importance of addressing the question of how "collective and individual actors engage in struggles to transform authoritarian states and build democracy but also how they are enabled and constrained by structured environments." Their call for a more explicit focus on the mediating effects of local politics is supported by a growing number of studies that question decentralization as a panacea for good governance (for example, see Avritzer 2002; Bardhan and Mookherjee 2000; Platteau 2004; Ostrom 2001).

Collectively, the Democratic Decentralization scholars offer a compelling argument about why local politics matter in the creation of participatory-governance institutions. They argue that one should not expect such institutions to emerge automatically as a consequence of decentralization reforms. In oligarchic and clientelistic societies, decentralization reforms may exacerbate existing asymmetries of power and resources between regular citizens and the local elite, making participatory governance *less* likely to occur. In this sense, this argument is consistent with the Modernization scholars' view, since social and economic inequalities are particularly grave in developing, nonindustrial nations. According to the Democratic Decentralization scholars, the formation of downwardly accountable local governments requires direct and democratic elections of political representatives (Agrawal and Ribot 1999; Crook and Manor 1998) as well as competitive local elections, since these encourage political parties to reach out to previously ignored groups (Harriss et al. 2005; Cleary 2004; Hirschman 1970). But the promotion of downwardly accountable local governments seems meaningful only if governments actually devolve substantial political decision-making powers to the local level (Oakerson 1999; Ribot 1999a).

We suggest that there is a fourth approach that combines some of the key insights from all of the three schools outlined above. According to this approach—the new institutionalism—decentralization outcomes are best understood by studying the incentive structures of local politicians (Andersson et al. 2004; Gibson and Lehoucq 2003). Because it is to the local politicians that power and resources are being devolved through the reforms, they constitute the "linchpins" of the decentralized regime. Because local politicians worry about staying in power, they are unlikely to follow blindly what the central government asks them to do and will perform only those tasks that are congruent with their interests. Rather than looking for the origins of participatory governance institutions *either* in the streets *or* in the town halls, we focus on the interactions among local politicians, central-government officials, and groups of local farmers. Our approach recognizes that citizens may or may not demand inclusion in the political decision-making process, central governments may or may not encourage participation, and local governments may or may not pay attention to these signals. Understanding these parallel and partially intertwined incentive structures then becomes crucial for disentangling the relationship between decentralization reforms and participatory local governance.

Our institutional approach employs contextually grounded analysis of incentives. We define institutional incentives as the expectations of future rewards and penalties associated with one's actions. We view these incentives as components of human interactions that take place in particular and institutional contexts. This emphasis on the importance of context specificity in incentive analysis makes our institutional approach compatible with some aspects of each of the theoretical contributions from the Modernization, New Left, and Democratic Decentralization scholars. The Modernization scholars' concern with the broader socioeconomic prerequisites of democracy and the New Left's focus on the political ideology, leadership, and macroinstitutional design, as well as the Democratic Decentralization scholars' emphasis on electoral competition, downward accountability, and the power relationships between local politicians and other actors within the governance system, all have a place in the institutional incentive framework. These variables help to characterize the context in which local interactions take place. Our institutional analysis assesses the influence that each of these, as contextual factors, has on the likelihood of local politicians engaging in participatory municipal governance.

There are two particular limitations in the existing research on the emergence of participatory governance that we seek to improve on in this chapter. First, by comparing local-governance processes in four countries with different degrees of decentralization, we are in a position to analyze the possible effects of national decentralization policies on the conditions for civic engagement at the local level. Second, we seek to add to the existing set of studies—most of which rely on qualitative case studies of selected local-government success stories—by broadening the scope of case selection to include a representative sample of local-governance experiences from a large number of localities. In addition, we aim to provide a more rigorous set of tests of the existing theories, potentially leading to more generalizable results.

Hypotheses

Drawing on the new institutionalist approach, we propose a context-sensitive theory about what would make a local government participatory. Consequently, our analytical approach zeroes in on the relationship between the decentralization reforms and resource-user participation from the perspective of local politicians. We argue that elected local politicians will support participatory-governance institutions as long as they serve their social, political, and financial interests.

Consistent with the New Left and Democratic Decentralization literature, we also suggest an interactive effect between local politics and the macrolevel policy context, including both formal rules and cultural norms that shape the governance style of the national government. The idea here is that the incentive structures of local politicians are derived partly from the formal institutional constraints imposed by the central government's selective transfer of power and resources. These formal constraints set the stage for the relationship between the local-government representatives, the municipal electorate, and central-government actors, and it is within these local interactions that the institutional incentives arise.

According to our line of reasoning, for participatory governance to happen it is crucial that, among other things, community-based organizations (CBOs) demand municipal action. We argue that participatory municipal governance is very unlikely to occur unless CBOs demand specific municipal actions, even if it is official central-government policy that municipal governments should plan their activities together with CBOs. If there is a strong local demand for municipal action, local officials face the decision of whether they should rely on the traditional, hierarchical chain of command within the municipal administration for planning activities or if they should invite representatives from the CBOs to take some part in the decision making.

If the local politicians choose to pursue a participatory-governance strategy, this may generate combinations of three different rewards for the local politicians. First, inviting CBOs into the decision making could serve to transmit an image of resolve to face up to the problems in the rural sector, hence possibly scoring important political points among farmers. Second, participatory decision making can mitigate criticism from the opposition and may work as a strategy to shift blame (onto nongovernmental participants). Finally, if CBOs have been involved in the decision process, it will make cost-sharing for implementation of activities and investments more feasible. As such, participatory governance has the potential to allow local politicians to be more efficient in their campaigns to stay in office—receiving more political credit for money spent on public services. The incentives to create municipal spaces for participatory governance are likely to be strengthened even further if civic participation is promoted by the central government's political party elite, regardless of the party's ideological orientation.

The Empirical Approach

We test the potential influence of these sources of institutional incentives on municipal decision making in 390 local governments in Brazil, Chile, Mexico, and Peru. We compare the conditions for participatory municipal-government decision making in each of these localities and analyze how the institutional constraints imposed by the national governments in each country may affect the likelihood of participatory governance.

We employ a regression model that incorporates several factors that the existing theories consider to be important determinants. We use logit estimators for the pooled sample of all 390 observations and employ a dummy variable to denote whether any given municipality is located in Peru—our control group. Table 9.1 describes all variables included in the model, and table 9.2 provides the descriptive statistics.

Dependent Variables

We use three indicators for participatory governance as dependent variables, each reflecting a different aspect of participatory decision making. Coprovision[3] is a binary variable indicating whether the municipal government hosts a municipality-wide forum where community-based organizations are allowed a seat and where natural-resource sector activities are planned. Coproduction[4] measures whether the municipality has engaged in any joint implementation of activities together with CBOs in the natural-resource sectors, and field presence[5] is a binary variable indicating to what extent the municipal government staffs actually get out into the field to work with local farmers.[6] All dependent variables are derived from the FAO municipal surveys with CBO representatives. Figure 9.1 presents the percentage of municipalities in each country that, according to our three indicators, practice participatory municipal governance.

Independent Variables

The factors influencing local politicians' choice for governance strategy may be divided into three broad categories: (1) institutional incentives, (2) political structure, and (3) socioeconomic context.

We include two major sources of institutional incentives as independent variables. Demand from CBOs on the local politicians is a continuous variable, measured by the frequency of reported interactions between those CBOs that have solicited municipal action in the natural-resource sectors and the municipal government. We include both formal and informal ways that the CBOs used to express their demands. We expect that municipal governments that are subject to relatively frequent interactions with such CBOs are more likely to engage in participatory-governance activities. Central-government support and supervision is a continuous variable that represents the frequency of reported contacts between the municipal and central governments regarding central supervision, technical support, and training. We expect that more contact with the central government will increase the probability of achieving participation—especially in Brazil, Chile, and Mexico—where participatory planning in the natural-resource sectors is part of the official national-government policy.

Several independent variables are concerned with the political structure of the municipal government that other researchers have suggested are influential. First, as suggested by the New Left scholars, if the elected mayor is a member of a leftist political party that actively promotes participatory governance, occurrences of civic participation are thought to be more likely.[7] Also, according to the Democratic Decentralization scholars, local politicians are assumed to be more likely to promote participatory-governance institutions when the electoral competition is relatively high, since this will motivate incumbent politicians to reach out and appeal to previously ignored groups, offering them a seat at the decision-making table. Third, because participatory governance can be time-consuming to organize, it is important to consider variation in the continuity of office. Administrations with higher continuity of office generally have lower turnover rates among staff and officials, and thus have more time to organize participatory governance. Finally, the national government's policy concerning the role of the municipal government in the natural-resource sectors is likely to have an effect on how the relationships between farmers and local governments develop and whether the municipal-government officials perceive any net gains from opening up their public affairs to civic participation. In our regression models, we capture this effect by adding a dummy variable for Peru, which had a largely centralized provision and production of most public goods and services. We would expect, for instance, that the local politicians in Brazil are more likely to engage in participatory governance than those in Peru because of the relatively strong official support from Brazilian federal and state governments to participatory local governance in the natural-resource sectors. If such a difference actually exists, the dummy variable will pick it up.

The third category of independent variables deals with the socioeconomic characteristics of the local context. Based on the modernization literature, we would expect participation to be more likely if a

Table 9.1
Description of variables included in the statistical analysis

Variables	Description	Comments	Source
Dependent variables			
Coprovision	Binary variable indicating whether the municipality has an active participatory forum for decision making	If at least half of the CBOs and the mayor said such a forum existed, we assigned a 1, otherwise 0	FAO 2002 (CBO)
Coproduction	Binary variable describing whether the municipal government and CBOs implemented joint activities	If at least half of the CBOs and the mayor said they had coproduced, we assigned a 1, otherwise 0	FAO 2002 (CBO)
Field presence	Binary variable measuring the relative presence in the field by the municipal government's technical staff	For each country, we ranked and classified the variable into two categories of equal size (high, low)	FAO 2002 (Mayor)
Independent variables			
CBO demands	Measures the strength of the demand from CBOs on the municipal government to take action in agricultural and natural resource (ANR) sectors	Frequency of interactions between municipal government staff and CBOs that, at some point, had requested municipal intervention in the sector	FAO 2002 (CBO)
Central supervision	Frequency of interactions between central and municipal government reps related to ANR services	Number of personal encounters related to technical support, training, and supervision in ANR sectors	FAO 2002 (Mayor)

Continuity of office	Number of years that the current mayor has held office	FAO 2002 (Mayor)
Municipal budget/cap	Size of the 2002 municipal budget, including all central-government transfers and local taxes	To normalize, we converted the budget amounts to 2002 USD equivalents and divided it by the U.S. State Department's per diem rates for each country	National census
Population density	Number of inhabitants per square kilometer		National census
Literacy rate	Percentage of population who can read and write		National census
Leftist party	Orientation of mayor's political party (binary)		National electoral data
Electoral competitiveness	The difference between the first and second place in the local elections for mayor (continuous)	The lower the percentage, the more competitive the electoral process	National electoral data
Ruling party	Mayor's and central ruling party are the same (binary)		National electoral data

Sources: FAO 2002, IBGE 2005, BANAMEX 2001, ONPE 2002, INE 2002, INEGI 2000

Table 9.2
Descriptive statistics

	Brazil (n = 100)		Chile (n = 40)		Mexico (n = 150)		Peru (n = 100)	
	Mean	SD	Mean	SD	Mean	SD	Mean	SD
Dependent variables								
Institutions for coprovision	0.70	0.46	0.33	0.47	0.20	0.40	0.08	0.28
Institutions for coproduction	0.72	0.45	0.70	0.46	0.62	0.49	0.47	0.50
Municipal field presence	0.58	0.50	0.66	0.48	0.40	0.49	0.21	0.41
Independent variables								
CBO demand	4.39	3.77	4.98	6.81	6.50	8.31	5.55	9.47
Central support and supervision	7.98	2.86	5.73	2.53	8.13	3.48	7.41	3.23
Continuity of office	4.34	1.75	5.61	3.44	3.14	2.46	4.39	1.56
Leftist party	0.22	0.42	0.45	0.50	0.74	0.44	0.04	0.20
Ruling party	0.08	0.27	0.45	0.50	0.08	0.28	0.17	0.38
Literacy rates	74.77	15.12	89.32	2.89	81.52	11.14	74.08	12.99
Population density	36.73	34.36	23.26	27.21	93.36	192.91	40.16	57.36
Electoral competitiveness	0.15	0.16	0.17	0.14	0.17	0.17	0.10	0.09
Municipal budget	12.52	5.97	5.66	2.76	10.46	6.47	1.32	1.16

municipality enjoys relatively high literacy rates and financial endowments. In analyzing the effect of these potential determinants of participatory municipal governance, we control for the population density of each locality.

Results

Table 9.3 presents the results of three different regression models. For all three models, institutional incentive variables perform consistently better than both structural and electoral variables in explaining variation in participatory municipal governance in the four countries. Demands from community-based organizations have a positive and statistically

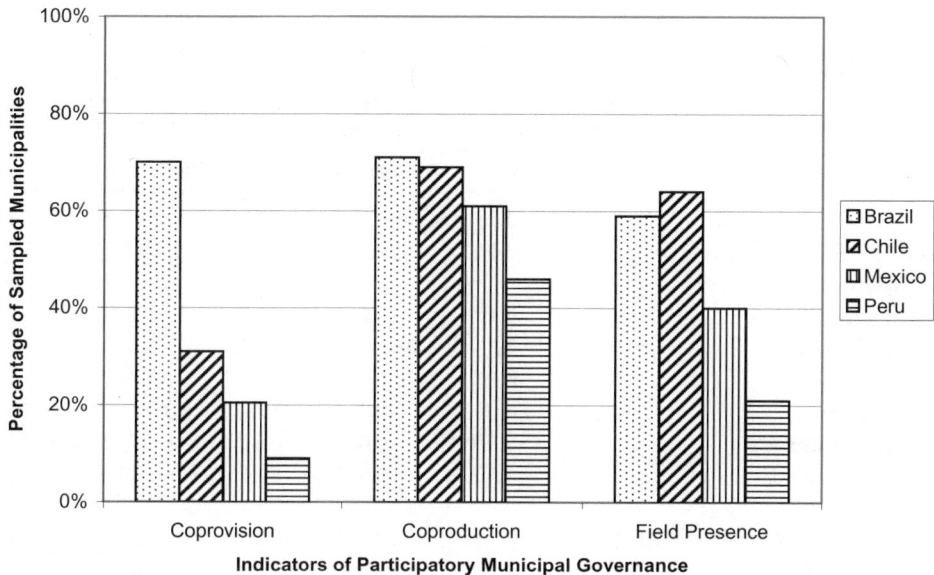

Figure 9.1 Participatory municipal governance in four Latin American countries (FAO Municipal Survey 2002).

significant effect ($p < 0.05$) on all three measures of participatory governance. The predicted probabilities presented in table 9.4 indicate that when CBO pressure is zero, the probability for coprovision among municipal governments in all four countries is only 19.3 percent, holding all other variables constant at their means. It jumps to over 80 percent, however, when local pressure is at its maximum.

The effects of the central governments' support and supervision are more ambiguous. The variable has a significant and positive effect on the probability of municipal-government staff working with farmers in the field as well as being involved in coproduction activities ($p < 0.01$), but a significantly negative effect on the probability of coprovision ($p < 0.05$). Holding all other variables constant at their means, the municipalities that receive most central-government attention are almost 30 percent less likely to create institutions for coprovision compared to colleagues in municipalities who receive the least support and supervision. We attribute this seemingly contradictory result to a "crowding-out" effect of central-government involvement in local public-service provision.

Table 9.3
Determinants of participatory municipal governance

Independent variables	Model 1 Coprovision		Model 2 Coproduction		Model 3 Field presence	
	Coefficient	z	Coefficient	z	Coefficient	z
CBO demand	0.705***	3.47	0.567***	2.68	0.371**	1.96
Central support and supervision	−0.113**	−2.26	0.118***	2.89	0.140***	3.27
Continuity of office	0.010	0.19	−0.051	0.96	0.157**	2.48
Leftist party	−0.949***	−3.35	−0.945***	3.25	−0.435	−1.6
Ruling party	−0.341	−0.84	1.166***	3.11	0.693**	2.06
Literacy rates	−0.006	−0.61	−0.011	1.23	−0.021**	−2.35
Population density	−0.005**	−2.13	−0.001	0.81	−0.001	−0.68
Electoral competitiveness	−1.082	−1.20	−0.537	0.64	−0.772	−0.98
Municipal budget	0.089***	3.50	0.011	0.49	−0.042*	−1.84
Peru	−1.933***	−4.03	−1.372***	−3.73	−2.304***	−5.75
Constant	0.504	0.53	0.949	1.04	0.625	0.69
N	371		370		371	
Pseudo r^2	0.193		0.1033		0.1379	
Prob > chi^2	0.000		0.000		0.000	

* $p < 0.10$
** $p < 0.05$
*** $p < 0.01$

When a municipal government receives strong central-government support to provide public services, it likely perceives less need to invite local farmers to participate in shaping public policy, especially if the municipal budget relies more on central-government transfers than on locally raised taxes. When it comes to the probability of actually implementing activities jointly with CBOs and sending out municipal staff to the field, having strong central-government support is likely to make such activities less costly for the local politicians (e.g., sharing costs for vehicles, fuel, equipment, personnel, etc.). This would explain why this variable's coefficient changes its sign from negative to positive in the second and third models.

Apart from the two institutional incentive variables, party politics also seem to matter a great deal when it comes to explaining the existence

Table 9.4
Changing probabilities for statistically significant coefficients

Independent variables	Model 1 Coprovision	Model 2 Coproduction	Model 3 Field presence
CBO demand			
Minimum ($x = 0$)	0.193	0.568	0.278
Maximum ($x = 57.6$)	0.800	0.927	0.728
Difference	0.607	0.359	0.450
Central support and supervision			
Minimum ($x = 0$)	0.459	0.414	0.198
Maximum ($x = 12$)	0.180	0.744	0.568
Difference	−0.279	0.330	0.370
Leftist party			
Minimum ($x = 0$)	0.337	0.722	
Maximum ($x = 1$)	0.164	0.502	
Difference	−0.173	−0.220	
Central rule			
Minimum ($x = 0$)		0.601	0.402
Maximum ($x = 1$)		0.829	0.573
Difference		0.228	0.171
Continuity of office (years)			
Minimum ($x = 1$)			0.314
Maximum ($x = 33$)			0.986
Difference			0.672
Literacy rates			
Minimum ($x = 43.8$)			0.609
Maximum ($x = 97.32$)			0.332
Difference			−0.277
Municipal budget			
Minimum ($x = 44$)	0.145		0.511
Maximum ($x = 50{,}252$)	0.935		0.113
Difference	0.790		−0.398
Population density			
Minimum ($x = 0.39$)	0.308		
Maximum ($x = 1{,}485$)	0.003		
Difference	−0.305		
Peru			
Minimum ($x = 0$)	0.367	0.720	0.579
Maximum ($x = 1$)	0.078	0.395	0.121
Difference	−0.289	−0.325	−0.458

of institutions for participatory governance. When the political party of the mayor is the same as the national government's ruling party, the likelihood of both coproduction and field presence increases by about 20 percent. This result likely reflects pork-barrel politics as the distribution of scarce central-government resources is likely to follow party lines. This is consistent with our earlier finding that central-government support and supervision have a positive effect of about the same magnitude on both of these variables.

Contrary to the claims by the New Left scholars—that political leaders from leftist parties are more supportive of participatory-governance institutions—we find the opposite relationship for two of our three measures of participation. In fact, mayors who are members of leftist parties are about 20 percent less likely to engage in coprovision and coproduction than mayors from nonleftist parties ($p < 0.01$). This result is more consistent with the view that leftist parties are more prone to governmental production of public services because it is the supposed duty of the state to secure the social welfare for its citizens, providing and producing all necessary public services, and asking only for taxes in return (Tilton 1990; de Swaan 1988). However, this result turns out to be quite sensitive to the definition of the "left." When coding the Mexican Institutional Revolutionary Party (PRI) as a nonleftist party—which some would argue is a more appropriate designation—the coefficient remains negative but loses its statistical significance.

There is mixed evidence on the relationship between financial endowments and participatory governance depending on which indicator of participatory governance is considered. As suggested by the Modernization literature, we find that the richer a municipality is, the more likely it will engage in coprovision ($p < 0.01$). The poorest municipalities in the region are 79 percent less likely to engage in coprovision (all other variables held constant at their means). When considering the effect of municipal finances on field presence, however, the relationship is the opposite: poorer municipalities are actually more likely to send their personnel to work together with local people in the field ($p = 0.065$). When mayors in poorer municipalities are under pressure to take action in the natural-resource sectors, they have little choice but to rely on the contributions from local people. Wealthier municipalities, however, have the option to offer unilateral, in-house production of the solicited services.

One of the most interesting results of the empirical analysis is that several of the frequently cited drivers of civic participation do not have a discernible effect in our analysis. We found no consistent evidence regarding the claimed effects of electoral competitiveness, population density, literacy rates, or the continuity of political office on the likelihood of participatory municipal governance.

In all three models, the dummy variable for Peru is negative and highly significant ($p < 0.01$). The predicted probabilities in table 9.4 indicate that a municipal government in Peru is 29 percent less likely to organize coprovision, 32 percent less likely to engage in coproduction, and more than 45 percent less likely to dispatch municipal personnel to work with local people in the field. These results appear to support the idea that a centralized-governance structure is less propitious for building participatory local-governance institutions. It is possible, however, that other factors that are not directly related to decentralization policies also contribute to the apparent differences between national contexts. In the next section, we seek to sort out the nature of the relationship between decentralization policies and participatory municipal governance.

Discussion

Why would local politicians in Brazil, Chile, and Mexico be more interested in participatory governance than their colleagues in Peru? One possibility is that local politicians in countries that have passed decentralization reforms have become politically and financially empowered and would therefore be more inclined to organize coprovision and coproduction in response to pressure from both central and local actors. In a decentralized-policy context, it is the local government's official and legitimate role to facilitate such actions. In Peru, although the mayors are democratically elected, they are not empowered to respond to problems in the natural resource and agricultural sectors. At the time of our study, Peruvian mayors had no officially recognized role to intervene in the sector. They were not authorized to levy taxes, and they did not receive central-government funding and technical support to carry out activities in the sector. Hence, there were relatively few direct benefits for local politicians to decide to invest in the coprovision and coproduction of natural-resource governance activities. Apart from the costs to facilitate the participatory-governance process within the municipal governments, local politicians also risk being reprimanded by the central government for overstepping the agreed-upon boundaries of policy jurisdiction. As a result, community-based organizations in Peru that would like assistance to address a particular problem in the natural-resource sectors are likely to request support from the organizations that *do* have an official mandate in this area, and not the municipal government. But even if Peruvian CBOs were to demand action from their municipal government in the natural-resource sector, it would be easy for local politicians to hide behind their restricted mandate and thus avoid organizing the participatory process.

According to this line of reasoning, centralized-governance structures make local politicians less likely to be participatory. If this is true, one would expect two things to occur in the case of Peru. First, both CBOs and central governments in Peru would interact less with municipal governments in the natural-resource management sector relative to the other countries because local governments were not a key player there. Second, the effect of these interactions on the likelihood for participation should be weaker in Peru, where mayors had no formal obligation to organize any activities in the sector. We proceeded to carry out simple statistical tests to see if any such differences actually exist.

Contrary to the expectations posited above, we found no significant differences between the absolute values of the CBO demand variable or the central support and supervision variable in Peru compared to the other three countries. To rule out the possibility that Chile and Mexico, which are in the middle of the continuum of decentralized countries in this sample, drive these results, we compare Brazil—the most decentralized nation among the four—with Peru. Again, we find no significant differences between levels of central-government support and supervision to local governments between the two countries. We do detect a significant difference between the absolute values of CBO pressure between Peru and Brazil. Contrary to expectations, however, the average level of CBO pressure among Peruvian municipal governments is actually significantly *higher* than in the Brazilian equivalents ($p = 0.02$). Only when combining the two independent variables into one (by adding the central and local pressure variables together) is the mean value of this variable significantly higher in the decentralized countries than in the centralized ($p = 0.05$). Although this last result lends some support to the idea that decentralization promotes interactions with local governments, the two test results taken together reject the proposition that decentralization reforms are necessary for local governments to be regarded as legitimate governance actors. It may be that even though local governments in Peru are not officially recognized as key players in natural-resource governance, CBOs may still turn to them when they need assistance. When considering the small, rural municipalities that this study focuses on, local organizations in Peru are likely to have a limited number of alternative organizations to turn to with their problems. The question as to why CBOs would demand to participate in local-governance issues is beyond the scope of this chapter but is an intriguing topic for future research.

The second test gauges whether there are any differences in the effects that the two institutional incentive variables have on the three measures of participatory governance between Peru and the other three countries. We let the country dummy variables interact with each of the independent variables and then use a Wald test to check whether the coefficients are significantly different for each of the countries. When considering the two institutional incentive sources separately, we find no differences in the strength of their effects on any of the three dependent variables. When combining the two incentive variables into one, the Wald test does indicate that the effect on coprovision is significantly stronger in the decentralized countries than in the centralized ($\chi^2 = 4.13$, df = 1; $p = 0.04$). For the other two dependent variables, however, there are no discernible differences between the responses to the institutional incentives by mayors in different national contexts.

One would also expect the effect of central-government support and supervision on participation to be stronger in Brazil than in Peru since participatory municipal governance of natural resources is part of national policy in Brazil. The results of the Wald tests support this prediction for two of the three models, suggesting that effective top-down control may actually increase the chances of local politicians to become more participatory.[8]

Taken together, however, there is rather mixed empirical support for the idea that decentralization policies make local government more welcoming of civic engagement in municipal affairs. We find that differences in the observed levels of participatory municipal governance among the four countries cannot be explained solely by the degree of decentralization. Other factors, related to deeper societal characteristics, might provide better explanations. For instance, the lack of participatory governance among municipal governments in Peru could very well be a manifestation of the greater social and economic inequalities that exist in Peruvian rural societies compared to Brazil, Chile, and Mexico. Future studies would therefore benefit from including variables that somehow capture such inequalities in each municipality. It is also entirely possible that the indiscernible differences of institutional incentives and their effects in the centralized versus decentralized countries have to do with the way we measure the dependent variables. The so-called Mesas de Concertación that exist in several Peruvian municipalities represent spaces for participatory governance, albeit not under the auspices of the municipal governments. Our measures of participation considered only municipally organized participation. It is conceivable that the existence of these nongovernmental forums explains why there are relatively high levels of interactions among local politicians, central-government representatives, and CBOs in Peru, without these having a statistically significant impact on the probability of participatory governance, as defined by our study. In fact, when coding coprovision differently—including nongovernmental roundtables as coprovision in Peru—the dummy variable for Peru loses its statistical significance in the first model. This result suggests that the influence of decentralization policies is limited to municipal *governments*, but the nongovernmental realm may be more important for organizing participatory *governance* in Peru.

Conclusions

Few contemporary researchers question the idea that locally organized institutions for coprovision and coproduction of public services can lead to increased transparency in public affairs, improved legitimacy of government, enhanced downward accountability, and even improved quality of public services. The literature on local governance has accumulated an impressive collection of case studies that document the many benefits of participatory governance. This chapter adds a new contribution to this collection: a quantitative, institutional approach to the analysis of the conditions that enhance civic engagement in public affairs. We utilized a natural experiment-of-kind to shed light on the ostensible link between decentralization policies and the likelihood of participatory municipal governance.

Our analysis provides mixed evidence regarding the effect of decentralization reforms on local efforts to organize participatory-governance institutions. The results question the existing assumptions that democratic local governance would be an automatic consequence of decentralization policies. We show that the low incidence of participatory municipal governance in Peru is not necessarily related to its (pre-2002) national policy of *centralized* decision making. Likewise, the significantly higher occurrence of civic engagement in municipal affairs in Brazil, Chile, and Mexico is not necessarily a result of the national decentralization policy. What we do show is that, regardless of the local governments' official role and mandates, participatory municipal governance is more likely to occur when community-based organizations frequently demand action from their elected municipal officials. Under some circumstances, but not always, national governments may affect the likelihood of participation in the municipal affairs by offering technical support, opportunities for training, and direct supervision. We also show, however, that strong central-government support and supervision can also lead to a "crowding-out" of local initiatives to create participatory decision-making forums.

Finally, our current understanding of the effects of national-policy reforms would benefit from more empirical studies that systematically study how local actors respond to decentralization policies. In future studies, it would be particularly useful to collect and analyze longitudinal data on local politicians' incentive structures *before* and *after* the decentralization reforms. The fact that Peru recently passed such reforms presents an opportunity for revisiting the sampled Peruvian municipalities, which are now operating under an officially decentralized-government structure. Such a study would provide additional evidence on the conditions that may or may not affect the transformation of local strongmen into modern facilitators of increased civic engagement and deliberative democracy.

10
Conclusions

During the last decade, we have witnessed renewed interest in rural-development research among policy scholars, practitioners, and diplomats concerned with development issues. Members of the international community have shown renewed commitment to addressing rural poverty in developing countries, as evidenced by increased support to initiatives such as the UN's Millennium Development Project and the World Bank's Highly-Indebted, Poor-Country program. These programs recognize that rural poverty is one of the major constraining factors for any nation's human development potential (UN 2005; World Bank 2003). These international-policy initiatives have increased the demand for new knowledge about rural-development policy and poverty alleviation strategies. Responding to this demand, the policy-research community has developed new approaches to the study of the causes and consequences of rural poverty. For rural-development studies focusing on Latin America, several recent studies by both international organizations (World Bank 2005 and 2008; Inter American Development Bank 2001; Food and Agriculture Organization 2002; International Institute for Cooperation and Agriculture 2004; International Fund for Agriculture and Development 2001) and academics (Quijandría et al. 2001; Reardon et al. 2001; Echeverria 2001; De Janvry and Sadoulet 2003; Schejtman and Berdegué 2004; Gordillo et al. 2006; Bresciani and Valdez 2007) have contributed to a more nuanced understanding of the complexities of rural development in this region. A number of the core findings of these studies relate directly to the results of our own study.

What has become clear from this new literature is that, first, the rural sector seems to be larger than what official statistics depict, both in terms of its share of GDP and in terms of the number of people who earn their livelihoods in rural areas (World Bank 2005; IICA 2004; OECD 2002). This result points to the importance of analyzing the challenges associated with public policies designed to support rural development in the region, the main purpose of our book. Second, the World Bank (2005) states that in Latin America the estimated contribution of agricultural growth (forestry and fisheries included) to national development is about twice as much as could be expected based on the sector's share of GDP. In fact, nonagricultural sectors contribute less to growth in most countries in the region. In Latin America as a whole, the World Bank calculates that for each 1 percent growth in the rural sector, national GDP increases 0.22 percent while the incomes of the poorest families increase 0.28 percent. This is more than twice the growth that would be expected based on the sector's share of GDP (0.12 percent) (World Bank 2005).

A third aspect emerging from recent studies on rural development that merits attention is the importance of nonfarm incomes for rural families' livelihoods. According to Reardon et al. (2001), rural households receive more than 40 percent of their total income from activities not directly related to agriculture (55 percent in Mexico; 50 percent in Peru; 41 percent in Chile; and 39 percent in Brazil). This means that rural-development policies must go beyond an exclusive focus on agriculture and pay more attention to the interaction of a variety of economic and social activities in the rural sector. Also according to the World Bank (2005), about 37 percent of the poor in Latin America and the Caribbean live in rural areas, and in countries like Bolivia, Guatemala, Honduras, Nicaragua, Paraguay, and Peru, about 70 percent of the rural population lives in poverty. Paradoxically, in Mexico—which is considered one of the richest nations in the region—more than 35 percent of the rural population does not earn enough money to pay for a minimum food basket (the monetary value of the food items that would provide the minimum number of calories per capita per day to be healthy). This number is well above the regional average of 20 percent. In urban areas, "only" 11 percent of the population lives in conditions of extreme poverty (World Bank 2005; ECLAC 2006).

Public expenditures in rural areas are frequently biased in favor of individual farm subsidies and against public goods and services. According to estimates from the Inter-American Development Bank, between 1985 and 2000, more than 54 percent of total rural expenditures were allocated through subsidies, the vast majority provided to large and medium-sized producers, rather than through the provision of public goods and services that would aid the rural poor (Echeverria 2001). It seems that public resources in the countryside are to a considerable extent captured by people who are less needful of such support (World

Bank 2005; Gordillo et al. 2006). But even if public policies were reoriented to spend more public funds on services for rural communities that need these services the most, such investments would not deliver the intended benefits automatically. There are a number of factors—political, social, economic, and biophysical—that influence the effectiveness of service delivery to the rural poor. In this study, we identify and analyze these factors.

In sum, careful policy design and implementation of rural-development policy are of the utmost importance, due to the size of the rural sector (both in terms of population and economic impact), the fact that poverty is strongly associated with rural conditions, the diversity of productive activities and sources of income, and the propensity of public expenditures for rural development to be captured by special-interest groups.

Throughout this book, we have argued that the success of agricultural policies as a tool to fight rural poverty is closely linked to how public policies affect local-governance patterns. Because of their expressed intent to empower local-governance structures, our analysis pays particular attention to the effect of decentralization reforms. The results of our study have demonstrated the relevance of institutional arrangements and the extent to which they foster cooperation and complementarity among the governance actors who may affect rural-development outcomes at the municipal level. We find that these institutions help explain the varying levels of performance of municipal-governance systems in the region's agricultural sectors. One of the most significant conclusions from this analysis is that, even though legal reforms and economic resources are often necessary components of effective municipal governance, they are insufficient to generate improved outcomes. In addition to those components, a successful municipal-governance regime requires either formal or informal local institutional arrangements that are capable of addressing the three municipal governance dilemmas always present in local-governance efforts: motivation dilemmas, information problems, and power asymmetries.

Municipal-Governance Dilemmas

The quality of agricultural public services in rural municipalities throughout the region, we have shown, is associated with the role played by the municipal government within public-service governance systems. When municipal governments are capable of creating institutions that can effectively respond to motivation, information, and power issues, they are better positioned to achieve better-quality services. Below, we present a summary of the results of our analysis regarding each of these governance dilemmas.

Motivational Dilemmas

The book's first hypothesis is that the stronger the incentives a mayor perceives resulting from relationships with higher levels of government, local-level constituents, and community-based organizations (CBOs), the higher the probability that he or she will dedicate time, effort, and resources to address their demands. This hypothesis puts the institutional incentives of decentralized governance at center stage of the analysis. We proposed four sources of incentives to which we expected local governments to respond when considering the provision of services to the agricultural sector: effective central-government monitoring of municipal commitments; the potential for financial gain; demands from an organized electorate; and pressures from CBOs. The empirical evidence presented here suggests that the role of local institutions in the coprovision of agricultural services is a relevant factor that can explain why some municipalities decide to promote actions in the agricultural sector while others do not. It is more likely that a local government, in any of the four countries under study, will take action in the agricultural sector when the relevant actors, both at the municipal level and at other levels of government, interact more frequently.

Our analysis also shows that strengthening decentralized governance is not merely a matter of training municipal staff or of assigning more economic resources. This does not imply that such forms of support lack significance, but rather, that such support could be even more effective if the municipal administration's incentive structures were taken into consideration when designing support programs. Our analysis further demonstrates that a strong, demanding central government makes local governmental action more likely. This finding underscores the importance of multilevel governance arrangements through which actors at multiple levels may coordinate their corresponding actions and decisions.

In our cross-national comparative analyses, we find that it is unreasonable to expect locally elected political officials to engage in participatory governance unless they can expect a financial or political payoff from doing so. Contrary to conventional wisdom, we show that the degree of decentralization seems to matter very little when it comes to the likelihood of local politicians seeking participatory forms of governance. Instead, we find that the presence of institutional incentives—which seem virtually unaffected by the decentralization process—is what best explains the variation in participatory leadership across the 390 local governments in the four countries.

In Brazil, stronger pressure from local farmer organizations is associated with higher levels of municipal investment in agricultural activities. As for the relationship between the level of municipal action in the agricultural sector and the effective commitment of the central government, it is evident that the municipalities with a closer interaction with the central government offer more services.

In Chile, the relation between the strength of the local government's performance in the agricultural sector and the pressure it perceives from the central government is not very strong. We believe this outcome is related to the Chilean administrative structure, which establishes very little space for municipal decision making in the agricultural sector. However, the relationship with the central government is in general a very significant factor in determining municipal action in the agricultural sector, second only to the pressure exerted by CBOs.

In the case of Mexico, about 65 percent of the variation in municipal performance of agricultural services is explained by combining the four sources of incentives into one index. The outcome is significant for both the north-central and the southern region of the country, although the degree of correlation seems to be greater in the north-central subsample.

In Peru, the two subsamples generate two different outcomes. The fifty coastal municipalities show a positive and significant relationship between three of the four incentives and the probability of municipal action in the agricultural sector. Of the four incentives listed above, the most significant and strongest predictor of municipal action is the degree of interaction with the central government. In the highlands and rain-forest subsample, none of the four incentives is linked to the potential for municipal action in agriculture. We attribute this result to a "low-number problem" in the analysis: there are few local governments in this subsample that have a sufficient number of staff, much less staff specialized in agricultural development. Hence, as a result of insufficient variation in the dependent variable, our statistical model does not uncover any statistically significant relationships in this region of Peru. Also, the outcome in the inland regions subsample could be explained by the geographical conditions of highland and rain-forest municipalities. Great distances prevent frequent interactions among local actors, such as central-government agents residing in the area, community-based organizations, and local politicians.[1] But it is also possible that our result for Peru as a whole is driven by a policy bias toward the coastal areas. This region happens to possess a richer and more modernized agricultural sector and is also the base of one of the most powerful groups of political elites. As a consequence, for the Peruvian sample as a whole, the municipalities that receive the most support from the central government are those that also demonstrate the highest level of motivation to carry out their own, independently defined programs and activities.

These results highlight the importance of the four institutional incentives in explaining why a given municipality's leadership would decide to take action in the agricultural sector. It also describes the conditions that would make this leadership more likely to engage civil society in the decision-making process. But our analysis falls short in explaining why a municipality that has already invested resources in personnel and agricultural activities would succeed in producing high-quality services.

In our analysis, we find that motivation and policy success are not as closely connected as might be expected. Bureaucratic motivation is likely to increase the chances for policy success, but we find that motivation is not a good predictor of quality. In fact, the Chilean case is the only one in which a significant correlation is visible between municipal human resources earmarked for the agricultural sector and farmers' perception of the quality of local services. Municipal staff's technical capacity does not explain why the quality of the services in some municipalities is better than in others. Once motivational dilemmas are overcome, the municipality has to contend with information and power asymmetry issues that stand in the way of an efficient, effective, and equitable system for the provision and production of agricultural services. In the next section, we present our findings about the factors that we found increase the probability of producing and providing these services at a high level of quality.

Information Problems

Our statistical analysis of the factors that affect the likelihood of successful service production concludes that local institutions created for information exchange are of vital importance. As discussed in chapter 1, this study proposes that an effective exchange of information is essential for

(1) the operation of accountability mechanisms; (2) the adaptation of political interventions to the local conditions and needs; and (3) the coordination and exchange of learning experiences with other actors.

The frequency of opportunities for information exchange among actors involved in municipal governance is positively correlated with a favorable opinion of community-based organizations regarding the quality of the agricultural services offered at the local level. Institutions that promote the exchange of information are key components of an effective municipal-governance system in all four countries.

In Brazil, the frequency of interactions between farmer organizations and the municipality is strongly correlated with the quality of agricultural services. This correlation is strengthened when the interaction between the municipality and the central government is added. In other words, in those municipalities where the exchange of information among all three actors is greater, a better quality of service is likely.

In Chile, two factors related to the exchange of information in municipal governance stand out in terms of their relevance for achieving good agricultural-service management: the interaction between municipal administration and community-based organizations, and the existence of comanagement activities between the municipal government and the rural community. However, there are relatively few municipalities that engage in such comanagement activities, a fact that we link to the highly centralized administrative structure in Chile's agricultural sector.

In Mexico, the combination of two factors is closely correlated to the opinion of farmers regarding the quality of public services in the territory. The first of these is the frequency of interactions between municipality and central government, and the second is the interaction between municipality and community-based organizations. High levels of interaction mean positive ratings by farmers. Nonetheless, when the interaction between municipality and community-based organizations is excluded, the statistical significance of this association disappears. It is probable that the recent democratization process in Mexico, which ended 70 years of single-party politics,[2] has also enhanced the importance of CBOs and other forms of citizens' organizations.

In Peru, the relation between information-exchange arrangements among local actors and the quality of agricultural services is not statistically significant for the overall sample. However, in the subsample of the fifty highlands and rain-forest municipalities, a positive and significant relation does exist. A possible explanation is that a byproduct of highly biased public policies toward the coastal region has made municipalities in the highlands and the rain-forest areas more decisive in terms of service delivery, because no other levels of government provide services in those locations.

One of the positive implications of the analysis of local institutions for information exchange is that local actors have the potential to improve the performance of the services produced in their territories. They can do so through the creation of institutions that facilitate the exchange of information related to (1) government initiatives in agriculture at both central and municipal levels, (2) the lessons from different local community initiatives, and (3) the rural-development experiences of different farmer and peasant organizations, NGOs, and other municipalities. Our analysis suggests that technical assistance provided by the central government and international-development organizations could be made more effective if these actors would take into consideration the relevance of initiatives that promote the exchange of information among a variety of governance actors in the local sphere.

One way to support more effective municipal governance would be to promote the creation of neutral or nonpartisan forums to encourage cooperation among actors involved in the municipal-governance system. Direct support to municipal-government administrations could actually hinder the achievement of this goal, since external income is frequently subject to the economic interests of municipal officials without any input from other governance actors (such as farmer representatives and central-government program officials). The allocation of support funds to an association of municipal actors representing diverse interests has the potential—at least in part—to address the negative incentives that engender opportunistic behavior. The logic behind the promotion of institutional arrangements that emphasize shared responsibility and checks and balances is that such arrangements can lessen information asymmetries among actors.

Power Asymmetries

The third argument that we have tested in this study relates to the importance of local institutional arrangements in mitigating problems of patronage and corruption through the promotion of broad participation in the provision of public agricultural services. We began by noting that the existence of neutral consensus-building forums is not very common in three of the four countries. Only in the southern region of Brazil do most municipalities have such forums (see also Oliveira 2005; J. Ortega 2005). Ironically, it is only in Brazil that we do not observe a systematic relationship between the existence of forums and a favorable opinion of the quality of agricultural services. More than one-third of those municipalities where a forum is present fail to provide an adequate service response to their farmers—as per the farmers' own opinions. However, we find that coproduction—in contrast with the coprovision practiced in the mandatory forums—is a stronger predictor of municipal performance in Brazil. There is strong evidence of a positive association between broad participation by the intended beneficiaries of services and the quality of those services across all four countries.

In Chile, although social consensus-building forums are present in only 30 percent of the municipalities, we found that the performance of local agricultural services is strongly linked to the existence of those spaces.

In Mexico, the mere existence of consensus-building forums seems to be strongly linked to farmers' favorable opinions of quality of local agricultural services. Nonetheless, these forums are present in only 25 percent of the country's municipalities.

In Peru, we found a positive and significant correlation between the quality of public services and the level of farmers' involvement in the municipal governance of the agricultural sector. Municipalities offering more opportunities to participate in coprovision and coproduction activities also obtain better ratings in terms of user satisfaction with agricultural services, according to the small-scale farmers interviewed. The relation is particularly strong in the highlands and in the rain-forest region, where the Mesas de Concertación had been active for a longer period of time.

The degree of participation by community-based organizations in municipalities' budgetary planning processes may be used as another indicator of equitable power relationships and institutional openness. Worth noting is that in those countries where the ratio of municipalities with municipal consensus-building forums is higher, i.e., Brazil and Peru, the degree of citizen participation in municipal planning processes is also broader. We found that 68 percent of the Brazilian municipalities promote the participation of local farmer groups in budgetary planning related to agricultural activities. The corresponding ratios for Peru, Mexico, and Chile are 39 percent, 34 percent, and only 8 percent, respectively. The statistics for Chile are surprising, because even though 29 percent of Chilean municipalities organize consensus-building forums, only a fraction of these facilitate the participation of community-based organizations in their economic decisions. The Chilean case shows that, beyond the existence of consensus-building forums, the actual mandate and attributes of these forums are important in enhancing democratic and equitable municipal governance. The relatively high showing of CBO participation in municipal-budget decisions in Peru compared to the more decentralized rural-development sectors of Mexico and Chile also indicates that decentralization reforms alone are insufficient to promote equitable forms of governance, and that such reforms may not even represent a necessary condition for addressing power asymmetries at the municipal level.

The Effects of National Policies on Municipal Performance

Recent studies have found that the centralized public agricultural services in many countries in the region have failed to improve most indicators of agricultural productivity among small-scale farmers (Gordillo et al. 2006; World Bank 2005; Litvack et al. 1998). Most public investment earmarked for rural development and agricultural promotion still resides in the ministries in the capital. In general, the design, implementation, supervision, and evaluation of development funds, promotion instruments, and social policy programs do not fall under the jurisdiction of local governments. When asked if the national government intervenes in the agricultural arena, 71.43 percent of the mayors in Peru said yes. In Chile, Mexico, and Brazil, this percentage is 92.50, 98.63, and 98.00, respectively. These figures contrast with the low numbers of municipal professionals active in the agricultural sector. In Chile, an average of 2.08 professionals work at the municipal level. In Mexico, this average is 1.41, in Brazil it is 1.16, and in Peru the average is only 0.15 professionals hired by the municipality to work in the agricultural sector.

In response to the perceived failures of central governments' efforts to offer much-needed services to support rural-development efforts in the region, essentially all countries have embarked on a process of decentralization of their public sectors, although the structure and context may vary from country to country. Our comparative study addresses how these different decentralization reforms help solve agricultural-production issues that plague the poorest farmers in the region.

In our cross-national comparisons examining how the degree of decentralization might affect the likelihood of participatory municipal leadership as well as any leadership achieving high-quality services, we find mixed evidence. Our findings in both chapters 8 and 9 show that there is a much higher likelihood for Brazilian municipalities to have more democratic and participatory-governance styles, as well as to achieve high-quality services, when compared to municipalities in Peru. However, it would be a stretch to attribute these differences to the degree of decentralization alone. There are many other things that are different in the two countries that provide alternative explanations for the observed differences. For example, if the degree of decentralization is the decisive factor in determining differences in the extent of participatory governance as well as differences in levels of perceived service quality, one would expect that the effect of CBO pressure (the strongest determinant of participatory governance in all four countries) would be stronger in a decentralized regime (Brazil) than in a more centralized one (Peru), but our statistical tests reject such a relationship.

When it comes to explaining differences in the quality of public services, the degree of decentralization does seem to matter. We find that the presence of participatory governance institutions is the strongest determinant of high-quality services, and that these institutions (coprovision and coproduction) are significantly more common in decentralized regimes (such as Brazil) than in centralized ones (such as Peru). One would also expect that the effect of these participatory institutions on service quality would be stronger in a decentralized regime because of the relatively greater level of autonomy at the local level, which permits local governments to be more responsive to the decisions made in the forums for coprovision. Our Wald tests in chapter 9 confirm that this is indeed the case. Also, one would expect that the effect of interaction with central-government officials on service quality would be stronger in a centralized country like Peru than in the other three countries, since it is the central government that is responsible for delivering services throughout the country. Statistical tests demonstrate that this hypothesis holds for our sample.

Because of this mixed evidence regarding the effects of these national-level reforms, we conclude that it is not appropriate to attribute differences in municipal performance to decentralization reforms alone. We cannot rule out the possibility that other factors, such as the cross-national differences in socioeconomic inequalities within societies, and the level of trust that citizens place in public-governance institutions at all levels in a given society could also contribute to the observed differences in governance outcomes between countries. We leave the exploration of these issues for future research.

Questions for Future Research

In light of our main findings, we identify three important issues for future research related to the local institutional dynamics of rural-development policies: (1) The origins of effective local institutions, (2) Factors that make participatory municipal forums work, and (3) The economic, social and environmental outcomes of rural development efforts.

What Are the Origins of Effective Local Institutions?

Our study is not the first to suggest that local institutions matter for rural development. But we have taken the local institutional argument one step further by analyzing which type of institutions seems to account for the biggest differences in outcomes, both in terms of motivating local politicians and in terms of making municipal interventions responsive to local needs and expectations. Across all four countries, institutions for coprovision and coproduction seem to be of the utmost importance for achieving high-quality public services for rural development. We also show some evidence that these institutions are most likely to emerge in decentralized regimes, especially when there is ample support and strong collaboration ties between the municipality and external organizations at both lower and higher levels of governance. We conclude that the density of these local networks, consisting of actors from different governance levels, plays a central role for both the formation and functioning of effective local institutional arrangements. This is the limit of our analysis. However, if dense local networks are so crucial for local governance, under what conditions are such networks more likely to emerge? Can public policy help their creation?

These are important questions for future research, as answers might help shed new light on the origins of effective local institutions and provide new ideas as to how public policy can help create such institutions. The research agenda that we propose is closely related to that of the social-capital literature. Indeed, social-capital scholars see networks as one important aspect of social capital (Ostrom and Ahn 2003; Putnam 1993; Woolcock 1998). Looking at the origins of social capital for the benefit of rural development, several studies have made important contributions. We summarize some of these below, as they are important references for the design of new studies on local governance and rural development.

Fafchamps (1996) points to the importance of education aimed at the creation of a culture of cooperation. Such a culture, Fafchamps argues, enhances the compliance of contracts, reduces avoidance of payment delays, and improves the fulfillment of conditions of production and delivery. Fisman and Khanna (2004) argue that the promotion of clusters and agglomerations of businesses is an effective way of nourishing social capital. According to this study, such an approach could help to overcome the potential shortcomings of basic services and governance. Gertler and Wolfe (2004) propose to promote the exercise of regional foresight as a socially organized learning process documented in a dynamic strategy that should be translated into concrete projects.

A number of studies suggest that favorable local environments (Putnam 1993; Bagnasco 1988; Carmagnani and Gordillo 1997) are capable of creating certain kinds of social capital that result in improved economic welfare for communities and regions. However, it has also been suggested that in places with a long tradition of exclusionary development and with a low endowment of entrepreneurship—particularly policy entrepreneurship—specific interventions may be needed to spur the development of social capital (North et al. 2000; Gordillo and Andersson 2004).

We propose that future research in this area should examine socioeconomic and biophysical factors, as suggested by the theoretical framework presented in chapter 1, which may influence the formation of social capital. It would be particularly interesting to revisit some of the 390 local governments in our study, to gather systematic data on these hypothesized drivers of social capital formation. Such data could be used for comparative analysis, to examine how socioeconomic inequalities related to income, property rights, and education affect changes in the density of local-governance networks over time. The passage of a Peruvian decentralization reform shortly after our first visit to one hundred municipalities there in 2002 presents a unique opportunity to analyze the effects of the reform by revisiting the same local governments some five years after the reforms (and our first visit).

What Makes Participatory Municipal Forums Work?

Local institutions for coprovision and coproduction seem to make a large difference for the performance of municipal rural-development programs. This finding resonates with much of the existing development literature on people's participation and downward accountability (Blair 2000; Ackerman 2004; Fung and Wright 2001; Ribot 2002). While there is now a relatively firm consensus among rural-development scholars that participatory decision-making forums are good for rural development, few studies have looked deeper into the specific characteristics that determine the effectiveness of these policy forums. This is a problem because it is now evident that the introduction of participatory forums has resulted in very mixed outcomes (Rydin and Pennington 2000; van Laerhoven chap. 4 in this book). Some cases have been successful, but many have not lived up to expectations. Given the increased prevalence of these forms of decision making, not to mention the importance that international-development organizations put on the creation of such institutions in rural-development projects, it is important to analyze what factors influence variation in outcomes. Previous research points to several factors that may complicate the functioning of participatory forums, including insufficient economies of scale (Vogelgesang 2000), "window-dressing" councils that are created merely to capture subsidies (Oliveira 2005; J. Ortega 2005), the absence of sufficient support from central-government authorities (Andersson 2003), managerial problems, monitoring and enforcement problems (Agrawal and Ostrom 2001), lack of decision-making power on the part of participants (Ribot 2002), and disconnection between the committees and the operational level of activities undertaken (Andersson and van Laerhoven 2007). It would be appropriate to note here that our collective knowledge of participatory municipal councils would be well-served by future studies that systematically test the influence of each of the factors mentioned in previous studies.

What Are the Economic, Social, and Environmental Outcomes of Rural Development Efforts?

Most of the outcome measures used in this study are based on perceptions of incentives and public-service performance by particular local actors—either resource users or local politicians. We see an opportunity to improve the use of outcome measures by broadening the types of outcomes measured and by improving the way in which these outcomes are measured. In addition to the quality of public services, it would be worthwhile to collect data on other policy outcome variables such as changing levels of rural poverty, modified investment yields for farmers participating in rural-development programs, changing income from agricultural activities, and changes in land-use patterns. Regarding measurement methods, we recognize the limitations of relying primarily on interviewee perceptions, especially when these perceptions were recorded by the same survey instruments that also measure causal factors. This limits the validity of the analysis as the relationships discovered in our analysis may, at least in part, be an artifact of measurement. Because perceptions are not true representations of actual outcomes, it is important for future studies to complement these measures with independently measured outcomes. The problem is that such data is rarely available for local governments in most Latin American countries. This means that such data would need to be collected by field researchers, which can be quite expensive. Creative use of modern technology, however, may reduce these costs. For example, the increased availability of satellite images may benefit future studies by using time-series observations of land cover change to infer changes in land use, agricultural productivity, soil erosion, and deforestation. Such an approach would require a shift toward a more interdisciplinary research program for the study of rural-development policy.

Having identified these three areas for future research, we conclude our final chapter with a discussion of the implications of our findings in terms of public-policy options for rural development in Latin America.

Policy Implications

The results of this study are not unequivocal. For instance, despite the proliferation of participatory municipal councils in Brazil, it is precisely in this country where we fail to find a systematic correlation between the existence of forums and a favorable opinion about the quality of the agricultural services. In Peru, neither the demands of the central government, the constituency, or CBOs, nor the potential agricultural gains for the municipality motivate the local governments of the inland municipalities to take action in the agricultural sector. Consequently, even though we identified some key elements of the decentralization-policy design, we are not in a position to prescribe a unique "recipe" for success. In fact, one of the main findings of our study is that there are a number of paths leading to success.

To deal with the specific characteristics and conditions of each region and locality, specific interventions should be designed with the potential for serving as public-policy experiments that might be monitored so that policy actors may learn how policies may be adjusted for the best possible results. National governments may carry out pilot projects in the area of municipal governance of rural development programs for a select number of municipalities to experiment with particular institutional designs. One way for national governments to create improved conditions for horizontal learning and cooperation among municipalities would be to allocate some financial resources for larger-scale services, such as research and extension programs, to clusters of municipalities rather than transferring smaller amounts to individual administrations. Through such programs, the members of each cluster would have the opportunity to exchange ideas and experiences in other areas and might even be asked to participate in peer monitoring and evaluation.[3]

Although such horizontal cooperation may be extremely beneficial in terms of improving the performance of public services in the agricultural sector, many rural-development problems in Latin America require more than effective local governance. Some problems—such as the inequalities related to access to education, healthcare, and stable employment—have such deep and complex roots that even the most effective local governments would not be able to address them single-handedly. It would seem that the more complex the collective problem at hand, the more sophisticated the institutional response must be. If collective-action institutions at multiple levels of governance—from local communities to municipal governments to the national and international arenas—are able to coordinate their efforts in order to attack a problem from multiple fronts simultaneously, resolution seems more likely.[4]

Our study has also shown that municipal institutions for co-production and co-provision play an important role in efforts to improve the quality of public agricultural services in rural areas of Latin America. Based on the results presented here, we would argue that carefully designed public policies have the potential to strengthen this role considerably. Favorable conditions that support the role of municipal governments in their efforts to promote rural development include at least three basic elements of public policy.

First, central-government policies should recognize the specific comparative advantages of local governments in the provision and production of certain goods and services in the agricultural sector, emphasizing the importance of coprovision and coproduction. Local governments enjoy several advantages compared to central governments when it comes to knowledge about the particular conditions of localities, residents, and residents' needs and concerns. These advantages suggest that local governments can play a crucial role in shaping policy responses in their territory to make sure these responses are appropriate, given the local conditions. These advantages do not mean, however, that local governments are always able to play the role of an effective local facilitator of public goods and services on their own. As our study notes, local governments often face incentives that are incompatible with the goals of investments in rural-development activities. To strengthen positive incentives to prioritize rural development, mechanisms for both upward and downward accountability are needed. Effective mechanisms would permit other governance actors, including the business community, to articulate their expectations regarding the decisions and actions of the local public officials. In other words, institutions for coprovision and coproduction are key components of an amplified mandate of municipal governance.

Second, regional programs supporting the formation of municipal networking activities in which municipal governance actors have an opportunity to share experiences related to agricultural service provision and production have the potential to strengthen the overall local-government capacity in the rural-development sectors. A common problem among local governments in Latin America is their limited financial and human resources. The lack of resources often prevents them from being effective, regardless of their level of motivation. Such programs would provide a forum for sharing experiences and would aid the dissemination of new ideas and technology that would improve the potential performance of all participating local governments. As such, increased communication and cooperation may help offset the problems presented by insufficient resources, by combining resources and know-how with other local governments in a similar position.

Finally, central and regional authorities should implement programs that involve both vertical and horizontal supervision, monitoring, and evaluation mechanisms. These programs should primarily be designed to provide opportunities for follow-up and organizational learning from policy experiments. This would require moving away from the traditional focus in which monitoring and evaluation programs in government are used as mechanisms for vertical control and punishment. Such a focus is likely to prevent local-governance actors from revealing information about the problems they face for fear of being sanctioned. An effective learning environment is one in which the emphasis is on the identification of the causes of observed outcomes and on the exploration of possible adjustments in the governance process that addresses these causes. In this context, the discussion by Ostrom (1996a) and Ackerman (2004) of voucher systems and cogovernance seems relevant. So does the discussion presented in Tendler and Alves-Amorim (1996), which describes how to facilitate policy entrepreneurship in a sustainable fashion. Finally, Hirschman's notion of "exit" and "voice" is relevant (Hirschman 1970).

Local institutions for participatory governance have a good chance of improving the transparency of public affairs and, therefore, of making citizen monitoring of local government performance less costly. However, as useful as these institutions are, they are unlikely to suffice for producing good governance. Local-policy actors themselves need to monitor, enforce, evaluate, and continuously adjust the institutional arrangements they have agreed upon in participatory forums, in order to produce good governance. On the one hand, centralized governance arrangements lack sufficient information about local preferences and capacities. On the other hand, however, localized governance arrangements may be disadvantaged by the absence of economies of scale. Decentralized local governance is not a panacea: Decentralization reforms must be designed carefully with a nation's contextual diversity in mind, especially when it comes to institutional arrangements for facilitating collective action at the local level.

Notes

Chapter 1. Poverty, Rural Development, and Local Governance in Latin America

1. Brazilian towns with fewer than 20,000 inhabitants have an average Human Development Index (HDI) of 0.692, whereas larger municipalities have an average HDI of 0.718 (UNDP Brazil 2000). In Mexico, the average HDI for municipalities with fewer than 20,000 inhabitants is 0.675, compared to 0.736 for larger towns (SAGARPA 2001). The difference is statistically significant.

2. *Collective action* is any effort made by a group of two or more individuals aimed at achieving a collective benefit (Ostrom 1990).

3. When the benefits of a public service benefit all, regardless of contributions, service providers have an incentive to discontinue such services. For instance, if municipal governments are made accountable for biodiversity conservation—a public asset that benefits all human beings on the planet—the assumption is that the cost of such conservation will be shouldered by the citizens of those municipalities with a high biodiversity, and that the other beneficiaries will not share in the cost. Under such circumstances, one cannot expect an adequate provision of services related to biodiversity conservation unless positive incentives are in place to persuade the local government to provide such services.

4. Singleton (1998, 10) agrees with this point of view in her study on local institutions for the comanagement of fisheries in the northeastern United States: "In theory, a successful management system is made possible by the creation of (local) institutions, but since said institutions are also public assets, their creation and conservation becomes a collective dilemma in itself."

Chapter 2. Framing the Comparative Study of Decentralization in Latin America

1. We checked the representativeness of the sampled municipalities by comparing the means and variance for a series of socioeconomic variables relevant to the topic of our study—such as the ratio of urban/rural population, literacy rates, and the proportion of inhabitants whose livelihood depend on agriculture—with the entire population of small, rural municipalities in each country. Using student t-tests and F-tests, we found no statistically significant

differences between our sample and the general population of these kinds of municipalities (assuming unequal variation across samples and a 95 percent confidence interval).

2. The fieldwork was carried out by DESER (south Brazil), SEI (northeast Brazil), Centro Ideas (Peru; Sierra and Selva regions), Instituto APOYO (Peru; coastal region), Gestión y Desarrollo (Chile), INDESO (Mexico; center and northern states), and Instituto MAYA (Mexico; southern states).

3. Two community-based organizations were identified and interviewed in all municipalities. In Chile, representatives of three CBOs were interviewed.

Chapter 4. Brazil: At the Decentralization Forefront

This chapter should be cited as van Laerhoven, F. 2009. Brazil: At the Decentralization Forefront. In *Local Governments and Rural Development: Comparing Lessons from Brazil, Chile, Mexico, and Peru,* ed. Krister Andersson, Gustavo Gordillo de Anda, and Frank van Laerhoven. Tucson: University of Arizona Press.

1. Formal criteria are established to determine eligibility for government-support programs.

2. Since 2000, mandates can be extended, in the event of re-election, for one additional four-year term.

3. We adopt the term *Participatory Publics,* which was coined by Wampler and Avritzer (2004).

4. In this study, which targets a specific segment of all Brazilian municipalities, higher percentages were found than the 68 percent reported by Favareto and de Marco. In the southern states, 92 percent of the municipalities possessed a CMDR. For the northeastern states this percentage was 84.

5. The results of the 2000 Census had not yet been published at the time that the municipalities for this study were selected.

6. Using a t-test to compare means between the sample and the sample pool, no significant difference between the selected localities and the total sampling pool was found regarding indicators such as literacy rate, income, life expectancy, and population. It is therefore reasonable to assume that the sample used in this analysis is representative for all rural municipalities in the states included in the study.

7. Departamento de Estudos Sócio-Econômicos Rurais (DESER) was the entity responsible for the fieldwork in the southern states. The Superintendência de Estudos Econômicos e Sociais da Bahia (SEI) was the institute responsible for the fieldwork in the northeastern states.

8. The confidence interval (95 percent) for the low values of this variable is narrower. We are more confident about the relation between low numbers of field visits and the likelihood of finding agricultural extension workers in a given municipality.

9. The confidence interval for low values is wider than for high values.

10. The confidence interval (95 percent) for high values is narrower than for low values.

11. Due to biophysical, climatic, and historic reasons, the average size of the farms varies according to region. In the sample, the average size of the southern farms is 35 hectares, while the average size of the northeastern farms is 22 hectares. A t-test reveals that this difference in means is significant ($p < 0.05$). However, the *dummy* differentiating between south and northeast is not statistically significant in this segment of the analysis.

12. The confidence interval (95 percent) for $x = 1$ is narrower than for $x = 0$.

13. The estimated probabilities at high values of x are quite imprecise: the confidence intervals (95 percent) are relatively wide.

Chapter 5. Chile: A Free-Market Model of Decentralization

This chapter should be cited as Lewin, P., and Andersson, K. 2009. Chile: A Free-Market Model of Decentralization. In *Local Governments and Rural Development: Comparing Lessons from Brazil, Chile, Mexico, and Peru*, ed. Krister Andersson, Gustavo Gordillo de Anda, and Frank van Laerhoven. Tucson: University of Arizona Press.

1. The HDI is a summary measure of human development. It measures the average achievements in three basic dimensions of human development: a long and healthy life, as measured by life expectancy at birth; knowledge, as measured by the adult literacy rate (with two-thirds weight) and the combined primary, secondary, and tertiary gross enrollment ratio (with one-third weight); a decent standard of living, as measured by GDP per capita (PPP US$).

2. Ratio of Economically Active Population that works in the agricultural sector, rurality index, population density, literacy, etc.

3. Due to some problems in filling out the survey, the data of one municipality were incomplete, and the decision was made to exclude this municipality from the analysis. Therefore, the final sample includes thirty-nine municipalities.

Chapter 6. Mexico: A Case of Limited Decentralization

This chapter should be cited as González, F., Ochoa, J. J., and Andersson, K. 2009. Mexico: A Case of Limited Decentralization. In *Local Governments and Rural Development: Comparing Lessons from Brazil, Chile, Mexico, and Peru*, ed. Krister Andersson, Gustavo Gordillo de Anda, and Frank van Laerhoven. Tucson: University of Arizona Press.

1. The Plan stipulated for President Zedillo's six-year term.

2. According to Mexico's National Institute of Geographic Statistics and Informatics (INEGI), *rural population* refers to those communities with fewer than 2,500 inhabitants.

3. As per data from SAGARPA (2001, 23), of the 3.8 million production units, 54 percent have an extension of less than five hectares and 30 percent, of less than two hectares.

4. According to the 2000 Population and Housing Census XII of INEGI, a total of 8,381,314 individuals are over five years of age and fluent in an indigenous language.

5. The opposition gains the first state government in 1989, and the PAN (Partido de Acción Nacional) gains access to the government of Baja California. The PAN also gains access to the government of Guanajuato in 1991, and to the government of Chihuahua in 1992.

6. This concerns especially the controversial (in terms of democratic legitimacy) presidential elections of 1988, through which Carlos Salinas de Gortari became president.

7. For more information on factors that have had a bearing on the Mexican territorial disparities, we recommend Rodriguez-Pose and Sánchez-Reaza (2002).

8. For a description of the selection process and the results of the statistical tests on representativeness, see chapter 3.

Chapter 7. Peru: The Pre-Decentralization Baseline Case

The author wishes to express his gratitude for the outstanding assistance provided by César Cancho in drafting this document, as well as by Regina Cortez and Claudia Benavides during the first stages of the project.

This chapter should be cited as Jaramillo, M. B. 2009. Peru: The Pre-Decentralization Baseline Case. In *Local Governments and Rural Development: Comparing Lessons from Brazil, Chile, Mexico, and Peru,* ed. Krister Andersson, Gustavo Gordillo de Anda, and Frank van Laerhoven. Tucson: University of Arizona Press.

1. A detailed account of economic reforms in this period can be found in Jaramillo and Saavedra (2005).

2. At the coastal departments, the survey was conducted by the Instituto APOYO, whereas at the highlands and forest departments, by the Centro Ideas.

Chapter 8. Comparative Analysis of the Institutional Conditions for Effective Rural-Development Services

1. This classification represents a mean value per municipality of 4 or higher in a scale from 1 to 6.

2. Worthy of notice is the fact that in Brazil, where decentralization has advanced the most, the mayors did not always show a positive attitude vis-à-vis the pragmatic impact of these policies.

Chapter 9. Does Decentralization Promote Participatory Governance?

An extended version of this chapter was published by Sage as Andersson, K., and van Laerhoven, F. 2007. From Local Strongman to Facilitator: Institutional Incentives for Participatory Municipal Governance in Latin America. *Comparative Political Studies* 40(9): 1085–1111.

1. "Strongmen" are indeed "men" most of the time. According to FAO (2002), more than 95 percent of all mayors in rural municipalities in Brazil, Chile, Mexico, and Peru are male. The traditional leaders—often referred to as either *caciques, caudillos,* or *coroneles,* depending on which Latin American country is concerned—were even more likely to be men than the modern-day mayors.

2. Fieldwork was done in 2002 (Peru, south Brazil, Mexico, and Chile) and 2003 (northeast Brazil). Our analysis does not take into account policy changes that occurred after this period (i.e., in Peru and Chile).

3. The question we asked was: "Is there, to your knowledge, in this municipality a policy-planning or discussion platform in which citizens participate?" Mexican, Chilean, and Brazilian local governments all have the mandate to create some form of public policy forum (COPLADEMUN, CESCO, and CMDR, respectively). There exists, however, considerable variation in the actual presence of such forums.

4. The question asked to CBO representatives was: "Did your organization ever participate in an activity together with the municipality?" If yes, which activities? The replies included activities such as the drilling of wells, road maintenance, legal advice, help with central government–related administrative matters, etc.

5. We asked all CBO respondents whether municipal staff ever visited and met with them in the field.

6. We reason that field presence is closely related to our measure of coproduction, but it also captures a more down-to-earth form of interaction between the local government and citizens that is not necessarily manifested through our coproduction variable. As such, field presence constitutes a complementary measure to coproduction.

7. By "leftist party," we mean the segment of the political spectrum typically associated with any of several strains of socialism, social democracy, or social liberalism. To code any particular party as either leftist or nonleftist, we first consulted the *World Encyclopedia of Political Systems and Parties,* by George E. Delury (1999) and then established whether the party in question considers itself to be leftist or has its origins in leftist movements. If Delury did not list a particular party, we consulted the Web site of the "Leftist Parties of the World" (http://www.broadleft.org). Though both of these sources list PRI of Mexico as a leftist party, many scholars have raised doubts about their true political orientation. In

our empirical analysis, we therefore run our model two times: first with PRI coded as leftist party and then as nonleftist.

8. $\chi^2 = 5.48$, df = 1; $p = 0.01$ for coproduction, and $\chi^2 = 4.76$, df = 1; $p = 0.02$ for field presence.

Chapter 10. Conclusions

1. The analysis of the importance of interaction in the Peruvian case suffers from a "small numbers" problem, which often makes it difficult to detect a statistically significant correlation between two variables.

2. Presidential elections in 2000 ended the one-party system at the national executive branch. However, since the beginning of the 1990s and certainly after the 1997 legislative elections, a plurality of political options has been elected at municipal and state governments and at federal and local legislatures.

3. FAO in Latin America launched a regional cluster of programs with the participation of national, state, and local governments as well as regional and local NGOs and private corporations in five regions of Brazil, four regions in Mexico, and one region in Chile in 2005. On the strategy of these programs see Gordillo de Anda, Wagner, and Lewin (2005).

4. For more on multilevel, multiorganizational governance arrangements, particularly in Europe, see Culpepper 2003.

References Cited

Abramovay, R. (2001). Conselhos além dos Limites. Paper presented at the seminar "Desenvolvimento Local e Conselhos Municipais de Desenvolvimento Rural," organized by EMATER/RS, FETAG/RS and GTZ.

Abramovay, R., and da Vega, J. E. (1999). *Novas Instituições para o Desenvolvimento Rural: O Caso do Programa Nacional de Fortalecimento da Agricultura (PRONAF)*: FIPE/IPEA discussion paper no. 641.

Ackerman, J. (2004). Co-Governance for Accountability: Beyond "Exit" and "Voice." *World Development* 32 (3): 447–63.

Affonso, R. (1996). *Os Municípios e os Desafios da Federação no Brasil* (Vol. 10, nr. 3). São Paulo: Fundação SEADE.

Agranoff, R., and McGuire, M. (1998). Multinetwork Management: Collaboration and the Hollow State in Local Economic Policy. *Journal of Public Administration Research and Theory: J-PART* 8 (1): 67–91.

Agrawal, A., and Ostrom, E. (2001). Collective Action, Property Rights, and Decentralization in Resource Use in India and Nepal. *Politics and Society* 29 (4): 485–514.

Agrawal, A., and Ribot, J. C. (1999). Accountability in Decentralization: A Framework with South Asian and African Cases. *Journal of Developing Areas* 33 (4): 473–502.

Alvarado, J., and Ugaz, F. (1998). *Retos del Financiamiento Rural: Construcción de Instituciones y Crédito Rural*: Centro Peruano de Estudios Sociales (CEPES); Centro de Investigación y Promoción del Campesinado (CIPCA): Centro de Estudios Sociales Solidaridad (CESS).

Ames, B. (1987). *Political Survival: Politicians and Public Policy in Latin America*. Berkeley: University of California Press.

Andersson, K. (2001). *An Institutional Assessment of Two Cornerstones of Bolivia's Decentralized Forestry Regime: Municipal Governments and Indigenous Territories*. Rome, Italy: The Food and Agriculture Organization of the United Nations.

———. (2002). *Can Decentralization Save Bolivia's Forests? An Institutional Analysis of Municipal Forest Governance*. Unpublished dissertation, IU, Bloomington, IN.

———. (2003). What Motivates Municipal Governments? Uncovering the

Institutional Incentives for Municipal Governance of Forest Resources in Bolivia. *Journal of Environment and Development* 12 (1): 5–27.

———. (2004). Who Talks with Whom? The Role of Repeated Interactions in Decentralized Forest Governance. *World Development* 32 (2): 5–27.

Andersson, K., Gibson, C. C., and Lehoucq, F. E. (2004). The Politics of Decentralized Natural Resource Governance. *Political Science and Politics* 37 (3): 421–26.

———. (2006). Municipal Politics and Forest Governance: Comparative Analysis of Decentralization in Bolivia and Guatemala. *World Development* 34 (3): 576–95.

Andersson, K., and van Laerhoven, F. (2007). From Local Strongman to Facilitator: Institutional Incentives for Participatory Municipal Governance in Latin America. *Comparative Political Studies* September.

Asís Nassif, A. (1994). Municipio y Transición Política: Una Pareja en Formación. In M. Merino, ed., *En Busca de la Demicracia Municipal, Participación Ciudadana en el Gobierno Local Mexicano*. Mexico: El Colegio de México.

Avritzer, L. (2002). *Democracy and the Public Space in Latin America*. Princeton, NJ: Princeton University Press.

Bagnasco, A. (1988). *La Costruzione Sociale del Mercato: Studi Sullo Sviluppo di Piccola Impresa in Italia*. Bologna: Il Mulino.

Baiocchi, G. (2001). Participation, Activism, and Politics: The Porto Alegre Experiment and Deliberative Democratic Theory. *Politics and Society* 29:43–72.

———. (2005). *Militants and Citizens. The Politics of Participatory Democracy in Porto Alegre*. Stanford, CA: Stanford University Press.

Baland, J.-M., and Platteau, J.-P. (1996). *Halting Degradation of Natural Resources. Is There a Role for Rural Communities?* Oxford: Clarendon Press.

Banco Nacional de México (BANAMEX). (2001). *México Electoral: Estadísticas Federales y Locales, 1970–2000*. Mexico City: BANAMEX.

Bardhan, P. K., and Mookherjee, D. (2000). Capture and Governance at Local and National Levels. *American Economic Review* 90 (2): 135–39.

Bartley, T. Andersson, K. Jagger, P. and van Laerhoven, F. 2008. The Contribution of Institutional Theories to Explaining Decentralization of Natural Resource Governance. Society and Natural Resources 21 (2): 160–174.

Bartra, A., and Paz, L. (2002). *Desempeño de los Servicios Públicos y el Rol del Gobierno Local en la Región Sur-Sureste de México*. Santiago, Chile: FAO (http://www.fao.org/Regional/LAmerica/prior/desrural/servagrop [accessed August 9, 2006]).

Bazdresch Parada, M. (1994). Gestión Municipal y Cambio Político. In M. Merino, ed., *En Busca de la Democracia Municipal, Participación Ciudadana en el Gobierno Local Mexicano*. Mexico: El Colegio de México.

Bebbington, A., and Carroll, T. (2000). *Induced Social Capital and Federations of the Rural Poor*. Washington, DC: World Bank.

Belik, W. (1999). *Avaliação da Operacionalização do Programa PRONAF*. Campinos: Universidade de Campinos (Instituto de Economia).
Birk, G. (2000). *Dueños del Bosque. Manejo de los Recursos Naturales por Indígenas Chiquitanos de Bolivia*. Santa Cruz de la Sierra, Bolivia: Apoyo para el Indígena-Campesino del Oriente Boliviano-Central Indígena de la Comunidades Originarias de Lomerío.
Bittencourt, G. A. (2000). O Novo Retrato da Agricultura Familiar. In *Os Desafíos da Pobreza Rural*. Brasilia, Brazil: IPEA-NEAD/MDA–World Bank.
Blair, H. (2000). Participation and Accountability at the Periphery: Democratic Local Governance in Six Countries. *World Development* 28:21–39.
Boone, C. (2003). Decentralization as Political Strategy in West Africa. *Comparative Political Studies* 36 (4): 355–80.
Booth, J. A., and Seligson, M. A. (2005). Political Legitimacy and Participation in Costa Rica: Evidence of Arena Shopping. *Political Research Quarterly* 58 (4): 537–50.
Bratton, M. (1999). Political Participation in a New Democracy. Institutional Considerations from Zambia. *Comparative Political Studies* 32 (5): 549–88.
Bresciani, F., and Valdez, A., eds. (2007). *Beyond Food Production: The Role of Agriculture in Poverty Reduction*. Cheltenham, UK: Edward Elgar.
Bruce, I., ed. (2004). *The Porto Alegre Alternative. Direct Democracy in Action*. London and Ann Arbor: Pluto Press.
Burki, S. J., Perry, G. E., and Dillinger, W. R. (1999). *Beyond the Center: Decentralizing the State*. Washington, DC: World Bank.
Burns, P. (2002). The Intergovernmental Regime and Public Policy in Hartford, Connecticut. *Journal of Urban Affairs* 24 (1): 55–73.
Cabrero, E. (1995). *Los Dilemas de la Modernización Municipal*. Mexico: Porrúa, Miguel Ángel.
———, ed. (2000). Hacia la Construcción de una Agenda para la Reforma Administrativa Municipal en México (http://www.municipio.org.mx/agenda_adm1.htm [accessed August 9. 2006]).
Campbell, T. (2003). *The Quiet Revolution. Decentralization and the Rise of Political Participation in Latin American Cities*. Pittsburgh, PA: University of Pittsburgh Press.
Carmagnani, M., and Gordillo, G. (1997). *Desarrollo Social y Cambios Productivos en el Mundo Rural Contemporaneo*. Mexico City: Fondo Cultura Economica.
Casas, C. (1997). *Descentralización Fiscal: El Case de Perú*. Santiago, Chile: CEPAL.
Centro Nacional de Desarrollo Municipal (SEGOB), and Instituto Nacional de Estadísticas Geografía e Informática (INEGI). (1997). *Los Municipios de México*. Mexico.
Chambers, R. (1994). Participatory Rural Appraisal (PRA): Challenges, Potentials and Paradigm. *World Development* 22 (10): 1437–54.

Cleary, M. R. (2004). *Electoral Competition and Democracy in Mexico*. Chicago: University of Chicago.

Cohen, J., and Rogers, J. (1995). *Association and Democracy*. London, UK: Verso.

Conrad, C. (2002). *Strategic Organizational Communication in a Global Economy*. Belmont, CA: Thomson/Wadsworth.

Contreras, H., and Vargas, T. (2001). *Dimensiones Sociales, Ambientales y Económicas de las Reformas en la Política Forestal de Bolivia*. Santa Cruz, Bolivia: Proyecto de Manejo Forestal Sostenible and the Center for International Forestry Research (CIFOR).

Contreras Suárez, E. (2000). Una Visión Crítica de los Programas Actuales de Combate a la Pobreza. In R. Cordera and A. Ziccardi, eds., *Las Políticas Sociales de México al Fin del Milenio. Descentralización, Diseño y Gestión*. Mexico: Porrúa, Miguel Ángel.

Cordera Campos, R. (1994). Los Municipios y las Discontinuidades Nacionales. In M. Merino, ed., *En Busca de la Democraqcia Municipal, Participación Ciudadana en el Gobierno Local Mexicano*. Mexico: El Colegio de México.

Crook, R., and Manor, J. (1998). *Democracy and Decentralization in South East Asia and West Africa: Participation, Accountability, and Performance*. Cambridge, MA: Cambridge University Press.

Culpepper, P. (2003). Institutional Rules, Social Capacity and the Stuff of Politics: Experiments in Collaborative Governance in France and Italy. *Research Working Paper RWP 03–29*. Cambridge, MA: John F Kennedy School of Government, Harvard University.

Davies, J. S. (2003). Partnerships Versus Regimes: Why Regime Theory Cannot Explain Coalitions in the UK. *Journal of Urban Affairs* 25 (3): 253–69.

de Janvry, A., Gordillo de Anda, G., and Sadoulet, E. (1997). *Mexico's Second Agrarian Reform: Household and Community Responses, 1990–1994*. Boulder, CO: Lynne Rienner.

de Janvry, A., and Sadoulet, E. (2003). Rural Poverty in Latin America: Determinants and Exit Paths. In *Agricultural Research and Poverty Reduction: Some Issues and Evidence*, S. Mathur and D. Pachico, eds., 105–30. Economics and Impact Series no. 2. Cali, Colombia: Centro Internacional de Agricultura Tropical (CIAT).

Delury, G. E., and Kaple, D. A., eds. (1999). *World Encyclopedia of Political Systems and Parties*. New York: Facts on File.

Dessler, G., Frederick, A., and Cyr, D. J. (2001). *Management: Leading People and Organizations in the 21st Century*. Toronto: Pearson Education.

de Swaan, A. (1988). *In Care of the State : Health Care, Education, and Welfare in Europe and the USA during the Modern Era*. New York: Oxford University Press.

Diamond, J. (2004). *Collapse: How Societies Choose to Fail or Succeed*. New York: Viking Penguin Group.

Doornbos, M. (2001). "Good Governance": The Rise and Decline of a Policy Metaphor? *The Journal of Development Studies* 37 (6): 93–108.

Eaton, K. (2004). Designing Subnational Institutions. Regional and Municipal Reforms in Postauthoritarian Chile. *Comparative Political Studies* 37 (2): 218–44.

Echeverria, Ruben, ed. (2001). *Development of Rural Economies in Latin America and the Caribbean*. Washington, DC: IADB.

Economic Commission for Latin America and the Caribbean (ECLAC).(2006). *Social Panorama of Latin America*. Santiago, Chile: ECLAC.

Escobar, J., and Torero, M. (2000). *Cómo Enfrentar una Geografía Adversa? El Rol de los Activos Públicos y Privados*. Lima, Peru: Grupo de Análisis para el Desarrollo (GRADE).

Espinoza, J., and Marcel, M. (1993). *Decentralización Fiscal: El Caso de Chile*. Santiago, Chile: CEPAL.

Evans, P. (1996). Government Action, Social Capital and Development: Reviewing the Evidence on Synergy. *World Development* 24 (6): 1119–32.

Eyzaguirre, H. (2001). *Municipal Decision Making Process: Sensitivity to the Needs and Preferences of Local Residents*. Lima, Peru: Instituto Apoyo.

Fafchamps, M. (1996). The Enforcement of Commercial Contracts in Ghana. *World Development* 24 (3): 427–48.

Falleti, T. G. (2005). A Sequential Theory of Decentralization: Latin American Cases in Comparative Perspective. *American Political Science Review* 99 (3): 327–46.

Favareto, A., and de Marco, D., eds. (2002). *Políticas Públicas, Participação Social e as Instituições para o Desenvolvimento Rural Sustentável. Uma Avaliação dos Conselhos Municipais de Desenvolvimento Rural*. São Paulo, Brasilia.

Fisman, R., and Khanna, T. (2004). Facilitating Development: The Role of Business Groups. *World Development* 32 (4): 609–28.

Fiszbein, A. (1997). The Emergence of Local Capacity: Lessons from Colombia. *World Development* 25 (7): 1029–43.

Food and Agriculture Organization (FAO). (2001). *Formulación de Hipótesis Centrales sobre el Desempeño de los Servicios Públicos y el Rol del Gobierno Local*. Santiago, Chile (http://www.fao.org/Regional/LAmerica/prior/des rural/servagrop/).

———. (2002). *Encuestas Municipales en Brasil, Chile, Mexico y Peru*. Santiago, Chile: FAO Regional Office for Latin America and the Caribbean.

Fornos, C. A., Power, T. J., and Garand, J. C. (2004). Explaining Voter Turnout in Latin America, 1980 to 2000. *Comparative Political Studies* 37 (8): 909–40.

Forza, C., and Salvador, F. (2001). Information Flows for High-Performance Manufacturing. *International Journal of Production Economics* 70 (1): 21–36.

Fox, J. (1994). The Difficult Transition from Clientelism to Citizenship: Lessons from Mexico. *World Politics* 46 (2): 151–84.

———. (1996). How Does Civil Society Thicken? The Political Construction of Social Capital in Rural Mexico. *World Development* 24 (6): 1089–1103.

Fox, J., and Aranda, J. (1998). Decentralization and Rural Development in Mexico: Community Participation in Oaxaca's Municipal Funds Program. Monograph Series 42. San Diego, CA: Center for US-Mexican Studies at the University of California at San Diego.

Frisken, F. (2001). The Toronto Story: Sober Reflections on Fifty Years of Experiments with Regional Governance. *Journal of Urban Affairs* 23 (5): 513–41.

Fukuyama, F. (1996). The Primacy of Culture. *Journal of Democracy* 6 (1): 7–14.

Fulk, A., and Wright, E. O. (2001). Emerging Theories of Communication in Organizations. *Journal of Management* 12 (2): 407–46.

Fuller, C., Bennet, R., and Ramsden, M. (2004). Local Government and the Changing Institutional Landscape of Economic Development in England and Wales. *Environment and Planning C: Government and Policy* 22:317–47.

Fung, A. (2001). Accountable Autonomy: Toward Empowered Deliberation in Chicago Schools and Policing. *Politics and Society* 29:73–103.

Fung, A., and Wright, E. O. (2001). Deepening Democracy: Innovations in Empowered Participatory Governance. *Politics and Society* 29:5–42.

García del Castillo, R. (1999). *Los Municipios en México. Los Retos ante el Futuro*. Mexico: Porrúa, Miguel Ángel.

Garnett, R. T. (2003). Bowling Ninepins in Tocqueville's Township. *American Political Science Review* 97 (1): 1–16.

Geddes, B. (1994). *Politician's Dilemma: Building State Capacity in Latin America*. Berkeley: University of California Press.

Gertler, M. S., and Wolfe, D. A. (2004). Local Social Knowledge Management: Community Actors, Institutions and Multilevel Governance in Regional Foresight Exercises. *Future* 36 (1): 45–65.

Gibson, C. C., Andersson, K., Ostrom, E., and Shivakumar, S. (2005). *The Samaritans' Dilemma: The Political Economy of Development Aid*. Oxford, UK: Oxford University Press.

Gibson, C. C., and Lehoucq, F. E. (2003). The Local Politics of Decentralized Environmental Policy in Guatemala. *Journal of Environment and Development* 12 (1): 28–49.

Gibson, C. C., McKean, M., and Ostrom, E., eds. (2000). *People and Forests. Communities, Institutions, and Governance*. Cambridge, MA: MIT Press.

Gibson, C. C., Williams, J. T., and Ostrom, E. (2005). Local Enforcement and Better Forests. *World Development* 33 (2): 273–84.

Goldfrank, B. (2002). The Fragile Flower of Local Democracy: A Case Study of Decentralization/Participation in Montevideo. *Politics and Society* 30:51–83.

Gordillo de Anda, G. (2001). Grandes Emociones y Pensamientos Imperfectos: Agricultura Familiar y Seguridad Alimentaria. Paper presented at the International Seminar on Sustainable Family Agriculture, Brasilia, Brazil.

Gordillo de Anda, G., and Andersson, K. (2004). From Policy Lesson to Policy

Actions: Motivation to Take Evaluation Seriously. *Public Administration and Development* 24:305–20.

Gordillo de Anda, G., Lopez, J. F., and Rivera, R. (2006). *Desafíos para el desarrollo rural en América Latina y el Caribe*. Santiago, Chile: Food and Agriculture Organization.

Gordillo de Anda, G., Wagner, R., and Lewin, P. (2005). *Una Transición Permanentemente Trunca: Estado y Sociedad Rural en México (1975–2000) en 25 Años de Desarrollo Social en México*. Mexico City: Banco Nacional de México/Citibank.

Government of Chile. (1980). Political Constitution of the Republic of Chile.

Government of Mexico. (2001). Law on Sustainable Rural Development: Official Gazette of the Federation.

Government of Peru. (1984). The Organic Law of Municipalities (LOM), No. 23853.

Greene, K. F. (2002). Opposition Party Strategy and Spatial Competition in Dominant Party Regimes. A Theory and the Case of Mexico. *Comparative Political Studies* 35 (7): 755–83.

Gret, M., and Sintomer, Y. (2005). *The Porto Alegre Experiment. Learning Lessons for Better Democracy*. London and New York: Zed Books.

Grindle, M. S. (2000). *Audacious Reforms. Institutional Invention and Democracy in Latin America*. Baltimore and London: Johns Hopkins University Press.

Habermas, J. (1998). *The Inclusion of the Other: Studies in Political Theory*. Cambridge, MA: MIT Press.

Hardee, K., Bronfman, M., Valenzuela, T., and McGreevey, W. (2000). *Promoting Partnerships and Participation in the Context of Decentralization to Improve Sexual Reproductive Health in Latin America and the Caribbean*. Washington, DC: USAID.

Hardin, G. (1968). The Tragedy of the Commons. *Science* 162:1243–48.

Harriss, J., Stokke, K., and Törnquist, O., eds. (2005). *Politicizing Democracy: The New Local Politics of Democratization*. New York: Palgrave Macmillan.

Hayek, F. A. V. (1948). *Individualism and Economic Order*. Chicago: University of Chicago Press.

Hirschman, A. (1970). *Exit, Voice, and Loyalty. Responses to the Decline in Firms, Organizations, and States*. Cambridge, MA: Harvard University Press.

Hooghe, L., and Marks, G. (2003). Unraveling the Central State, but How? Types of Multi-level Governance. *American Political Science Review* 97 (2): 233–43.

Houtzager, P. P. (2003). *Changing Paths: International Development and the New Left of Inclusion*. Ann Arbor: University of Michigan Press.

INCRA/FAO. (2000). *Novo Retrato da Agricultura Familiar: O Brasil Redescoberto*. Brasília, Brazil: Projeto de Cooperação Técnica INCRA/FAO.

INCRA/SADE. (2000). Banco de Dados da Agricultura Familiar (Database of small-scale (family) agriculture).

Inglehart, R. (1989). *Culture Shifts in Advanced Industrial Countries*. Princeton, NJ: Princeton University Press.

Inman, R. P., and Rubinfeld, D. L. (1997). The Political Economy of Federalism. In D. C. Mueller, ed., 73–105, *Perspectives on Public Choice. A Handbook*. Cambridge: Cambridge University Press.

Instituto Brasileiro do Geografia e Estadisticas (IBGE). (1995). *Censo Agropecuario 1995* (http://www.ibge.gov.br/home/estatistica/economia/agropecuaria/censoagro/default.shtm [accessed August 9, 2006]).

——. (2005). *Cidades en Linea*. Ministerio do Planejamento, Orçamento en Gestão do Brasil.

Instituto de Desarrollo Agropecuario (INDAP). (2005). *Cuenta Pública 2004. Instituto de Desarrollo Agropecuario*. Santiago, Chile: INDAP.

Instituto de Gestión para el Desarrollo Social (INDESO), González, F., and Ochao, J. J. (2002). *Desempeño de los Servicios Públicos y el Rol del Gobierno Local en la Región Centro-Norte de México*. Santiago, Chile: FAO (http://www.fao.org/Regional/LAmerica/prior/desrural/servagrop [accessed August 9, 2006]).

Instituto Nacional de Estadísticas (INE). (2001). *Informe Provisional del Censo Nacional de 2001*. Santiago, Chile: INE.

Instituto Nacional de Estadísticas Geografía e Informática (2000). *XII Censo General de Población y Vivienda*. Mexico City: INEGI.

Inter American Development Bank (IADB). (2001). *Poverty and Inequality in Latin America and the Caribbean*. Washington, DC: IADB.

International Fund for Agricultural Development (IFAD). (2001). *Rural Poverty Report 2001: The Challenge of Ending Rural Poverty*. Rome, Italy: IFAD.

International Institute for Cooperation and Agriculture (IICA). (2004). *More Than Food on the Table: Agriculture's True Contribution to the Economy*. San José, Costa Rica: IICA.

IPARDES. (2001). *Caracterizacao dos Conselhos de Desenvolvimento Rural da Paraná: Sintese dos Principais Resultados da Pesquisa da Campo*. Curitíba, Brazil: EMATER-PR/DESER/PRONAF.

Jacobs, A. J. (2004). Federations of Municipalities: A Practical Alternative to Local Government Consolidation in Japan? *Governance* 17 (2): 247–74.

Jacobs, J. (1961). *The Death and Life of Great American Cities*. New York: Vintage Books.

Jaramillo, M. (1999). *El Potencial de Generación de Empleo de la Agricultura Peruna*. Lima, Peru: International Labour Organization (ILO), Oficina de Área y Equipo Técnico Multidisciplinario para los Países Andinos.

——. (2003). *Políticas de Rercursos Humanos para la Agricultura Comercial Costeña*. Lima, Peru: Consorcio de Investigación Económica y Social. Red de Políticas de Empleo.

Jaramillo, M., and Saavedra, J. (2005). Governability, Reforms and Economic

Performance in 1990s Peru. In A. Solimano, ed., *Political Crises, Social Conflict and Economic Development: The Political Economy of the Andean Region.* New York: Edward Elgar Publishing.

Johnson, N. (1999). Diversity in Decentralized Systems: Enabling Self-Organizing Solutions. Paper presented at the Decentralization II Conference, University of California at Los Angeles.

Johnson, N., and Minis, H. (1996). *Toward Democratic Decentralization: Approaches to Promoting Good Governance.* Research Triangle Park, NC: TRI International.

Kaimowitz, D., and Angelsen, A. (1998). *Economic Models of Tropical Deforestation. A Review.* Bogor, Indonesia: Center for International Forestry Research (CIFOR).

Kaimowitz, D., Flores, G. J., Johnson, J., Pacheco, P., Pavez, I., Roper, J., et al. (2000). *Local Government and Biodiversity Conservation: A Case from the Bolivian Lowlands. A Case Study for Shifting the Power: Decentralization and Biodiversity Conservation.* Washington, D.C.: Biodiversity Support Program.

Kaimowitz, D., Pacheco, P., Johnson, J., Pavez, I., Vallejos, C., and Velez, R. (2000). Gobiernos municipales y bosques en las tierras bajas de Bolivia. *Ciencias Ambientales* 19:82–92.

Khadiagala, L. S. (2001). The Failure of Popular Justice in Uganda: Local Councils and Women's Property Rights. *Development and Change* 32:55–76.

Kickert, W. J. M., Klijn, E.-H., and Koppenjan, J. F. M., eds. (1997). *Managing Complex Networks.* London: Sage.

King, G., Keohane, R. and Verba, S. (1994). *Designing Social Inquiry: Scientific Inference in Qualitative Research.* Princeton, NJ: Princeton University Press

Klijn, E.-H., and Koppenjan, J. F. M. (2000). Public Management and Policy Networks. Foundations of a Network Approach to Governance. *Public Management* 2 (2): 135–58.

Kooiman, J., and van Vliet, M. (1993). Governance and Public management. In K. Eliassen and J. Kooiman, eds., *Managing Public Organizations.* London: Sage.

Koonings, K. (2004). Strengthening Citizenship in Brazil's Democracy: Local Participatory Governance in Porto Alegre. *Bulletin of Latin American Research* 23 (1): 79–99.

Lake Frank, Z. (2001). Elite Families and Oligarchic Politics on the Brazilian Frontier. *Latin American Research Review* 36 (1): 49–74.

Langston, J. (2003). Rising from the Ashes? Reorganizing and Unifying the PRI's State Party Organization after Electoral Defeat. *Comparative Political Studies* 36 (3): 293–318.

Larson, A. M. (2002). Natural Resources and Decentralization in Nicaragua: Are Local Governments Up to the Job? *World Development* 30 (1): 17–31.

Law Decree No. 575. (1974). Regionalization of the Country.

Law Decree No. 3063. (1979). Rules Related to Municipal Revenues.
Law Decree No. 18.695. (1988). Ley Orgánica Constitucional de Municipalidades.
Law Decree No. 19.175. (1993). Ley Orgánica Constitucional sobre Gobierno y Administración Regional.
Lee, K. N. (1993). *Compass and Gyroscope: Integrating Science and Politics for the Environment*. Washington, D.C.: Island Press.
Light, S., Serafin, R., Blann, K., O'Riordan, T., Bochniarz, Z., and Sendzimir, J. (2002). The Role of Biodiversity Conservation in Rural Sustainability: Using Adaptive Management, Institutional Analysis, and Sustainability Appraisal to Understand Experience from North America and Europe. Paper presented at the NATO Advanced Research Workshop, Krakow, Poland.
Lipset, S. M. (1959). Some Social Requisites of Democracy: Economic Development and Political Legitimacy. *American Political Science Review* 53 (1): 69–105.
Litvack, J. I., Ahmad, J., and Miller Bird, R. (1998). *Rethinking Decentralization in Developing Countries*. Washington, D.C.: World Bank.
Long, J. S. (1997). *Regression Models for Categorical and Limited Dependent Variables*. Thousand Oaks, CA: Sage Publication.
Lyon, F. (2000). Trust, Networks, and Norms: The Creation of Social Capital in Agricultural Economies in Ghana. *World Development* 28 (4): 663–81.
Manin, B. (1987). On Legitimacy and Political Deliberation. *Political Theory* 15:338–68.
Maro, P. (1990). The Impact of Decentralization on Spatial Equity and Rural Development in Tanzania. *World Development* 18:673–93.
Martin, S., and Sanderson, I. (1999). Evaluating Public Policy Experiments: Measuring Outcomes, Monitoring Processes. *Evaluation* 5:245–58.
Martinez Assad, C., and Ziccardi, A. (2000). Límites y Posiblidades para la Descentralización de las Políticas Sociales. In R. Cordera Campos and A. Ziccardi, eds. *Las Políticas Sociales de México al fin de Milenio*. Mexico: Miguel Ángel Porrúa.
McGinnis, M. D., ed. (1999a). *Polycentricity and Development. Readings from the Workshop in Political Theory and Policy Analysis*. Ann Arbor: University of Michigan Press.
———. (1999b). *Polycentricity and Local Economies. Readings from the Workshop in Political Theory and Policy Analysis*. Ann Arbor: University of Michigan Press.
McGlynn, E. A. (1997). Six Challenges in Measuring the Quality of Health Care. *Health Affairs* 16 (3): 7–21.
Meso, P., Datta, P., and Mbarika, V. (2006). Moderating Information and Communication Technologies' Influences on Socioeconomic Development with Good Governance: A Study of the Developing Countries. *Journal of the American Society for Information Science and Technology* 57 (2): 186–97.
Meyer, L. (1994). El Municipio Mexicano al Final del Siglo XX. Historia, Obstáculos, y Posibilidades. In M. Merino, ed., *En Busca de la Democracia Mu-*

nicipal, la Participación Ciudadana en el Gobierno Local Mexicano. Mexico City: El Colegio de México.

Miller, G. J. (1992). *Managerial Dilemmas: The Political Economy of Hierarchy*. New York: Cambridge University Press.

Ministry of Agriculture (Chile) (2000). *Una Política de Estado para la Agricultura Chilena, Período 2000–2010*.

Moe, T. M. (1984). The New Economics of Organization. *American Journal of Political Science* 28 (4): 739–77.

Mohar, A. (1998). *La Nueva Institucionalidad Rural: El Caso de México*. Santiago, Chile: FAO.

Muñoz, D. E. (2000). *Políticas Públicas y Agricultura Campesina: Encuentros y Desencuentros*. La Paz, Bolivia: Plural Editores.

Musgrave, R. A. (1959). *The Theory of Public Finance*. New York: McGraw-Hill.

———. (1997). Devolution, Grants, and Fiscal Competition. *Journal of Economic Perspectives* 11:65–72.

Nagayets, O. (2005). Small Farms: Current Status and Key Trends. Paper presented at the Future of Small Farms Research Workshop, Wye College, UK.

Nickson, A. R. (1995). *Local Government in Latin America*. Boulder, CO: Lynne Rienner.

Nicod, C. (1999). *Proceso de Concertación Público-Privado: Una Oportunidad para el Desarrollo Económico Local: Estudio de Casos en Bolivia, Chile y Perú*. Santiago, Chile: ILPES.

North, D. C., Summerhill, W., and Weingast, B. R. (2000). Order, Disorder, and Economic Change: Latin America vs. North America. In Bruce Bueno de Mesquita and Hilton Root, eds., *Governing for Prosperity*. New Haven: Yale University Press.

Nygren, A. (2005). Community-Based Forest Management within the Context of Institutional Decentralization in Honduras. *World Development* 33 (4): 639–55.

Oakerson, R. J. (1999). *Governing Local Public Economies: Creating the Civic Metropolis*. Oakland, CA: ICS Press.

Oates, W. E. (1999). An Essay on Fiscal Federalism. *Journal of Economic Literature* 37 (3): 1120–49.

Oficina Nacional de Procesos Electorales (ONPE). (2002). *Historia y Estadística Electoral*. Lima, Peru: ONPE.

Oliveira, R. (2005). *Desarrollo Territorial en Brasil: Limitaciones de la promoción del desarrollo al nivel micro y potencialidades al nivel meso*. Santiago, Chile: Food and Agriculture Organization.

Olson, M. (1965). *The Logic of Collective Action. Public Goods and the Theory of Groups* CXXIV. Cambridge, MA: Harvard University Press.

O'Neill, K. (2003). Decentralization as an Electoral Strategy. *Comparative Political Studies* 36 (9): 1068–91.

Organization for Economic Co-operation and Development (OECD). (2001). *The OECD Territorial Outlook 2001*. Paris, France: OECD.

———. (2002). *Territorial Indicators of Socio-Economic Patterns and Dynamics*. OECD: DT/TDPC 23. Paris, France: OECD.

———. (2003). *Territorial Reviews: Mexico*. Paris, France: OECD.

———. (2005). Designing and Implementing Rural Policies. Policy Paper. Paris, France: OECD.

O'Riordan, T., ed. (2001). *Globalism, Localism, and Identity: Fresh Perspectives on the Sustainability Transition in Europe*. London: Earthscan.

Ortega, A. C., and Petrelli Corréa, V. (2002). PRONAF: Program Nacional de Fortalecimento da Agricultura Familiar: Qual o Seu Real Objectivo e Público Alvo? Paper presented at the XL Congreso de Sociedade Brasileira de Economía e Sociología Rural.

Ortega, J. (2005). *Desenvolvimento Territorial e Descentralização da Gestão Pública no Brasil: Limites e Potencialidades dos CONSADs*. Santiago, Chile: CLAD.

Ostrom, E. (1990). *Governing the Commons: The Evolution of Institutions for Collective Action*. New York: Cambridge University Press.

———. (1996a). Crossing the Great Divide: Coproduction, Synergy, and Development. *World Development* 24 (6): 1073–87.

———. (1996b). Incentives, Rules of the Game, and Development. Paper presented at the Annual World Bank Conference on Development Economics 1995, Washington, DC.

———. (2001). Decentralization and Development: The New Panacea. In K. Dowding, J. Hughes and H. Margetts, eds., *Challenges to Democracy*. New York: Palgrave.

———. (2005). *Understanding Institutional Diversity*. Oxford: Princeton University Press.

Ostrom, E., and Ahn, T. K., eds.. (2003). *Foundations of Social Capital*. Cheltenham, UK: Edward Elgar.

Ostrom, E., Gardner, R., and Walker, J. (1994). *Rules, Games, and Common-Pool Resources*. Ann Arbor: University of Michigan Press.

Ostrom, E., Gibson, C. C., Shivakumar, S., and Andersson, K. (2002). *Aid, Incentives, and Sustainability. An Institutional Analysis of Development Cooperation*. Stockholm, Sweden: Sida.

Ostrom, E., Schroeder, L., and Wynne, S. (1993). *Institutional Incentives and Sustainable Development*. Boulder, CO: Westview Press.

Ostrom, V., Tiebout, C. M., and Warren, R. (1961). The Organization of Government in Metropolitan Areas: A Theoretical Inquiry. *American Political Science Review* 55:831–42.

Pacheco, P. (2000). *Avances y Desafíos en la Descentralización de la Gestión de los*

Recursos Forestales en Bolivia. Santa Cruz, Bolivia: Center for International Forestry Research (CIFOR).

Pacheco, P., and Kaimowitz, D., eds. (1998). *Municipios y Gestión Forestal en el Trópico Boliviano.* La Paz, Bolivia: Centro de Estudios para el Desarrollo Laboral y Agrario / Taller de Iniciativas en Estudios Rurales y Reforma Agraria / Center for International Forestry Research (CIFOR).

Peterson, G. E. (1997). *Decentralization in Latin America: Learning through Experience.* Washington, DC: World Bank.

Peterson, P. E. (1995). *The Price of Federalism.* New York: Twentieth Century Fund.

Petro, N. (2001). Creating Social Capital in Russia: The Novgrod Model. *World Development* 29 (2): 229–44.

Platteau, J.-P. (2004). Monitoring Elite Capture in Community-Driven Development. *Development and Change* 35 (2): 223–46.

Powell, G. B. (2000). *Elections as Instruments of Democracy: Majoritarian and Proportional Visions.* New Haven, CT: Yale University Press.

Pulgar Vidal, J. (1986). *Las Ocho Regiones Naturales del Perú.* Lima, Peru: OMEGA Edition.

Putnam, R. D. (1993). *Making Democracy Work: Civic Traditions in Modern Italy.* Princeton, NJ: Princeton University Press.

Quijandría, B., Monares, A., de Peña Montenegro, R. U. (2001). *Assessment of Rural Poverty: Latin America and the Caribbean.* Rome, Italy: International Fund for Agricultural Development.

Reardon, T., Berdegué, J. A., and Escobar, G. (2001). Rural Nonfarm Employment and Incomes in Latin America: Overview and Policy Implications. *World Development* 29 (3): 395–409.

Rhodes, R. A. W. (1996). The New Governance: Governing without Government. *Political Studies* 44:652–67.

Ribot, J. (1999a). Accountable Representation and Power in Participation and Decentralized Environmental Management. *Unasylva* 50 (4).

———. (1999b). Decentralization, Participation and Accountability in Sahelian Forestry: Legal Instruments of Political-Administrative Control. *Africa* 69 (1).

———. (2001). *Local Actors, Powers, and Accountability in African Decentralizations: A Review of Issues.* Geneva, Switzerland: United Nations Research Institute for Social Development.

———. (2002). *Democratic Decentralization of Natural Resources. Institutionalizing Popular Participation.* Washington, DC: World Resources Institute.

Riddell, R. C. (2007). *Does Foreign Aid Really Work?* Oxford, UK: Oxford University Press.

Rile Hayward, C. (2003). The Difference States Make: Democracy, Identity, and the American City. *American Political Science Review* 97 (4): 501–14.

Rodríguez, V. (1998). Recasting Federalism in Mexico. *Publius, Journal of Federalism* 28:235–54.

Rodriguez-Pose, A., and Sánchez-Reaza, J. (2002). Economic Polarization through Trade: Trade Liberalization and Regional Growth in Mexico. Paper presented at the Cornell/LSE/Wider Conference on Spatial Inequality and Development, London School of Economics, London.

Rosegrant, M. W., Paisner, M. S., Meijer, S., and Witcover, J. (2001) *2020 Global Food Outlook: Trends, Alternatives, and Choices*. Washington, DC: International Food Policy Research Institute.

Rydin, Y., and Pennington, M. (2000). Public Participation and Local Environmental Planning: The Collective Action Problem and the Potential of Social Capital. *Local Environment* 5 (2): 153–69.

Santa Cruz, F. (1999). *La Nueva Institucionalidad Rural. El Caso de Perú*. Santiago, Chile: FAO.

Schejtman, A., and Berdegué, J. (2004). *Desarrollo territorial rural*. Santiago, Chile: IFAD-IDB-RIMISP.

Schönwälder, G. (1997). New Democratic Spaces at the Grassroots? Popular Participation in Latin American Local Governments. *Development and Change* 28:753–70.

Secretaría de Agricultura, Ganadería, Desarrollo Rural, Pesca y Alimentación (SAGARPA). (2001). *Plan Sectorial Agropecuario*. Mexico City: SAGARPA.

———. (2002). Rules of Operation of Alianza para el Campo. *Official Gazette of the Federation*.

Secretaría de Medio Ambiente, R. N., y Pesca (SEMARNAP). (1999). *Agenda Municipal para la Gestión Ambiental*. Mexico City: Subsecretaría de Planeación, Coordinación General de Descentralización / SEMARNAP.

Singleton, S. (1998). *Constructing Cooperation: The Evolution of Institutions of Co-Management in Pacific Northwest Salmon Fisheries*. Ann Arbor: University of Michigan Press.

Smoke, P. (2003). Decentralization in Africa: Goals, Dimensions, Myths and Challenges. *Public Administration and Development* 23:7–16.

Sproull, L., and Kiessler, S. (1991). *Connections: New Ways of Working in the Networked Organization*. Cambridge, MA: MIT Press.

Stiglitz, J. E. (2000). The Contributions of the Economics of Information to Twentieth Century Economics. *Quarterly Journal of Economics* 115 (4): 1441–78.

Stoker, G. (1998). Governance as Theory: Five Propositions. *International Social Science Journal* 50 (1): 17–28.

SUBDERE. (2000). *Bases para una Política de Descentralización*. Santiago, Chile: SUBDERE.

———. (2001). *El Chile Descentralizado que Queremos. Un Proyecto de Todos*. San-

tiago, Chile: Ministerio del Interior / Subsecretaría de Desarrollo Regional y Adminstrativo.
Tendler, J. (1997). *Good Government in the Tropics*. Baltimore, MD: Johns Hopkins University Press.
Tendler, J., and Alves-Amorim, M. (1996). Small Firms and Their Helpers: Lessons on Demand. *World Development* 24 (3): 407–26.
Thirtle, C., Beyers, L., Lin, L., McKenzie-Hill, V., Irz, X., Wiggins, S., et al. (2002). *The Impact of Changes in Agricultural Productivity on the Incidence of Poverty in Developing Countries*. London: Department for International Development (DFID).
Tilton, T. A. (1990). *The Political Theory of Swedish Social Democracy: Through the Welfare State to Socialism*. New York: Oxford University Press.
Tocqueville, A. d. (1840 [2003]). *Democracy in America*. London: Penguin.
Toonen, T. A. J. (1998). Networks, Management and Institutions: Public Administration as "Normal Science." *Public Administration* 76:229–52.
Trivelli, C. (2001). *Crédito Agrario en el Perú: Qué Dicen los Clientes?* Lima, Peru: Consorcio de Investigación Económica y Social / Instituto de Estudios Peruanos.
Umali-Deininger, Dina. (1997). Public and Private Agricultural Extension: Partners or Rivals? *The World Bank Research Observer* 12 (2): 203–24
United Nations Development Program (UNDP). (2000) (http://www.undp.org).
———. (2002). *Human Development Report 2002*. New York: Oxford University Press.
———. (2004). *Human Development Report 2004*. New York: Oxford University Press.
United Nations Development Program Brazil. (2000). Human Development Index (http://www.undp.org.br [accessed January 2007]).
United Nations Millennium Project. (2005). *Investing in Development: A Practical Plan to Achieve the Millennium Development Goals*. New York.
Urioste, M., and Pacheco, D., eds. (2001). *Las Tierras Bajas de Bolivia a Fines del Siglo XX*. La Paz, Bolivia: Programa de Investigación Estratégica en Bolivia (PIEB).
Vanden, H. E., and Prevost, G., eds. (2002). *Politics of Latin America. The Power Game*. Oxford, UK: Oxford University Press.
Vogelgesang, F. (2000). Reformas Institucionales y Desarrollo Rural: Un balance a partir de las experiencias de seis países. Unpublished paper presented at the workshop "Políticas públicas, institucionalidad y desarrollo rural en América Latina y el Caribe", Mexico City, August.
Wade, R. (1989). Politics and Graft: Recruitment, Appointment, and Promotions to Public Office in India. In P. M. Ward, ed., *Corruption, Development, and Inequality: Soft Touch or Hard Graft?* New York: Routledge.

Wampler, B., and Avritzer, L. (2004). Participatory Publics: Civil Society and New Institutions in Democratic Brazil. *Comparative Politics* 36 (3): 291–312.

Ward, P. M., and Rodriguez, V. E. (1999). New Federalism, Intra-governmental Relations and Co-governance in Mexico. *Journal of Latin American Studies* 31:673–710.

Warman, A. (2001). *El Campo Mexicano en el Siglo XX*. Mexico City: Fondo de Cultura Económica.

Webster's Online Dictionary. (2004). (http://www.websters-online-dictionary.org).

Weimer, D. L., and Vining, A. R. (2004). *Policy Analysis: Concepts and Practice*. Englewood Cliffs, NJ: Prentice Hall.

Woolcock, M. (1998). Social Capital and Economic Development: Toward a Theoretical Synthesis and Policy Framework. *Theory and Society* 27 (2): 151–208.

World Bank. (1988). *World Development Report 1988*. New York: Oxford University Press.

———. (1996). *The World Bank Participation Sourcebook*. Washington, DC: World Bank.

———. (2003). *Inequality in Latin America and the Caribbean: Breaking with History?* Washington, DC: World Bank Group.

———. (2005). *Beyond the City: The Rural Contribution to Development*. World Bank Latin America and Caribbean Studies. Washington, DC: World Bank Group.

———. (2008). World Development Report: Agriculture for Development. Washington, DC: The World Bank.

Wyckoff-Baird, B., Kaus, A., Christen, C. A., and Keck, M. E. (2000). *Shifting the Power: Decentralization and Biodiversity Conservation*. Washington, DC: World Resources Institute.

Zack, M. H. (1993). Interactivity and Communication Mode Choice in Ongoing Management Groups. *Information System Research* 4 (3): 2007–2239.

Zaz Friz Burga, J. (2001). *El Sueño Obcecabo. La Descentralización Política en La América Latina*. Lima, Peru: Fondo Editorial Del Congreso de Perú.

Zegarra, E. (1996). Mercado de Tierras y Exclusión Social en el Agro Costeño. *Debate Agrario* 25:61–72.

Index

accountability, 6, 27, 37, 140, 142, 161, 164, 190; in Brazil, 47, 62–64; in Chile, 89; and decentralization, 166, 168, 182; and information, 14, 142; and institutions, 8, 15, 140, 166; in Mexico, 104; in Peru, 123, 125

agricultural services, 190; in Brazil, 51, 53; in Chile, 71; and coprovision, 153; in Mexico, 91; in Peru, 38, 118, 131

Agricultural State Councils, 36

agriculture, 5; agricultural management (quality of), 78; agricultural producers, 12; agricultural production in Mexico, 93–94; commitment to, 78; income from in Mexico, 93; Mexican productivity, 94; municipal officials in, 59; and rural development, 5–6, 23; size of properties, 106

Alianza para el Campo, 104, 110

Andes, 113

Antuco, Chile, 70, 71

asymmetrical relationships, 141

authoritarianism, 45

Banco Agrario, 118

Brazil, 19, 30, 143, 188, 190; agricultural research, 48; Annual Municipal Work Plan, 48; Brazilian Association for Credit and Rural Support (ABCAR), 48; Brazilian Company for Technical Support and Rural Extension (EMBRATER), 48; community-based organizations, 156; comparison to Mexico, 91; comparison to Peru, 159; Constitution of 1988, 45; institutional structure of, 31–35, 42–68; mayors, 46; municipal councils, 46; Municipal Councils for Rural Development, 46–47; National Program for Strengthening Family Farming (PRONAF), 47

businesses (clusters of), 196

Cajas Rurales, 118

Cândido de Abreu, 43

case selection, 22–25, 76–78, 126–127

Catholic Church, 25

central governments, 3, 180; agricultural services, 193; commitments, 72; "crowding out," 61, 66, 175, 183; and local governments, 200; monitoring, 13; number of programs, 67–68; and participatory fora, 197; pressure, 82, 102, 106, 181, 187; support, 153, 157, 159, 171, 175, 181

Chile, 19, 25, 30, 69–90, 143, 144, 188, 190; community-based organizations, 156; comparison to Mexico, 91; decentralization mandate, 70; institutional structure of, 32, 34–35; Ministry of Agriculture, 82; typical agricultural services, 70–71

civil society, 60–61, 66, 143, 155–156
clientelism, 15, 113
coffee, 92
collective action problems, 15, 89, 95, 115, 128, 136, 141, 142; definition, 203n2; endogeneity and, 129; institutions to resolve, 11, 15, 40, 88, 98, 109, 112, 129, 132, 135
Comala, Colima, Mexico, 92
comanagement activities, 190
Commission of Water Users, 127
Communal Committees, 123
Communal Economic and Social Council, 34
communication: between actors, 72, 99, 143; mechanisms, 142
community-based organizations, 15, 25–27, 154, 157, 158, 193; in Brazil, 61–67; budgeting, 192; in Chile, 70–71, 74, 76, 78, 87; demands, 169, 180, 183, 187, 194; in Mexico, 92, 97, 99–100, 104, 105, 106–107, 109; municipal cooperation, 43–44, 51–53; organizational capacity, 155, 156; in Peru, 135, 180, 199; as variables, 55, 60, 170, 174
consensus-building fora, 19, 143, 191–193; in Brazil, 66; in Chile, 88–89; in Mexico, 102, 107; in Peru, 115, 124, 125, 129, 132, 136–137
consumers (of public services), 8–9, 74
continuity (of office), 143, 157, 171
control variables, 25–26
cooperation, 8, 99, 122–125
coordination, 8, 14, 190
coprovision and coproduction, 7–15, 20, 195, 197, 199–200; in Brazil, 60–62; and central governments, 10; in Chile, 73–74, 87, 88; as a condition for rural development, 140–142, 154, 156, 159; and decentralization, 194; in Mexico, 106; in Peru, 192; as variables, 170, 175, 192
corruption, 15, 113, 124, 163, 191
cost-sharing, 169
cross-national differences, 19, 39–41
Cuautitlán de García Barragán, Jalisco, Mexico, 92

data; in Brazil, 49–55
decentralization, 3, 158, 182–183, 193–195; and democratization, 45, 162; national policies, 23; and participatory governance, 179, 181, 182, 188; and poverty reduction, 6, 30
decentralized public organizations, 119
decision-making authority, 10, 37, 90, 161, 166, 193, 197
degraded soils, 74, 76, 86–87, 102, 104
demands (citizen), 38–39, 61, 98, 107, 111, 142, 187
democratic decentralization, 166, 167, 168, 171
dependent variables, 26–27, 51–52; 78–79, 129, 146–147, 170–171
descriptive statistics: for all four countries, 145, 147, 150, 174–175; for Brazil, 52, 54; for Chile, 79; for Mexico, 98, 100–101;
developmental state, the, 45
downward accountability, 5, 168

economic crises, 116
economies of scale, 10, 33, 37, 117, 135, 197, 201
education: for cooperation, 196; mayors', 25; mayors', in Chile, 74–75, 82, 85, 89; mayors', in Mexico, 106; mayors', in Peru, 131, 135; policy, 31, 34, 46, 110, 121, 122
electoral politics, 12, 13, 132, 168, 171
elites, 14–15, 111, 162

empowerment (of municipal officials), 179
entrepreneurship, 196
exclusionary development, 196
Export Promotion Commission, 118

family farming, 44–45
Farmers' Direct Support Program (PROCAMPO), 104
farms, number of, 24, 53, 73–75, 78
field presence of government officials, 76, 86, 143, 157, 158, 175; as variables, 170, 178
fieldwork, 25
financial gain, 13, 187; in Chile, 72–73, 84; in Mexico, 99; in Peru, 132, 135
financial resources, 7, 85, 109
Fujimori, Alberto, 115, 118
funding, 143
future research, 195

gender, 143, 153
generalizability, 19
"governance," 3, 140, 141, 186–187

horizontal cooperation, 199
Human Development Index, 74, 75, 85, 86, 203n1

ideology, 168
incentives, 9, 13, 167, 169; political and economic, 187
indigenous communities, 94
inequalities, 163, 199
information, 8, 13–14, 18, 142, 187, 189–190, 190–191
infrastructure, 116
Institutional Analysis and Development (IAD), 17, 143
institutional capacity, 7, 19
institutions, 143, 186, 189, 201; for accountability, 190; for collective action, 129, 131, 132, 135, 141, 154, 156, 201; as constraints, 169; creation of, 160; formal and informal, 141, 144; for information exchange, 191; local, 146; looking beyond formal arrangements, 140, 150, 155; macro-level, 168; nestedness, 4, 140; origin of, 195–197; for participatory governance, 164, 191, 201; structuring incentives, 163; study of, 141; as variables, 170, 181
Instituto Maya, 111
interactions, 167, 182, 190; and distance, 189
International Fund for Agricultural Development, 5
international organizations, 162
irrigation associations, 25

Jaliso, 112
joint planning and implementation, 99

La Joya, Peru, 123
Law on the Basis of Decentralization, 125
leadership, 168
Licaten, Chile, 70, 71
literacy, 165
local conditions, 14, 74, 190, 200, 201
local government, 186
local political actors, 17, 162
logit regression, 82, 102, 147, 170
longitudinal data, 183

macroeconomic policies, 117
managerial problems, 197
mandates, legal, 13, 144, 156; mismatch to resources, 159
Mariana Pimentel, 43
mayors: age, 131, 134; characteristics, 128;

measurement, 25
Mesas de Concertación, 182, 192
methodology, 7, 19–20, 27–28
Mexico, 19, 25, 30, 91–112, 143, 188, 190; agricultural services, 188; Committee for Municipal Development Planning, 105; community-based organizations, 156; decentralization mandate, 91–92; as example to Chile, 90; Institutional Revolutionary Party (PRI), 95, 178; institutional structure of, 32, 35–37; Law on State and Municipal Planning, 112; Law on Sustainable Rural Development, 94, 105; Municipal Councils for Agricultural Development, 105; municipal self-sufficiency, 95; National Development Plan, 91; "new federalism," 35, 91
middle class, 165
modernization theory, 165, 167, 168, 178
monitoring and enforcement, 197
motivation, 8, 12–13, 18, 187, 189; in Brazil, 55–62; in Chile, 72–73
multivariate logit regression, 146
municipalities: altitude, 134; autonomy, 156; budget, 99; characteristics, 128; demographics, 128; fora, 99; governance in Mexico, 94–98; intermediaries, 89, 115, 136; Municipal Councils for Rural Development, 33; partnerships with community organizations, 144; relevance in agriculture, 146; role in economic development, 137
Municipal Plans, 33; size, 99

National Agrarian Health Service, 118
National Electoral Jury, 124
National Program of Watershed Management and Soil Conservation (PRONAMACHS), 114, 118
natural experiment, 182
neighborhood associations, 122
networks, 141, 200
New Institutionalism, 167
New Left, 165, 168, 171, 178
nongovernmental organizations (NGOs), 119, 168

Oaxaca, Mexico, 111
Ordinary Least Squares regression, 82
Organic Law of Municipalities, 121, 124, 125, 137

Paraná, Brazil, 42
participation: in Peru, 122–125; as a result of decentralization, 161, 162
participatory budgeting, 4, 124
participatory fora, 14, 153, 157; and accountability, 197; and autonomy, 194; in Brazil, 43, 46; in Chile, 87; functioning, 195, 197, 198–199; in Mexico, 102, 108; in Peru, 123, 125, 130
participatory governance, 165, 166, 179, 182; for shifting blame, 169
partnerships (between actors), 140
paternalism, 104, 113
peasants, 15
Peasants' Community, 127
Peru, 19, 25, 30, 143, 153, 188; agrarian reform, 117; agricultural income, 115; agricultural sector, 115–121; agricultural services, 114; as baseline case, 113; coastal region, 116; community-based organizations, 156; comparison to Brazil, 114, 117, 159; comparison to Chile, 113, 117; comparison to Mexico, 91, 113, 117; constitution, 121; decentralized structure, 121, 125–126, 146; District

Development Plans, 124; ecological diversity, 113–114; ecological-economic zoning plans, 118; forest law of 1997, 118; institutional structure of, 32, 37–38, 118; local development plans, 125; mandate, 179, 180–181; mayoral power, 123–124; Ministry of Agriculture, 119, 120; 131, 134; municipal mandate, 121, 135; organizations for agriculture, 135; oversight, 125; poverty, 132–134; public organizations in agriculture, 119–121; regional governments, 131; role of nontraditional agricultural products, 116; as a variable, 157, 179
perverse incentives, 8, 15
Poisson regression, 67
policy networks, 140
political affiliation, 74, 75
political demands: in Chile, 73; in Mexico, 99, 102, 106
political parties, 162; leftist, 171, 178; leftist vs. rightist, 165; as variables, 178
political structure, 170
popular vote, 73
population density, 99
Porto Alegre, Brazil, 4
poverty, 5, 135, 184; and agriculture, 6; rural, 185; unsatisfied needs, 134
power, 8, 168, 187; power asymmetries 14–19
probit analysis, 127
problem solving: in Brazil, 64–65
producers (of public services), 8
public services: provision and production, 5; quality of, 164

qualitative studies, 7

rain-fed regimes, 133
rational choice theory, 9

region (geographic), 75, 106
regional foresight, 196
relationships (between governments), 187
relevance (municipal government to agricultural sector), 79, 87, 156
representation: formal institutions, 164
research design, 22; in Brazil, 51
residence (of actors), 75, 85, 99, 143, 154, 156, 157
resolve, 169
resources (importance of), 159
Rio Grande do Sul, 43
rules-in-use, 142
rural development, 122, 185, 186; and accountability, 200; outcomes, 195, 198
rural sector, 185

sample size, 55
San Martin, Peru, 114
San Martin Municipalities Association, 114
satellite imagery, 198
Secretariat of Agriculture, Livestock, Rural Development, Fisheries, and Food (SAGARPA), 36, 93
services (agricultural), 108, 115, 119, 128, 132, 136, 144, 145–146; quality of, 154–156, 161
social capital, 196
socioeconomic dynamics, 168; as variables, 170, 171
soil degradation, 42–44
Special Land Titling and Cadastral Project, 118
statistical results: for all four countries, 151–152, 176–177; for Brazil, 55–62; for Chile, 81; for Mexico, 103; for Peru, 130, 133
strongmen, 162, 207n1

Subsectoral Program of Irrigation, 118
survey questionnaires, 126
sustainable development, 119

technical capacity, 144
technical staff, 74, 144, 158; number of, 78, 143, 153, 193
terrorism, 116
Tibaya, Arequipa, Peru, 123
titling program, 118
Total Institutional Linkages and Policy Implications Analysis (TILAPIA), 16
transaction costs, 142
Transitory Regional Administration Councils, 27

United Nations Millennium Development Project, 185
unit of analysis, 28–29

variables, 148–149, 172–173; in Brazil, 56–57; in Chile, 80–81; in four-country analysis, 172–173
varied outcomes, 7

Wald tests, 181, 194
water rights, 117
wealth, 74, 75
"window dressing" councils, 197
Workshop in Political Theory and Policy Analysis at Indiana University, 143
World Bank Highly Indebted Poor Countries initiative, 185

Yanahuara, Peru, 123

Zedillo, Ernesto, 91